Lecture Notes in Artificial Intelligence   2321

Subseries of Lecture Notes in Computer Science
Edited by J. G. Carbonell and J. Siekmann

Lecture Notes in Computer Science
Edited by G. Goos, J. Hartmanis, and J. van Leeuwen

Springer

Berlin
Heidelberg
New York
Barcelona
Hong Kong
London
Milan
Paris
Tokyo

Pier Luca Lanzi   Wolfgang Stolzmann
Stewart W. Wilson (Eds.)

Advances in Learning Classifier Systems

4th International Workshop, IWLCS 2001
San Francisco, CA, USA, July 7-8, 2001
Revised Papers

Springer

Volume Editors

Pier Luca Lanzi
Politecnico di Milano
Dipartimento di Elettronica e Informazione
Artificial Intelligence and Robotics Laboratory
Piazza Leonardo da Vinci 32, 20133 Milan, Italy
E-mail: pierluca.lanzi@polimi.it

Wolfgang Stolzmann
DaimlerChrysler AG
Research and Technology, Cognition and Robotics
Alt-Moabit 96A, 10559 Berlin, Germany
E-mail: wolfgang.stolzmann@daimlerchrysler.com

Stewart W. Wilson
Prediction Dynamics, Concord, MA 01742, USA, and
The University of Illinois
Department of General Engineering
Urbana-Champaign, IL 61801, USA
E-mail: wilson@prediction-dynamics.com

Cataloging-in-Publication Data applied for

Die Deutsche Bibliothek - CIP-Einheitsaufnahme

Advances in learning classifier systems : 4th international workshop ;
revised papers / IWLCS 2001, San Francisco, CA, USA, July 7 - 8, 2001.
Pier Luca Lanzi ... (ed.). - Berlin ; Heidelberg ; New York ; Barcelona ;
Hong Kong ; London ; Milan ; Paris ; Tokyo : Springer, 2002
  (Lecture notes in computer science ; Vol. 2321 : Lecture notes in
artificial intelligence)
  ISBN 3-540-43793-2

CR Subject Classification (1998): I.2, F.4.1, F.1.1

ISSN 0302-9743
ISBN 3-540-43793-2 Springer-Verlag Berlin Heidelberg New York

Springer-Verlag Berlin Heidelberg New York
a member of BertelsmannSpringer Science+Business Media GmbH

http://www.springer.de

© Springer-Verlag Berlin Heidelberg 2002
Printed in Germany

Typesetting: Camera-ready by author, data conversion by Christian Grosche, Hamburg
Printed on acid-free paper   SPIN 10846678   06/3142   5 4 3 2 1 0

Preface

The Fourth International Workshop on Learning Classifier Systems (IWLCS 2001) was held July 7-8, 2001, in San Francisco, California, during the Genetic and Evolutionary Computation Conference (GECCO 2001). We have included in this volume revised and extended versions of eleven of the papers presented at the workshop.

The volume is organized into two main parts. The first is dedicated to important theoretical issues of learning classifier systems research including the influence of exploration strategy, a model of self-adaptive classifier systems, and the use of classifier systems for social simulation. The second part contains papers discussing applications of learning classifier systems such as data mining, stock trading, and power distribution networks.

An appendix contains a paper presenting a formal description of ACS, a rapidly emerging learning classifier system model.

This book is the ideal continuation of the two volumes from the previous workshops, published by Springer-Verlag as LNAI 1813 and LNAI 1996. We hope it will be a useful support for researchers interested in learning classifier systems and will provide insights into the most relevant topics and the most interesting open issues.

April 2002

Pier Luca Lanzi
Wolfgang Stolzmann
Stewart W. Wilson

Organization

The Fourth International Workshop on Learning Classifier Systems (IWLCS 2001) was held July 7-8, 2001 in San Francisco (CA), USA, during the Genetic and Evolutionary Conference (GECCO 2001).

Organizing Committee

Pier Luca Lanzi   Politecnico di Milano, Italy
Wolfgang Stolzmann   DaimlerChrysler AG, Germany
Stewart W. Wilson   The University of Illinois at Urbana-Champaign, USA
     Prediction Dynamics, USA

Program Committee

Erik Baum   NEC Research Institute, USA
Andrea Bonarini   Politecnico di Milano, Italy
Lashon B. Booker   The MITRE Corporation, USA
Martin V. Butz   University of Würzburg, Germany
Lawrence Davis   NuTech Solutions, USA
Terry Fogarty   Southbank University, UK
John H. Holmes   University of Pennsylvania, USA
Tim Kovacs   University of Birmingham, UK
Pier Luca Lanzi   Politecnico di Milano, Italy
Rick L. Riolo   University of Michigan, USA
Olivier Sigaud   AnimatLab-LIP6, France
Robert E. Smith   The University of The West of England, UK
Wolfgang Stolzmann   DaimlerChrysler AG, Germany
Keiki Takadama   ATR International, Japan
Stewart W. Wilson   The University of Illinois at Urbana-Champaign, USA
     Prediction Dynamics, USA

Table of Contents

III   Appendix

Part I

Theory

Biasing Exploration in an Anticipatory Learning Classifier System

Martin V. Butz

Department of Cognitive Psychology, University of Würzburg
Röntgenring 11, 97070 Würzburg, Germany
butz@psychologie.uni-wuerzburg.de

Abstract. The chapter investigates how model and behavioral learning can be improved in an anticipatory learning classifier system by biasing exploration. First, the applied system ACS2 is explained. Next, an overview over the possibilities of applying exploration biases in an anticipatory learning classifier system and specifically ACS2 is provided. In ACS2, a *recency bias* termed *action delay bias* as well as an *error bias* termed *knowledge array bias* is implemented. The system is applied in a dynamic maze task and an hand-eye coordination task to validate the biases. The experiments exhibit that biased exploration enables ACS2 to evolve and adapt its internal environmental model faster. Also adaptive behavior is improved.

1 Introduction

Recently, anticipatory learning classifier systems (ALCS) (Butz, 2001) have gained an increasing interest in the learning classifier system (LCS) community (Lanzi, Stolzmann, and Wilson, 2001). An ALCS is an evolutionary rule learning system that represents anticipations in some form. The consequence is the evolution of an *environmental model* additional or even in contrast to the *payoff model* in other LCSs. The system is able to predict the perceptual consequences of an action in all possible situations in an environment. Thus, the system evolves a model that specifies not only what to do in a given situation but also provides information of what will happen after a specific action was executed.

The major concern in ALCS research during the last few years laid in the optimization of the model learning capabilities. It was intended to evolve a model that is *complete, accurate, and maximally general*. A model that *correctly* represents *all* possible action-effect relations with respect to situational properties with the *least number of maximally general* rules possible. For that, it is necessary to specify which environments are actually solvable with the pursued system. In ALCSs, usually deterministic and discrete Markov environments have been addressed (Gérard and Sigaud, 2001, Stolzmann, 2000). This, however, does not mean that ALCSs are generally limited to such environments as the application to noisy environments (Stolzmann and Butz, 2000), non-Markov environments (Stolzmann, 2000), and stochastic environments (Butz, Goldberg, and Stolzmann, 2001) has shown.

P.L. Lanzi, W. Stolzmann, and S.W. Wilson (Eds.): IWLCS 2001, LNAI 2321, pp. 3–22, 2002.

The exploitation of the evolving knowledge for an improved adaptive behavior has only been pursued to a limited extend so far. Previous model exploitation approaches in ALCSs were published in Stolzmann, Butz, Hoffmann, and Goldberg (2000), enhancing behavioral capabilities by internal reinforcement updates or lookahead action selection, and in Stolzmann and Butz (2000), enhancing model learning capabilities by planning.

In contrast to the global planning approach for improved model learning in Stolzmann and Butz (2000), the approach herein improves model learning by a local, computationally inexpensive method. Biasing exploration towards unknown regions or regions which have not been visited for a long time, model learning as well as adaptive behavior is improved.

The chapter is structured as follows. First, section 2 introduces the applied ALCS system ACS2 and points out the differences to the previous ACS system. Section 3 introduces two exploration bias approaches that are able to increase the model learning capabilities of the system. Section 4 shows that both biases work well in a maze environment. The combination of the two approaches proves to be most robust. Model learning and adaptive behavior is then investigated in an extended dynamic maze. A comparison of ACS2 with the biased exploration to the previous introduced planning approach (Stolzmann and Butz, 2000) in an hand-eye coordination task is presented as well, exhibiting the power of the approach. In this respect, ACS2 is now able to solve larger hand-eye problems much faster. Section 5 summarizes and concludes the chapter.

2   An Introduction to ACS2

Usually, anticipations in an ALCS are represented explicitly in each rule or classifier. That is, each rule consists of a condition-action-effect triple that specifies which perceptual effect takes place after executing the specified action under the specified conditions. Stolzmann (1997) developed a first ALCS (ACS) with an additional anticipatory part in each classifier. Another ALCS system with an explicit anticipatory part, YACS, has been published in Gérard and Sigaud (2001). Tomlinson and Bull (2000) published a cooperate learning classifier system (CXCS) in which cooperations between rules allow anticipatory processes. The ALCS used herein is derived from Stolzmann's work but comprises several important modifications and enhancements. This section introduces the derived system ACS2 and mentions the most important differences to ACS.

Generally, the name ACS2 is meant to introduce a new name for the current state of the ACS system rather than to draw any concrete distinctions. One major difference of ACS2 in comparison with ACS is that ACS2 evolves explicit rules for situation-action tuples in which no change occurs. Moreover, ACS2's anticipatory learning process, which results in a directed specialization pressure, as well as ACS2's genetic generalization mechanism are modified compared to the mechanisms in ACS improving the evolution of accurate, maximally general classifiers.

2.1   Agent Architecture

Similar to the agent architectures applied to reinforcement learning approaches or LCSs in particular, ACS2 interacts autonomously with an environment. In a behavioral act at a certain time t, the agent perceives a situation $\sigma(t) \in \mathcal{I} = \{\iota_1, \iota_2, ..., \iota_m\}^L$ where m denotes the number of possible values of each environmental attribute (or feature), $\iota_1, ..., \iota_m$ denote the different possible values of each attribute and L denotes the string length. Note that each attribute is not necessarily coded binary but can only take on discrete values. Moreover, the system can act upon the environment with an action $\alpha(t) \in \mathcal{A} = \{\alpha_1, \alpha_2, ..., \alpha_n\}$ where n specifies the number of different possible actions in the environment and $\alpha_1, ..., \alpha_n$ denote the different possible actions. After the execution of an action, the environment provides a scalar reinforcement value $\rho(t) \in \Re$. Figure 1 illustrates the basic interaction.

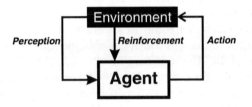

Fig. 1. The basic agent environment interaction

2.2   Knowledge Representation

As in other LCSs, the knowledge in ACS2 is represented by a population $[P]$ of classifiers. Each classifier represents a condition-action-effect rule that anticipates the model state resulting from the execution of the action given the specified condition. A classifier in ACS2 always specifies a complete resulting state. It consists of the following main components.

- *Condition part* (C) specifies the set of situations in which the classifier is applicable.
- *Action part* (A) proposes an available action.
- *Effect part* (E) anticipates the effects of the proposed action in the specified conditions.
- *Quality* (q) measures the accuracy of the anticipated effects.
- *Reward prediction* (r) estimates the reward encountered after the execution of action A in condition C.
- *Immediate reward prediction* (ir) estimates the direct reinforcement encountered after execution of action A in condition C.

The condition and effect part consist of the values perceived from the environment and '#'-symbols (i.e. $C, E \in \{\iota_1, ..., \iota_m, \#\}^L$). A #-symbol in the condition called *don't-care symbol* denotes that the classifier matches any value in this attribute. A '#'-symbol in the effect part, called *pass-through symbol*, specifies that the classifier anticipates that the value of this attribute will not change after the execution of the specified action. Non pass-through symbols in E anticipate the change of the particular attribute to the specified value in contrast to ACS in which a non pass-through symbol did not require a change in value. The action part specifies any action possible in the environment ($A \in \mathcal{A}$). The measures q, r, and ir are scalar values where $q \in [0, 1]$, $r \in \Re$, and $ir \in \Re$. A classifier with a quality q greater than the reliability threshold θ_r (usually set to 0.9) is called *reliable* and becomes part of the internal environmental model. A classifier with a quality q lower than the inadequacy threshold θ_i (usually set to 0.1) is considered as inadequate and is consequently deleted. The immediate reward prediction ir is separated from the usual reward prediction r in order to enable proper internal reinforcement learning updates. All parts are modified according to a reinforcement learning mechanism, and two model learning mechanisms specified in section 2.3.

Additionally, each classifier comprises a *Mark* (M) that records the values of each attribute of all situations in which the classifier did not anticipate correctly sometimes. The *mark* has the structure $M = (m_1, ..., m_L)$. Each attribute $m_i \subseteq \{\iota_1, ..., \iota_m\}$ records all values at position i of perceptual strings in which the specified effect did not take place after execution of action A. Moreover, each classifier specifies a *GA time stamp* t_{ga}, an *ALP time stamp* t_{alp}, an application average aav, an experience counter exp, and a numerosity num. The two time stamps record the time of the last learning module applications. The application average estimates the frequency the classifier is updated (i.e. part of an action set). The experience counter counts the number of applications. The numerosity denotes the number of micro-classifier this *macroclassifier* represents. Thus, one classifier can represent many identical micro-classifiers.

2.3   Environmental Model in ACS2

Interacting with an environment, ACS2 learns more and more about the structure of the environment. Usually, the agent starts without any prior knowledge except for the knowledge implicitly included in the coding structure and the competence in executing the provided actions. Initially, classifiers are mainly generated by a covering mechanism in the anticipatory learning process (ALP). Later, the ALP generates specialized classifiers while a genetic generalization process produces generalized offspring. Moreover, reinforcement learning techniques are applied to the evolving rules representing a behavioral policy in the evolving environmental model.

Figure 2 illustrates the interaction of ACS2 with its environment and its learning application in further detail. After the perception of the current situation $\sigma(t)$, ACS2 forms a match set $[M]$ comprising all classifiers in the population $[P]$ whose conditions are satisfied in $\sigma(t)$. Next, ACS2 chooses an action $\alpha(t)$ according to some action selection strategy. Usually, a simple ϵ-greedy strategy is applied as often used in reinforcement learning (Sutton and Barto, 1998). With respect to the chosen action an action set $[A]$ is generated that consists of all classifiers in $[M]$ that specify the chosen action $\alpha(t)$. After the execution of $\alpha(t)$, classifier parameters are updated by the ALP and the applied RL technique and new classifiers might be generated as well as old classifiers might be deleted by the ALP and genetic generalization. The different learning mechanisms and the various interactions of the mechanisms are explained in the following.

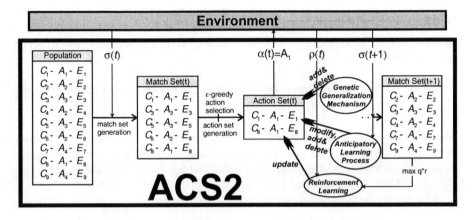

Fig. 2. During one agent/environment interaction, ACS2 forms a match set representing the knowledge about the current perceptions. Next, it generates an action set representing the knowledge about the consequences of the chosen action in the given situation. Classifier parameters are updated by RL and ALP. Moreover, new classifiers might be added and old classifiers might be deleted by genetic generalization and ALP

Anticipatory Learning Process. The ALP was originally derived from the cognitive theory of anticipatory behavioral control (Hoffmann, 1993). The process results in the evaluation and specialization of the anticipatory model in ACS2. Before the generation of offspring, classifier parameters are updated evaluating the anticipations of the classifiers in action set $[A]$. Next, offspring is generated and inaccurate classifiers are deleted.

Parameter Updates. The ALP updates the quality q, the mark M, the ALP time stamp t_{alp}, the application average aav, and the experience counter exp. The quality q is update according to the classifiers anticipation. If the effect part of the classifier correctly specified changes and non-changes, the quality is increased by the following formula.

$$q \leftarrow q + \beta(1 - q) \tag{1}$$

On the other hand, if the effect did not specify the correct outcome, the quality is decreased.

$$q \leftarrow q - \beta q \tag{2}$$

In the equation, $\beta \in [0,1]$ denotes the *learning rate* of ACS2. The smaller the learning rate, the more passive ACS2 updates its values and the less are the values biased towards recent environmental interactions. On the other hand, the larger the learning rate, the faster the parameters adapt to changes in the environment but also the more noisy are the parameters.

Situation $\sigma(t) = (\sigma_1, ..., \sigma_L)$ is added to the mark $M = (m_i, ..., m_L)$ if the classifier did not anticipate correctly. In this case, $\forall_i m_i = m_i \cup \{\sigma_i\}$.

The ALP time stamp is set to the current time t recording the last parameter update in the ALP. Before that, though, the application average aav is updated using the *moyenne adaptive modifiée* technique as introduced in Venturini (1994).

$$cl.aav \leftarrow \begin{cases} (cl.aav(cl.exp - 1) + (t - cl.t_{alp}))/cl.exp & \text{if } cl.exp < 1/\beta \\ cl.aav + \beta(t - cl.t_{alp}) & \text{otherwise} \end{cases} \quad (3)$$

The technique assures the fast adaptation of aav once the classifier is introduced and later assures a continues update according to the overall learning rate β. Note, this technique also introduces a possible high factor of noise in the young classifier. Thus, the technique is not applied in the quality updates.

Finally, the experience counter exp is increased by one.

Classifier Generation and Deletion. The ALP generates specialized offspring and/or deletes *inaccurate* classifiers.

Inaccurate classifiers are classifiers whose quality is lower than the inaccuracy threshold θ_i. When the quality of a classifiers falls below θ_i after an update, it is deleted.

More specialized classifiers are generated in two cases. In an *expected case*, in which a classifier anticipated the correct outcome, a classifier might be generated if the mark M differs from the situation $\sigma(t)$ in some attributes, i.e. $\exists_{i,j} \iota_j \in m_i \wedge \iota_j \neq \sigma_i$. Since the mark specifies the characteristics of situations in which a classifier did not work correctly, a difference indicates that the specific position might be important to distinguish the correct and wrong outcome case. Thus, the ALP generates an offspring whose conditions are further specialized. If there are unique differences in the mark compared to the current situation, i.e. $\exists_i \sigma_i \notin m_i$, then one of the unique difference is specialized in the offspring. However, if there are only positions that differ but σ_i is always part of m_i, i.e. $\forall_i \sigma_i \in m_i$, then all differing positions are specialized. The number of specialized positions in the conditions that are not specialized in the effects is limited to u_{max}.

In an *unexpected case*, a classifier did not anticipate the correct outcome. In this case, an offspring classifier is generate, if the effect part of the classifier can be further specialized (by changing pass-through symbols to specific values) to specify the perceived outcome correctly. All positions in condition and effect part are specialized that change from $\sigma(t)$ to $\sigma(t+1)$.

In both reproduction cases, the Mark M of the offspring is emptied, the experience counter exp is set to zero, ALP and GA time stamp are set to the current time t, the numerosity is set to one, and all other parameters are inherited from the parents. If the generated offspring already exists in the population $[P]$, the offspring is discarded and the quality q of the old classifier is increased applying equation 1.

A classifier is also generated if there was no classifier in the actual action set $[A]$ that anticipated the effect correctly. In this case, a *covering classifier* is generated that is specialized in all attributes in condition and effect part that changed from $\sigma(t)$ to $\sigma(t+1)$. The covering method was not applied in ACS since in ACS a completely general classifiers was always present for each action. The attributes of the Mark M of the covering classifier are initially empty. Quality q is set to 0.5 as well as the reward prediction r, while the immediate reward prediction ir as well as the application average avv are set to 0. The time stamps are set to the current time t.

Genetic Generalization Mechanism. While the ALP specializes classifiers in a quite competent way, over-specializations can occur sometimes as studied in (Butz, 2001). Since the over-specialization cases can be caused by various circumstances, a genetic generalization (GG) mechanism was applied that, interacting with the ALP, results in the evolution of a complete, accurate, and maximally general model. The mechanism works as follows.

After the application of the ALP, it is first determined if the mechanism should be applied. GG is applied if the average time since the last GA application in the current action set $[A]$ is larger than the threshold θ_{ga} (if $t - (\sum_{cl\in[A]} cl.t_{ga}cl.num)/\sum_{cl\in[A]} cl.num > \theta_{ga}$). If the mechanism is applied, θ_{ga} is set to the current time t. Next, two classifiers are selected with roulette wheel selection with respect to the qualities q. The two classifiers are reproduced where the attributes in the mark are emptied, and the qualities are halved. Next, the reproduced classifiers are mutated applying a generalizing mutation, that is, only mutating specified attribute in the condition part C back to don't care symbols. A specialized attribute is generalized with a probability μ. Moreover, conditions of the offspring are crossed applying two-point crossover with a probability of χ. In the case of a crossover application, quality, reward prediction, and immediate reward prediction are averaged over the offspring. Finally, the classifiers are inserted. If a generated offspring already exists in the population, the offspring classifier is discarded and if the existing classifier is not marked its numerosity is increased by one.

The GG mechanism also applies a deletion procedure inside the action sets. If an action set $[A]$ exceeds the action set size threshold θ_{as}, excess classifiers are deleted in $[A]$. The procedure applies a tournament selection process in which the classifier with the significant lowest quality, or the classifier with the highest specificity is deleted. Thus, deletion causes the extinction of low-quality as well as over-specialized classifiers.

Subsumption. To further emphasize a proper model convergence, subsumption is applied similar to the subsumption method in XCS (Wilson, 1998). If an offspring classifier was generated, regardless if by ALP or GG, the set is searched for a subsuming classifier. The offspring is subsumed if a classifier exists that is more general in the conditions, specifies the same effect, is *reliable* (its quality is higher than the threshold θ_r), is not marked, and is *experienced* (its experience counter exp is higher than the threshold θ_{exp}). If there are more than one possible subsumer, the syntactically maximally general subsumer is chosen. In the case of a draw, the subsumer is chosen at random from the maximally general ones. If a subsumer was found, the offspring is discarded and either quality or numerosity is increased dependent on if the offspring was generated by ALP or GG, respectively.

Interaction of ALP and GG. Several distinct studies in various environments revealed that the interaction of ALP and GG is able to evolve a complete, accurate, and maximally general model in various environments in a competent way (see e.g. Butz, Goldberg, and Stolzmann, 2000, Butz, 2001). The basic idea behind the interacting model learning processes is that the specialization process extracts as much information as possible from the encountered environment continuously specializing over-general classifiers. The GG mechanism, on the other hand, randomly generalizes exploiting the power of a genetic algorithm where no more additional information is available from the environment. The ALP ensures diversity and prevents the loss of information of a particular niche in the environment. Only GG generates identical classifiers and causes convergence in the population.

2.4   Policy in ACS2

The behavioral policy of ACS2 is directly represented in the evolving model. As specified above, each classifier includes a reward prediction estimate r and an immediate reward prediction estimate ir. Thus, as explained in Butz (2001), the environmental model needs to be specific enough to be able to represent a proper policy in the model. If this is not the case, *model aliasing* might take place.

In model aliasing a model is completely accurate in terms of anticipations but over-general with respect to reinforcement. For example, in a game such as checkers, ACS2 might be able to learn when it is possible to move a figure in some direction. However, the model will not be specific enough to evolve a proper strategy directly represented in the model. In checkers, it is sufficient to specify that the targeted position is currently empty in order to know the success of a simple movement. However, to be able to determine if the movement will payoff, more positions of the own as well as the opponents pieces need to be specified.

Policy Learning. After the action was executed, the next environmental situation was perceived and the subsequent match set was formed as visualized in figure 2, the reward related parameters r and ir are updated.

$$r \leftarrow r + \beta(\rho(t) + \gamma \max_{cl \in [M](t+1) \wedge cl.E \neq \{\#\}^L} (cl.q \cdot cl.r) - r) \qquad (4)$$

$$ir \leftarrow ir + \beta(\rho(t) - ir) \qquad (5)$$

As before, $\beta \in [0,1]$ denotes the learning rate biasing the parameters more or less towards recently encountered reward. $\gamma \in [0,1)$ denotes the discount factor similar to Q-learning (Watkins, 1989). In contrast to Q-learning, however, the rules may be applicable in distinct situations. The values of r and ir consequently specify an average of the resulting reward after the execution of action A over all possible situations of the environment in which the classifier is applicable.

Policy Execution. Usually, ACS2 applies a simple ϵ-greedy action selection strategy. An action is chosen at random with a probability ϵ and otherwise the best action is chosen. The action with the highest $q * r$ value in a match set $[M]$ is usually considered as the best action in ACS2.

While the reinforcement learning capabilities of ACS2 will be of minor interest in the following sections, the modification of the policy will be of major interest. The question is how the model learning progress can be further optimized by modifying the behavioral policy.

3   Model Exploitation

While diverse experiments have shown ACS2's capabilites of evolving a complete, accurate, and maximally general environmental model reliably (Butz, Goldberg, and Stolzmann, 2000), the approach herein optimizes the capability further. It is investigated, how the policy can be optimized to improve sampling of the environment and consequently optimize model learning in return.

The model building algorithm in ACS2 is basically an *implicitly supervised* learning algorithm. This means that the perceptual feedback of the environment can be regarded as a supervision but no explicit teacher is necessary for the supervision. In fact, the environment implicitly represents the supervisor. The agent does not ask for corrections but extracts information from the environment actively. Moreover, it manipulates the perception of environmental feedback by its own actions. Thus, an action policy that optimizes feedback can improve the model learning capabilities of ACS2. The optimization of the information extraction process by the means of an intelligent action selection process is the concern of the model exploitation approach herein.

3.1   Background

Previous intelligent situation and action selection approaches have been pursued in the RL literature. Sutton (1990) published the idea of an exploration bonus in his dynamical architecture *Dyna* that allowed the faster detection of environmental dynamics and a consequent faster adaptive behavior. In his approach, the agent is *positive* in that it believes that it is worth to explore unknown regions of its environment. In more behavioral terms, the agent might be said to be curious and feel save. Moore and Atkeson (1993) introduced a prioritized sweeping algorithm that further improved the internal update strategy in Dyna.

Their approach maintains a priority queue of to-be-updated states with the order of updating states in which previously large changes in the absorbing state prediction or the reward prediction values occurred. Dayan and Sejnowski (1996) systemize and extend Sutton's (1990) exploration bonus approach. By modeling the uncertainty of the world and providing the agent with additional goal information, their enhanced Dyna system is able to directly explore the existence of barriers and consequently detect possible shortcuts faster. Finally, Kaelbling (1993) applied an interval estimation strategy in which actions are selected according to prediction and the estimated error of the prediction.

Thrun (1992) as well as Wilson (1996) provide excellent overviews of the underlying exploration/exploitation dilemma and the different types of possible exploration. According to their frameworks, the model exploitation approach herein is a *directed* exploration approach pursuing *recency-based methods* as well as *error-based* methods. Directed exploration is compared to *undirected uniform random* exploration. The usual trade-off between exploration and exploitation does not apply in most of the experiments herein. In the trade-off problem, exploration usually inhibits the proper exploitation of the current knowledge for an optimal behavior. This work focuses on model learning optimization rather than policy learning optimization so that optimal behavior is purely defined as the behavior of optimizing knowledge, and not behavior, as fast as possible. However, the results in section 4.3 show that the direct bias is also able to positively influence policy learning in which behavior is realized by a simple *constant global* explore/exploit strategy.

3.2   Approach

The idea of the biased exploration is to decide before the execution of an action, from which action the system probably learns the most. To do that, the classifiers in the current match set $[M]$ are searched for indications which action might result in the highest knowledge gain. The action that promises the highest knowledge gain is then executed during exploration rather than a randomly chosen action.

Action Delay Bias. The first bias exploits the recency-based bias principle. The execution of actions which have been executed quite long ago in a given situation promises the detection of new situation-action-effect relations. This is similar to the exploration bonus approach pursued in Sutton (1990). In ACS2, such a bias needs to be adapted to the generalized evolving model representation.

To determine which action has been executed most long ago in ACS2, the mechanism takes advantage of the existing ALP time stamp t_{alp}. Given a current situation $\sigma(t)$ and the corresponding match set $[M](t)$, the action of the classifier with the lowest value t_{alp} in $[M]$ is assumed to denote the action that was chosen least recently in $\sigma(t)$. However, if there is an action that is not represented by any classifier in $[M]$, this action is assumed to be the one that was experienced most long ago (or not at all, yet) so that this action is chosen for execution.

Knowledge Array Bias. The second exploration bias is based on the error-based bias principle. Moore and Atkeson (1993) implemented this bias with respect to absorbing state prediction error and reward prediction error. Our bias however is concerned with optimizing model learning and consequently considers the anticipatory error.

The anticipatory error is actually expressed in the quality q of each individual classifier since the quality denotes the accuracy of the specified anticipations. Thus, a knowledge array bias application directly infers from the classifiers in the match set $[M]$, which action result is known the least. The bias uses the knowledge represented in all classifiers. Similarly to the prediction array PA in the XCS classifier system (Wilson, 1995) a knowledge array KA is generated in ACS2. KA has an entry for each possible action a that specifies the knowledge about the consequences of the action. It is determined as follows:

$$KA[a] = \sum_{cl \in [M] \wedge cl.A = a} cl.q \cdot cl.num / \sum_{cl \in [M] \wedge cl.A = a} cl.num \qquad (6)$$

Thus, each entry specifies the averaged quality of the anticipation for each possible action. The action with the lowest value in the knowledge array is chosen for execution. As in the action delay bias, actions that are not represented by any classifier are always chosen for execution first.

Interacting Biases. During exploration, an action is chosen according to the applied bias with a fixed biased exploration probability p_b while otherwise an action is chosen as before uniformly randomly. Section 4 validates the approach in a dynamic maze environment as well as an hand-eye coordination task.

Since the two approaches actually comprise different biases with the same objective, that is the optimization of model learning, action delay bias and knowledge array bias are also applied in combination. In this case, with a probability of p_b, action delay bias is executed with a probability of 0.5 and knowledge array bias is executed otherwise. Section 4.1 actually proves that the combined bias generates the best learning results as well as remedies possible misguiding effects.

4   Experimental Validation

The different exploration biases are now evaluated in a maze learning task as well as a hand-eye coordination task. Maze tasks have been studied widely in the LCS literature (see e.g. Lanzi, 1999) and RL literature (see e.g. Moore and Atkeson, 1993). The hand-eye coordination task was introduced in Birk (1995) and was previously studied with ACS in Stolzmann and Butz (2000). The accompanying results show that by biasing exploration ACS is able to achieve a complete, accurate, and compact knowledge of the environment faster.

Moreover, it is shown that behavior is adapted faster. All model learning curves are averaged over twenty runs. [1]

4.1 Exploration Bias in Maze5

The Maze5 environment has been studied before in Lanzi (1999) with XCS investigating the reinforcement learning capabilities of the system. The left hand side of figure 3 depicts Maze5. The environment is a discrete, deterministic environment. The agent perceives the eight adjacent cells so that $\sigma(t) \in \mathcal{I} = \{., O, F\}^8$. Moreover, the agent is able to move to those eight adjacent cells so that $\alpha(t) \in \mathcal{A} = \{N, NE, E, SE, S, SW, W, NW\}$. A movement towards an obstacle O has no perceptual effects and the animat remains in its current position. Movement into the food position F results in the provision of a reinforcement of 1000, the perception in the food position, and finally an end of trial and a consequent reset of the agent to a randomly chosen empty position. The experimental results in this and the following section display the model learning progress of the system. To evaluate the progress, all *reliable* classifiers of the current population are searched for a classifier that anticipates the correct changes in each situation-action tuple that actually does induce a change in the environment. Situation-action tuples that do not cause a change are not tested since the eight classifiers for these cases are learned very quickly. If those cases were included, the result would be an initial steep increase in knowledge in the beginning of a learning curve, which would only complicate the monitoring of the knowledge progress in the changing cases.

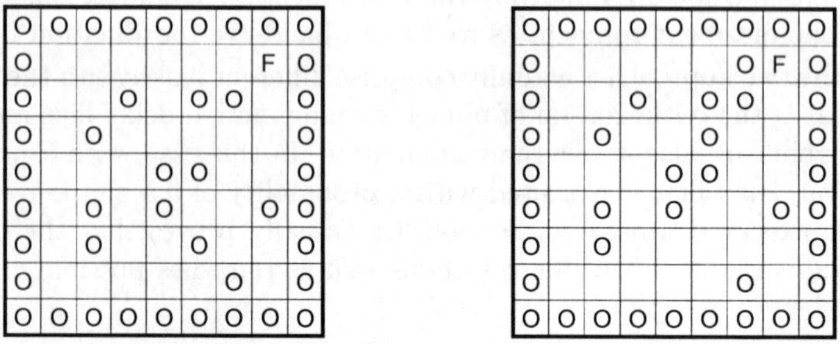

Fig. 3. Maze5 on the left-hand side and Maze7 on the right-hand side. Both mazes are discrete, deterministic Markov environments

Figure 4 shows that action delay bias, knowledge array bias, as well as the combination of the biases positively influence the shape of the learning curves. Knowledge array bias shows a stronger effect than action delay bias. However, in both cases the application of a completely biased exploration ($p_b = 1.0$)

---

[1] If not states differently, parameters were set to: $\beta = 0.05$, $u_{max} = \infty$, $\gamma = 0.95$, $\theta_{ga} = 100$, $\mu = 0.3$, $\chi = 0.8$, $\theta_{as} = 20$, $\theta_{exp} = 20$, $\epsilon = 1.0$.

disrupts the learning progress. In this case, a misguiding effect was observed that caused the system to neglect parts of the environment. Consequently, a complete knowledge of the environment was not achievable. The combination of the two biases however shows the best learning effect. It reliably generates a complete knowledge even with a $p_b = 1.0$. The remainder of this work consequently only shows results with the combined biases with $p_b = 1.0$.

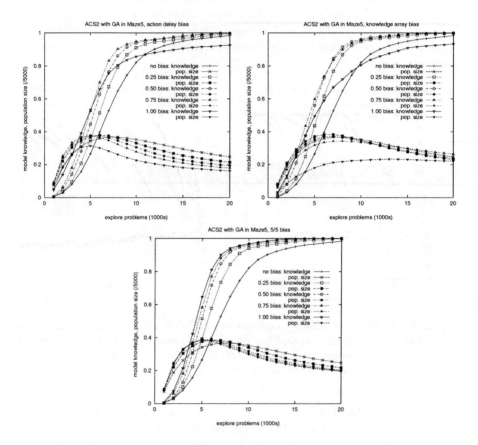

Fig. 4. Each bias causes a positive learning effect. Combining action delay bias and knowledge array bias, the best learning progress as well as the highest robustness is achieved

4.2 Model Learning in a Dynamic Maze

The next step in the investigation of the additional exploration bias is to change Maze5 to a dynamic maze. In figure 3, Maze7 is visualized on the right-hand side. Maze7 is more difficult in a reinforcement learning task, because longer chaining is necessary. The dynamics are simulated by switching back and forth between

Maze5 and Maze7 consequently always altering the maze structure slightly. The presented model learning experiments always start in the Maze5 environment and switch every 20000 steps to Maze7 and back to Maze5.

Figure 5 shows that the additional exploration bias always increases the model learning speed and the consequent knowledge adaptation in the dynamic environment. It is also observable that ACS2 is able to remember parts of the other environment in its classifier population since the knowledge loss is smaller and the recovery speed is faster in the later switches between Maze5 and Maze7. Note also that the peaks as well as the minima in the population size increasingly decrease indicating that the internal representation becomes increasingly compact.

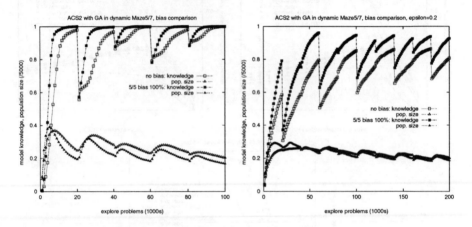

Fig. 5. In the dynamic Maze5/7 environment, ACS2 is able to adapt its knowledge faster with additional exploration bias. Although the knowledge is more complete, the population size is smaller than in the case where random action choice is applied. Decreasing the exploration probability ϵ, the model learning speed decreases in general

On the right hand side the model learning behavior of ACS2 is observable when ϵ is decreased. As would be expected, ACS2 builds up its environmental knowledge much slower in this case. The positive effect of exploration bias instead of random exploration is still observable, though. Note that in all curves the population size actually decreases more when the exploration bias is applied although a higher knowledge is achieved. The next section investigates the behavioral adaptation of ACS2 in Maze5/7 in which ϵ is altered as well.

4.3   Adaptive Behavior in the Dynamic Maze5/7

The behavior of ACS2 is directly represented in its classifiers. The reward prediction of each classifier combined with the quality determines the action choice during exploitation. Thus, it is clear that a proper model representation needs to be present, before an appropriate policy can be represented in the model. However, the model specifies all situation-action tuples whereas for a proper policy it might be sufficient to only represent the important situation-action tuples. The following results show how ACS2 is able to adapt its policy in the dynamic Maze5/7 environment. The first experiment was done according to the usually applied schema in LCSs with one pure exploration and one pure exploitation trial. During pure exploration, ϵ is set to one allowing for the strongest model and consequent policy learning. In the second experiment only one phase is executed during which ϵ is set to 0.2. The steps to food during these ϵ-greedy trials are recorded. Due to the slightly higher noise in the adaptive behavior tasks, the curves are averaged over 50 runs.

The left-hand side of figure 6 shows that ACS2 in the two phase experiment is able to adapt its behavior perfectly in the dynamic Maze5/7 environment. Especially in the switch from Maze5 to Maze7 a faster adaptation is observable when exploration bias is applied. The shortcut detection when switching back to Maze5 is detected nearly equally fast. However, in the ϵ-greedy experiment displayed on the right-hand side of figure 6, ACS2 is actually detecting the short cuts faster when biased exploration is applied. Improved adaptive behavior is observable in general. The curves also reveal that although the model might not yet be complete, behavior is already adapting indicating the simultaneous evolution of model and behavior. Note, the curves also expose that behavior is adapted faster in later environmental changes confirming the retention of previous knowledge.

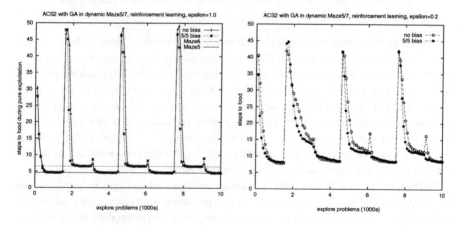

Fig. 6. In the reinforcement learning task in the dynamic Maze5/7 environment, ACS2 is also able to adapt its behavior faster with additional exploration bias. Applying an ϵ-greedy action selection policy, exploration bias enables a faster short cut exploitation and consequently adapts faster in the change from Maze7 to Maze5

4.4   Improved Performance in an Hand-Eye Coordination Task

To validate the general benefit of exploration bias, ACS2 was also applied in an hand-eye coordination task previously investigate in Stolzmann and Butz (2000). Figure 7 shows the problem on a 3×3 matrix. A camera is watching a plain on which one block is situated. A gripper acts upon the plain. The gripper is able to move to its four adjacent positions as well as execute a gripping and releasing action ($\mathcal{A} = \{N, E, S, W, G, R\}$). Perceived is the camera image which is discretized into the actual matrix size as well as an additional feeling sensor which indicates if there is currently no contact to the block (indicated by $'0'$), if the block is situated under the gripper (indicated by $'1'$), or if the gripper holds the block ($'2'$). Considering a problem with a matrix size of $l \times l$, the generally possible perceptions are in $\mathcal{I} = \{w, b, g\}^{l^2} \cdot \{0, 1, 2\}$.

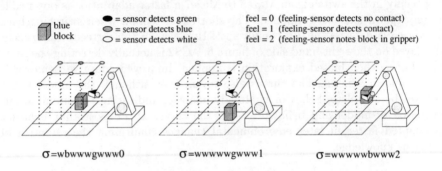

Fig. 7. The hand-eye coordination task exemplified in a 3x3 matrix

Tested in this environment is the environmental model. Thus, as before, only the reliable classifiers are tested. However, not all possible situation-action combinations are tested but randomly generated ones. In a test, 100 randomly chosen situations are generated with a 50% chance that the gripper is currently holding the block. Next, an action is chosen at random and the effect is generated. The resulting situation-action-effect triple is tested regardless if a change is caused by the chosen action or not. Note that in this problem the model size grows in $O(l^2)$ whereas the problem size grows in $O(l^4)$. Parameters were set as before and the curves are again averaged over twenty runs.

In Stolzmann and Butz (2000) planning was applied to improve model learning of ACS in the hand-eye scenario. In the planning approach, every 50 steps a goal is requested from a goal generator, a sequence is planned to the goal by a bidirectional search mechanism and if a sequence was found it is executed. Planning is executed as long as sequences are found and are successfully executed. The goal generator as well as the whole planning approach are implemented as specified in (Stolzmann and Butz, 2000).

The left hand side of figure 8 shows performance of ACS2 in the hand-eye task with $l = 5$ comparing the pursued additional exploration bias approach with the previous planning approach, and random exploration. As in the previous work, the curves confirm that the high-level planning approach is able to improve performance compared to simple continuous random exploration. However, planning is an expensive procedure and the effect is rather small. The exploration bias approach on the other hand is able to significantly increase the learning progress compared to both random exploration and the planning approach. Thus, in this case a low-level intelligent action selection strategy was able to beat a high-level computationally expensive planning strategy.

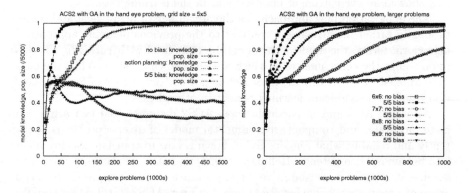

Fig. 8. The local direct exploration bias shows a stronger benefit than the planning strategy which again exhibits faster learning than simple random exploration. In larger problems displayed on the right hand side, ACS2 with exploration bias proves to be able to evolve its knowledge much faster

The right hand side of figure 8 exhibits performance of ACS2 in larger hand-eye problems. It can be observed that ACS2 strongly benefits from the exploration bias approach. Essentially, exploration bias helps to explore the cases *with contact to the gripper* and *holding the gripper* which occur only rarely when choosing actions at random. This helps ACS2 to learn the cases *transporting* and *releasing the gripper* which are tested during the test phase with a probability of 50%. Although also the planning approach was supposed to lead to the exploration of these cases, exploration bias works more effective and more reliable. A generalized environmental model is evolved much faster than with previous techniques.

5   Summary and Conclusions

Action delay bias as well as knowledge array bias demonstrated to be able to speed up the model learning process in ACS2. The combination of both exploration biases led to the fastest and most stable performance gain. The combination of the biases also showed the highest robustness achieving a complete knowledge with any parameter setting. The application of the combined bias to the dynamic maze environment exhibited further improvement. The dynamic maze task also confirmed that ACS2 is able to retain information as well as reuse information. Also adaptive behavior was improved due to exploration bias. In the dynamic maze task, ACS2 adapted its behavior faster regardless if testing behavior in a separate pure exploitation phase or online applying an ϵ-greedy action selection policy. The application in the hand-eye coordination task proved the robustness of the exploration bias as well as its broad applicability. Compared to the previous high-level planning approach, ACS2 appeared to improve performance significantly. In larger hand-eye problems, ACS2 with exploration bias showed an even stronger improvement in the learning rate.

The exploration bias approach has the advantage of being local and computationally rather inexpensive in contrast to the previous planning approach. In behavioral terms, the applied biases can be compared with *curiosity*, the drive to do things the consequences of which are not known for sure. While the biases were applied in an ALCS, the approach is not restricted to ALCSs and should also result in a significant learning benefit in other LCSs.

Although ACS and in particular now ACS2 demonstrated to learn a complete, accurate, and compact environmental model of diverse problems competently and reliably, what remains to be shown is how to translate this knowledge into behavioral competence. Hoffmann (1993) and other researchers in cognitive sciences emphasize more and more the importance of anticipations for the acquisition of a competent behavior. Right now, however, ACS2 is still rather stimulus-response driven in accordance with behaviorism and reinforcement learning. The applied exploration bias might be regarded as an anticipatory behavior—the anticipation of the (most unknown) consequences influences behavior and might be compared to curiosity, also an anticipatory driven behavior. However, other behaviors should be investigated such as further anticipatory driven action selection processes or the simulation of attentional processes. Future research will show in what way anticipatory learning mechanism like ACS2 can be exploited for the realization of anticipatory behavior in artificial agents.

Acknowledgments

I would like to thank the Department of Cognitive Psychology at the University of Würzburg for their ideas and thoughts provided with respect to this work. Moreover, I would like to thank Stewart W. Wilson for pointing out relevant literature and providing many useful comments. The work was sponsored by the German Research Foundation DFG.

References

[Birk (1995] Birk, A. (1995). *Stimulus Response Lernen [Stimulus response learning]*. Doctoral dissertation, University of Saarbrücken, Germany.

[Butz (2001] Butz, M. V. (2001). *Anticipatory learning classifier systems*. Genetic Algorithms and Evolutionary Computation. Boston, MA: Kluwer Academic Publishers.

[Butz, Goldberg, and Stolzmann (2000] Butz, M. V., Goldberg, D. E., and Stolzmann, W. (2000). Introducing a genetic generalization pressure to the anticipatory classifier system: Part 2 - performance analysis. In Whitely, D., Goldberg, D. E., Cantu-Paz, E., Spector, L., Parmee, I., and Beyer, H.-G. (Eds.), *Proceedings of the Genetic and Evolutionary Computation Conference (GECCO-2000)* pp. 42–49. San Francisco, CA: Morgan Kaufmann.

[Butz, Goldberg, and Stolzmann (2001] Butz, M. V., Goldberg, D. E., and Stolzmann, W. (2001). Probability-enhanced predictions in the anticipatory classifier system. In Lanzi, P. L., Stolzmann, W., and Wilson, S. W. (Eds.), *Advances in Learning Classifier Systems, LNAI 1996* pp. 37–51. Berlin Heidelberg: Springer-Verlag.

[Dayan and Sejnowski (1996] Dayan, P., and Sejnowski, T. J. (1996). Exploration bonus and dual control. *Machine Learning, 25*(1), 5–22.

[Gérard and Sigaud (2001] Gérard, P., and Sigaud, O. (2001). YACS: Combining dynamic programming with generalization in classifier systems. In Lanzi, P. L., Stolzmann, W., and Wilson, S. W. (Eds.), *Advances in Learning Classifier Systems, LNAI 1996* pp. 52–69. Berlin Heidelberg: Springer-Verlag.

[Hoffmann (1993] Hoffmann, J. (1993). *Vorhersage und Erkenntnis [Anticipation and cognition].* Goettingen, Germany: Hogrefe.

[Kaelbling (1993] Kaelbling, L. P. (1993). *Learning in embedded systems.* Cambridge, MA: MIT Press.

[Lanzi (1999] Lanzi, P. L. (1999). An analysis of generalization in the XCS classifier system. *Evolutionary Computation, 7*(2), 125–149.

[Lanzi, Stolzmann, and Wilson (2001] Lanzi, P. L., Stolzmann, W., and Wilson, S. W. (Eds.) (2001). *Advances in learning classifier systems, LNAI 1996.* Berlin Heidelberg: Springer-Verlag.

[Moore and Atkeson (1993] Moore, A. W., and Atkeson, C. (1993). Memory-based reinforcement learning: Converging with less data and less real time. *Machine Learning, 13*, 103–130.

[Stolzmann (1997] Stolzmann, W. (1997). *Antizipative Classifier Systems [Anticipatory classifier systems].* Aachen, Germany: Shaker Verlag.

[Stolzmann (2000] Stolzmann, W. (2000). An introduction to anticipatory classifier systems. In Lanzi, P. L., Stolzmann, W., and Wilson, S. W. (Eds.), *Learning Classifier Systems: From Foundations to Applications, LNAI 1813* pp. 175–194. Berlin Heidelberg: Springer-Verlag.

[Stolzmann and Butz (2000] Stolzmann, W., and Butz, M. V. (2000). Latent learning and action-planning in robots with anticipatory classifier systems. In Lanzi, P. L., Stolzmann, W., and Wilson, S. W. (Eds.), *Learning Classifier Systems: From Foundations to Applications, LNAI 1813* pp. 301–317. Berlin Heidelberg: Springer-Verlag.

[Stolzmann, Butz, Hoffmann, and Goldberg (2000] Stolzmann, W., Butz, M. V., Hoffmann, J., and Goldberg, D. E. (2000). First cognitive capabilities in the anticipatory classifier system. In Meyer, J.-A., Berthoz,

A., Floreano, D., Roitblat, H., and Wilson, S. W. (Eds.), *From Animals to Animats 6: Proceedings of the Sixth International Conference on Simulation of Adaptive Behavior* pp. 287–296. Cambridge, MA: MIT Press.

[Sutton (1990] Sutton, R. S. (1990). Integrated architectures for learning, planning, and reacting based on approximating dynamic programming. In *Proceedings of the Seventh International Conference on Machine Learning* pp. 216–224. San Mateo, CA: Morgan Kaufmann.

[Sutton and Barto (1998] Sutton, R. S., and Barto, A. G. (1998). *Reinforcement learning: An introduction.* Cambridge, MA: MIT Press.

[Thrun (1992] Thrun, S. B. (1992). The role of exploration in learning control. In White, D.A. adn Sofge, D. (Ed.), *Handbook of Intelligent Control: Neural, Fuzzy and Adaptive Approaches* New York, NY: Van Nostrand Reinhold.

[Tomlinson and Bull (2000] Tomlinson, A., and Bull, L. (2000). A corporate XCS. In Lanzi, P. L., Stolzmann, W., and Wilson, S. W. (Eds.), *Learning Classifier Systems: From Foundations to Applications, LNAI 1813* pp. 195–208. Berlin Heidelberg: Springer-Verlag.

[Venturini (1994] Venturini, G. (1994). Adaptation in dynamic environments through a minimal probability of exploration. In Cliff, D., Husbands, P., Meyer, J.-A., and Wilson, S. W. (Eds.), *From Animals to Animats 3: Proceedings of the Third International Conference on Simulation of Adaptive Behavior* pp. 371–381. Cambridge, MA: MIT Press.

[Watkins (1989] Watkins, C. J. C. H. (1989). *Learning from delayed rewards.* Doctoral dissertation, King's College, Cambridge, UK.

[Wilson (1995] Wilson, S. W. (1995). Classifier fitness based on accuracy. *Evolutionary Computation, 3*(2), 149–175.

[Wilson (1996] Wilson, S. W. (1996). Explore/exploit strategies in autonomy. In Maes, P., Matariac, M. adn Pollak, J., Meyer, J.-A., and Wilson, S. (Eds.), *From Animals to Animats 4: Proceedings of the Fourth International Conference on Simulation of Adaptive Behavior* pp. 325–332. Cambridge, MA: MIT Press.

[Wilson (1998] Wilson, S. W. (1998). Generalization in the XCS classifier system. In Koza, J. R., Banzhaf, W., Chellapilla, K., Deb, K., Dorigo, M., Fogel, D., Grazon, M., Goldberg, D., Iba, H., and Riolo, R. (Eds.), *Genetic Programming 1998: Proceedings of the Third Annual Conference* pp. 665–674. San Francisco: Morgan Kaufmann.

An Incremental Multiplexer Problem and Its Uses in Classifier System Research

Lawrence Davis[1], Chunsheng Fu[1], and Stewart W. Wilson[2]

[1] NuTech Solutions, 28 Green St., Newbury, MA 01951, USA
{david.davis,chunsheng.fu}@nutechsolutions.com
[2] Prediction Dynamics, 30 Lang St., Concord, MA 01742, USA
wilson@predictionDynamics.com

Abstract. This paper describes the *incremental multiplexer problem,* a new test problem for machine learning research. The incremental multiplexer problem is an extended version of the *multiplexer problem*, a well-known test problem for data mining systems that do classification. The multiplexer problem has been one of the testbed problems driving the development of classifier systems in the last 15 years, but it has one drawback: the number of different multiplexer problems that are interesting and solvable with current computers is very small. This paper describes a generalization of the multiplexer problem that has many instances that are accessible to today's researchers. The paper contains results showing how the performance of a classifier system with fixed parameter settings changes as the size of the message generated by incremental multiplexers increases, suggesting that the incremental multiplexer provides machine learning problems that "fill in the gaps" between the standard multiplexer problems.

1   The Incremental Multiplexer Problem

1.1   About the Multiplexer Problem

The multiplexer problem has been the subject of a good deal of research in the machine learning field in general and in the classifier system field in particular (Wilson 1995). There are many versions of the multiplexer problem, each with a different size of the form $n + 2^n$, for $n >= 1$. Examples of multiplexer sizes, beginning with the smallest and increasing in size, are the 3-multiplexer, the 6-multiplexer, the 11-multiplexer, the 20-multiplexer, the 37-multiplexer, the 70-multiplexer, etc. In this paper, these problems will be referred to as the "3-MP", the "6-MP", the "11-MP", and so forth.

The difficulty of a multiplexer problem is correlated with its size. The smaller multiplexer problems are fairly simple to solve. For researchers who have used classifier systems to solve the multiplexer problem, problems with interesting levels of difficulty begin with the 11-MP.

P.L. Lanzi, W. Stolzmann, and S.W. Wilson (Eds.): IWLCS 2001, LNAI 2321, pp. 23-31, 2002.

One topic of interest in the machine learning field is the rate at which learning system performance changes as problems become more difficult. A feature of the multiplexer problem that makes such studies difficult is the fact that examples are densest for sizes that are of little interest (the 3-MP and 6-MP), while the interval between standard multiplexer sizes increases rapidly from the 11-MP on. In fact, most researchers who have applied machine learning techniques to multiplexer problems have not solved a multiplexer problem larger than the 20-MP, because learning time for the 37-MP is prohibitively long, given contemporary learning algorithms and computer capabilities. (It is also the case that good XCS parameter settings for the 37-MP are different from those for the 20-MP, and very few researchers know what they are). Thus there are, in effect, only two multiplexer problems (the 11-MP and the 20-MP) that are both interesting and accessible to contemporary researchers, and there is a "parameter jump" between them and the next larger multiplexer size. Two interesting data points are not sufficient to provide a good characterization of the rate at which solution difficulty grows.

This paper addresses the problem of the paucity of interesting multiplexer instances by describing the *incremental* multiplexer problem (IMP), a generalization of the multiplexer problem that has an instance for each size greater than 1. To explain the generalization, let us first consider how the standard multiplexer works.

1.2   The Standard Multiplexer Problem

A multiplexer problem generates messages—lists of bits of length $n + 2^n$, where n is a positive integer. The *size* of a MP is the length of the messages it generates. An algorithm learning to solve a standard MP receives such messages from the MP and learns whether to respond with a "1" or a "0" to any messages it may receive. The MP decides what the correct reply is in this way:

1.   The MP treats the first n bits (called the *address bits*) of its message as the encoding of an integer in base 2. The MP converts the address bits of the message to i, the integer that the address bits encode in base 2.
2.   The MP treats the last 2^n bits (the *data bits*) of its message as a list of possible responses. Bit number i in this list is the data bit for a message with address bits encoding i in binary.
3.   If the learning algorithm provides a response equal to the value of signal bit number i, the MP provides positive reinforcement to the learning algorithm. If the learning algorithm provides a response different from the value of signal bit number i, the MP provides negative reinforcement to the learning algorithm.

Here are some examples of messages and the correct response to them for the 11-MP. (Note that 11 is of the form $3 + 2^3$, so each message generated by an 11-MP will have three address bits and eight data bits.) Note that here and in what follows, extra spaces are inserted to improve readability between the address bits and the data bits. These spaces are not represented in the signals themselves.

1 1 1   1 1 1 1 1 1 0: the 3 address bits encode 7 in base 2. The relevant data bit is the last one, so the correct response is "0". (Note that the counting starts from zero: the first data bit is bit number zero, and the last is data bit number 7).

0 1 1   1 1 1 1 0 0 0 0: the 3 address bits encode 3 in base 2. The relevant data bit is the final one of the initial block of 1s, so the correct response is "1".

0 0 1   0 1 0 1 0 1 0 1: the 3 address bits encode 1 in base 2. The relevant data bit is the first with the value of 1, so the correct response is 1.

The messages generated by a standard MP are randomly generated. A standard MP of size m will generate any message of length m with equal probability.

1.3   The Incremental Multiplexer Problem

An incremental multiplexer problem (hereafter, "IMP") is a generalization of the MP which "fills in the gaps" in size between the sizes of the messages generated by standard MPs. An IMP of size m works as follows:

1. if m is of the form $n + 2^n$, then the m-IMP works just like the standard multiplexer problem of size m. Thus, the set of MPs is a subset of the set of IMPs.
2. Otherwise, the m-IMP uses as many address bits as the next larger MP. The remaining bits are data bits.
3. To generate a message for a learning algorithm, an IMP with a address bits and d data bits does the following:
    a.   The IMP generates a random number p greater than or equal to 0 and less than d.
    b.   The IMP writes the first a bits of the message as the binary representation of p.
    c. The IMP fills the last d bits of the message with randomly-generated bits.
4. To compute the correct response to a bit string, an IMP follows the same procedure used by a standard MP: an IMP's first a bits encode an integer p, and a response to a message for such an IMP is correct if and only if the response to the message is equal to that message's signal bit number p.

Note that not all messages of length m will be generated by an m-IMP, unless m is the size of a standard MP, since the address bits will only address data bits available at that IMP's size.

Following are some examples of messages and correct responses for the 6-IMP, the 7-IMP, and the 8-IMP.

The 6-IMP:

This is a standard multiplexer with size of the form $2 + 2^2$, so its messages have two address bits and four data bits. Computation is done as for the standard 6-MP....

0 1   0 1 0 0   Address bits encode 1. The relevant data bit has the value 1.
1 1   1 0 1 0   Address bits encode 3. The relevant data bit has the value 0.
The 7-MP:

This is an IMP with size one greater than a standard MP, so this IMP has three address bits (the number of address bits for the 11-MP, the next larger MP) and four data bits (the number of remaining bits). Note that the address bits are restricted to encoding a number between 0 and 3, inclusive. The only difference between the 6-IMP and the 7-IMP is that an additional address bit has been added to the signal. The 7-IMP doesn't address any data bits that the 6-MP didn't address. In fact, the only value the new bit will take on during a run of the 7-IMP is "0".

Some examples of 7-IMP messages and correct responses:

0 0 1   0 1 0 0   The address bits encode 1. The relevant data bit has the value 1.

0 1 1   1 0 1 0   The address bits encode 3. The relevant data bit is the final one, with the value 0.

The 8-IMP:

0 0 0   1 0 0 0   The address bits encode 0. The relevant data bit has the value 1.

0 0 1   1 0 1 0   The address bits encode 1. The relevant data bit is the first with the value 0.

Table 1. Characteristics of the smallest IMPs

IMP Size	C-1*	C-2*	C-3*	Compact Solution Set Members
3 standard	8	54	4	0 0#-->0, 0 1#-->1, 1 #0-->0, and 1 #1-->1
4	8	162	4	as for 3-IMP, except "0" added at left
5	24	486	6	as for IMP-4, except "#" added at right, and two new classifiers: 10 ##0-->0 and 10 ##1-->1
6 standard	64	1458	8	as for IMP-5, except "#" added at right, and two new classifiers: 11 ###0-->0 and 11 ###1-->1
7	64	4374	8	as for 6-IMP, except "0" added at left
8	160	13122	10	as for IMP-7, except "#" added at right, and two new classifiers: 100 ####0-->0 and 100 ####1-->1
9	384	39366	12	as for IMP-8, except "#" added at right, and two new classifiers: 101 #####0-->0 and 101 #####1-->1
10	896	59049	14	as for IMP-9, except "#" added at right, and two new classifiers: 110 ######0-->0 and 110 ######1-->1
11 standard	2048	177147	16	as for IMP-10, except "#" added at right, and two new classifiers: 111 #######0-->0 and 111 #######1-->1
12	2048	531441	16	as for 11-IMP, except "0" added at left

(* C-1: Number of possible Signals; C-2: Number of Possible Classifiers; C-3: Compact Solution Set Size)

Table 1 shows various statistics about IMPs from size 3 to size 12. The first column is the IMP size, which grows by 1 as IMP size increases.

The second column in the table is the number of different messages that an m-IMP can generate. The number is $d * 2^d$, rather than 2^m, since address patterns addressing nonexistent signal bits will not occur. Thus, the number of signals possible for an IMP grows with the square of the size of the IMP.

The third column is the number of possible classifiers that could be produced to match messages from an IMP of this size. This number is $2*m^3$, since there are two possible actions, and for each position in a message, a classifier could have one of three values (0, 1, and #). Thus, the number of classifiers that could be generated to handle messages from an IMP grows with the cube of the size of the IMP.

The fourth column is the number of members of the compact solution set for XCS solving an IMP of this size. This number is two greater than the size of the compact solution set for the prior IMP except when the prior IMP was a standard MP, in which case the number is the same. Said differently, whenever a new data bit is added to an IMP, the compact solution set gains two new members, one to handle a "0" at the new position, and one to handle a "1" at the new position. Thus, the size of the compact solution set grows linearly with the size of the IMP.

The fifth column describes the growth of the set of compact classifiers. This column is a description of the compact classifiers whose count is given in the fourth column.

It is an interesting question whether a classifier system, which is capable of compacting its solutions into highly compressed sets of classifiers with perfect performance on the IMP, will have increases in run time, steps to solution, and so forth that are near-linear (like the increase in size of the compact solution sets and in the signal size), or exponential in the size of the IMP, like the rate of increase in size of the number of signals, or the rate of increase in the size of the search space of possible classifiers. The scarcity of testable points for the multiplexer problem makes this question difficult to study, since there are not enough interesting data points to determine what rate of growth in time to solution is being observed. Using the IMP, with a wider variety of interesting problems and problem sizes, researchers will be able to use their versions of XCS designed for multiplexer use to study this question in more detail.

2   Fixed-Parameter Performance of XCS on the IMP

In order to learn about the performance of XCS on IMP problems of different sizes, and to verify that increases in IMP size were correlated with increases in solution difficulty, a version of XCS with fixed parameter settings was applied to IMP problems of increasing size. The parameter settings used are similar for the most part to those published in the literature for the 11-MP, and are displayed in Table 2. In what follows, these parameter settings will be referred to as the "fixed parameter settings." It should be clearly noted that among the fixed parameter settings is the population size of XCS, which is fixed at size 2000. This size is far too small to solve IMP problems larger than the 15-IMP effectively. The results of runs on problems larger than the 15-IMP are presented only to show that, for fixed parameter settings, IMP difficulty increases for the most part as problem size increases, and IMP difficulty is consonant with the difficulty of standard MP problems. That is, the performance of XCS on IMPs transitions smoothly between its performance on MPs.

Table 2. XCS fixed parameter values

Parameter	Value
popsize	2000
learningRate	0.2
alpha	0.1
epsilonZero	1
nu	5
DiscountFactor	0.71
DiscountFactor	0.71
GAThreshold	40
CrossoverProb	0.5
MutationProb	0.03
DeletionThresholdExperience	20
DeletionThresholdFitness	0.1
SubsumptionThresholdExperience	20
CoveringDontCareProb	0.6
RandomActionChoiceProb	0.5
MinimumActionSetActions	1
DoGASubsumption	1
DoActionSetSubsumption	1
FitnessReductionCoef	0.1
ErrorReductionCoef	0.25

The version of XCS used was similar to that described in (Butz and Wilson 2001). A few inessential modifications were made to improve efficiency. These changes do not affect the results shown below.

One additional parameter used in this version of XCS that is not found in the literature is called randomActionChoiceProb. This parameter describes the relative probability that XCS will use an exploration rather than an exploitation action selection regime on a given presentation of training data. This parameter has not been given a Greek name. The practice described in Butz and Wilson (2001) and in prior work is to train XCS only on exploration steps, and track the system's performance without doing any system training on exploitation steps—those in which the action with the highest prediction is chosen. Extensive experimentation showed us that training XCS with some proportion of exploitation steps can improve performance, at least on multiplexer problems. The system used here for tests on the IMP had a randomActionChoiceProb of .5; that is, about half the time XCS updated its classifiers after a random choice of actions, and about half the time XCS updated its classifiers after choosing what it determined was the best action. To produce results for the more standard version of XCS, one would set this parameter to 1.0.

The parameter settings that will be referred to in this paper as the "fixed parameter settings" are shown in Table 2, and their performance on a range of IMP problems is shown in Figure 1.

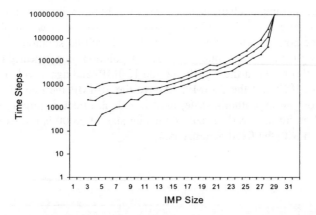

Fig. 1. Logarithmic graph of time steps to solution versus IMP size: max, min, and mean of 1,000 runs

It is an interesting question how to halt the training process when XCS is learning to solve an IMP. A number of criteria were tried, and the criterion of halting when 100 consecutive correct responses had been produced was the halting procedure used for the results reported here. The intent in choosing this halting criterion was to model a real-world situation, in which one would not know what the optimal solution is, and so would be required to use a performance criterion to halt learning. The authors intend in future work to study halting on the basis of finding some percentage of the minimal solution set for IMP problems. The set of classifiers produced using the last-100-responses-correct halting criterion sometimes does not have a large percentage of members of the minimal solution set, but it does get all of the responses right, and for real-world problems, this is a criterion that is accessible. (For real-world problems, it could be quite harmful to continue training too long after success, since there is the possibility that the machine learning system will "memorize" examples with loss of useful generality.)

Figure 1 shows the number of time steps to 100% accuracy on the last 100 exploitation presentations for XCS using the fixed parameter settings. The IMPs tested range from the 3-IMP to the 28-IMP. The figure shows the minimum number of time steps, maximum number of time steps, and mean number of time steps for each of the sets of runs of XCS at that IMP size. The data reflect 1,000 runs of XCS using the fixed parameter settings for each IMP size, except for IMP-27 and IMP-28. These results were produced in about 6 CPU-weeks for a Pentium 600MH desktop computer. The IMP-27 results consist of 300 runs, each on average over 1,000,000 time steps in duration. The IMP-28 results consist of two runs, each of which was terminated at 10,000,000 time steps, at which point both runs had recent performance in the neighborhood of 51% accuracy. The population size of 2,000 was clearly too small for XCS with the fixed parameter settings to solve the 28-IMP, and it had difficulty with the 27-IMP. For the version of XCS described here, with a population size of 2,000 and parameters as specified in Table 2, the 27-IMP is the largest IMP that can be solved in less than CPU-days. (Of course, with a larger population size, and perhaps some other parameter changes, these IMPs would be easily solved by XCS.)

Note that Figure 1 is a logarithmic graph. The final point was arbitrarily set at 10,000,000, the point at which the runs were halted with no solution. The graph has some interesting features. The rate of increase in solution time is nearly linear (on the logarithmic scale) between the 7-IMP and the 12-IMP, and again with a higher slope between the 12-IMP and the 20-IMP. Above the 20-IMP the rate of growth is no longer linear on the logarithmic scale, until it ends at effective infinity with the 28-IMP, at which point the overly small population size of 2,000 is not large enough to allow a solution with the fixed parameters.

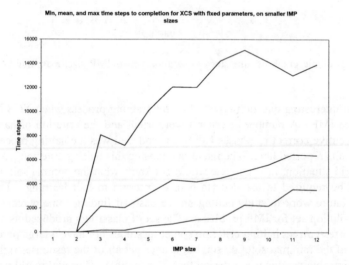

Min, mean, and max time steps to completion for XCS with fixed parameters, on smaller IMP sizes

Fig. 2. Graph of time steps to solution versus IMP size for smaller IMPs: max, min, and Mean of 1,000 runs

Note also an unexpected result occurring in the range from the 3-IMP to the 12-IMP, shown in more detail in Figure 2, which is not in logarithmic form. There we see that the IMPs that are one size larger than a standard MP (that is, the 4-IMP, the 7-IMP, and the 12-IMP) require smaller numbers of time steps to solution than the standard MPs that precede them in size. This effect is statistically significant, and it is not clear at present how to explain it. One would believe that adding a "dummy bit" whose value is always zero to the left side of each signal would slow down learning progress, or at best make learning occur at the same rate. Instead, for these smaller MP sizes, progress is faster with the dummy bit.

The purpose of applying XCS with fixed parameter settings to IMPs of different sizes was to show that the time to solution grows as the size of the IMP grows, and that the standard MP problems have times to solution that are consistent with the times to solution for the IMPs that lie between them. Aside from the anomalies just discussed, this is indeed the case. Thus, the IMP does appear to be a reasonable problem with which to study machine learning system performance as problem size increases, since there is an IMP problem for every interesting message size, and since the difficulty level of IMPs transitions smoothly between MPs.

3   Conclusions

This paper has described the incremental multiplexer problem, an extension of the classical multiplexer problem that has an instantiation at every size greater than 1. The paper has displayed empirical results demonstrating that a fixed version of XCS takes longer to solve an incremental multiplexer problem as the size of the problem increases, with the minor exception of the 4-IMP, 7-IMP, and 12-IMP. These results suggest that researchers studying the performance of their classifier systems on machine learning problems can use incremental multiplexer problems to gain better information about the responses of their system to increases in problem size.

References

1. Butz, M.V., Wilson, S.W. (2001). An Algorithmic Description of XCS. In Lanzi, P. L., Stolzmann, W., and S.W. Wilson (Eds.) Proceedings of the International Workshop on Learning Classifier System (IWLCS-2000). Springer-Verlag.
2. Wilson, S. W. Classifier Fitness Based on Accuracy. *Evolutionary Computation*, 3(2), 149-175 (1995).

A Minimal Model of Communication for a Multi-agent Classifier System

Gilles Énée and Cathy Escazut

Laboratory I3S, Les algorithmes / Bât. Euclide B
2000 Route des Lucioles - BP 121, 06903 Sophia-Antipolis CEDEX, France
{enee,escazut}@unice.fr

Abstract. Classifier systems are rule-based systems dedicated to the learning of more or less complex tasks. They evolve toward a solution without any external help. When the problem is very intricate it is useful to have different systems, each of them being in charge with an easier part of the problem. The set of all the entities responsible for the resolution of each sub-task, forms a multi-agent system. Agents have to learn how to exchange information in order to solve the main problem. In this paper, we define the minimal requirements needed by a multi-agent classifier system to evolve communication. We thus design a minimal model involving two classifier systems which goal is to communicate with each other. A measure of entropy that evaluates the emergence of a common referent between agents has been finalised. Promising results let think that this work is only the beginning of our ongoing research activity.

1 Introduction

Distributed artificial intelligence breaks complex problem into simplest ones. This decomposition into a multi-agent system involves that each agent is able to share its knowledge with the community. Two kinds of organisations can be considered: homogeneous and heterogeneous multi-agent systems [1]. In our context, agents are classifier systems. Classifier systems introduced by Holland [2] are machine learning systems using for their evolution genetic algorithms [3] . When learning is achieved, such systems know some of the best solutions and when they are integrated to an agent community in order to solve a complex task, exchanging information becomes the main difficulty to clear up. The next section of this paper describes classifier systems and multi-agent systems. The third section is devoted to the definition of the minimal model of communication we proposed. Results obtained with this minimal model are presented in section 4. Finally we discuss extensions of the model and the impacts we can expect.

2 Related Work

In this section we pay particular attention to explain how classifier systems can work while in community and overall how they can communicate.

P.L. Lanzi, W. Stolzmann, and S.W. Wilson (Eds.): IWLCS 2001, LNAI 2321, pp. 32–42, 2002.

2.1   Classifier Systems

A classifier system is a machine learning system that learns how to perform tasks having interactions with its environment. Such a system owns input sensors able to code the environment state. Based on these inputs, the system makes a choice between all the possible actions it can accomplish. The achievement of this action involves an alteration of the environment. Depending on this transformation the system is given a reward and the process is iterated.

Condition-action rules, called classifiers, are the elementary constituent of classifier systems. They are given a personal fitness that reflects their relevance in the achievement of the task. The population of a classifier system is filled with individuals. Each individual consists in one or several rules depending on the classifier system family. Usually, the condition part is defined on a ternary alphabet $\{0, 1, \#\}$, while action part is defined on a binary alphabet $\{0, 1\}$.

The general scheme of a classifier system (CS) is as follow : First, the population is randomly initialised except for the XCS described by Wilson [4] that may be empty. Then evaluation gives to each classifier a measure, named fitness, of its "usefulness" to the system. The genetic algorithm (GA) uses this fitness to evolve the population for the next generation. Thus, the GA selects parents that will be crossed-over and muted i.e. generating a new population of individuals ready to be evaluated.

The individuals of a CS are rewarded depending on their family. Hence, a Mich-style CS uses an apportionment of credit algorithm [5], a XCS-style CS uses a prediction variable and a Pitt-style CS [6] uses a collective reward.

We use a Pitt-style CS in our experimentation: an individual is a set of rules, thus solution is represented by the classifiers belonging to an individual. In other CS families solution is a population of chained individuals. Two interesting points are to be raised using a Pitt-style CS. First, the fitness will reward an individual allowing unused rules to be kept through generations. Second is that this fitness mechanism allows adaptation to more rapidly changing states [7]. This two points made us choose the Pitt-style CS.

2.2   Multi-agent Systems

Bull, Carse, and Fogarty [1] distinguished two sorts of multi-agent systems:

- Homogeneous multi-agent systems: Agents are physically identical and solve the same kind of problem.
- Heterogeneous multi-agent systems: Agents are usually physically distinct.

The decomposition of a complex problem into simple sub-tasks is insufficient if no information is exchanged between the agents. The next sub-section describes how communication can be performed within multi-agent classifier systems.

2.3   Communication

A first way to solve a problem with a multi-agent system is to use coordination [8]. As Miramontes and Fogarty developed an XCS approach [9] to the well-known "El farol" coordination problem [10], we successfully used the Pitt-style

CS [11] to solve the bar problem. Coordination can be applied to problems where other agents knowledge is not essential. When agents need much more informations from neighbours, coordination reaches its limits.

A second way to solve a problem with a multi-agent system is to use coevolution. In [12], Escazut and Fogarty used a map of traffic signals controllers to successfully test an endosymbiotic coevolution.

An other way to solve a problem with a multi-agent system is to communicate. A definition of communication has been proposed by Burghardt [13]:

"Communication is the phenomenon of one organism producing a signal that, when responded to by another organism, confers some advantage (or the statistical probability of it) to the signaller or his group."

In an earlier work, we studied how agents are able to communicate to others the knowledge they acquired. To make them force to share their learning, we have enlarged the elitism concept [14] applying it to the whole community instead of to a single agent. We then proposed the distributed elitism [15]. This mechanism can only be used with homogeneous multi-agent systems as we defined. Before establishing communication in an heterogeneous multi-agent systems, we need to study how communication emerges and how we can handle it in a minimal model of communication.

In this article we focus on the evolution of communication. We have thus defined a minimal model in order to force the communication between agents. The only task they have to learn is to communicate. The next section describes this minimal model.

3   A Minimal Model of Communication

Studying communication leads us to look at theories on the origins and evolution of language. Among the three definition proposed by Steels [16], we choosed the Baldwin approach [17] that is genetic assimilation: acquisition of language is the result of the synthesis between the genetic evolution and the individual adaptation.

3.1   Basic Principles

We stress that the unique aim of our work is to define the *minimum requirements* to have Pittsburgh-style CS agents communicating together. To study the best way the evolution of communication, we reduced the multi-agent system to two agents. All they have to do is to communicate with each other.

Each agent has a "view" of the world around it, i.e. it has a local environment. Agent cannot see other agent local environment but it needs this information in order to solve its part of the problem. Thus communication is the only way for agents to know things they cannot "see".

3.2   Agents' Structure

An agent A1 expresses its local environment using a word w_1. The agent A2 has to learn the meaning of the word w_1 so that it will correctly guess the local environment of A1.

The structure of a classifier of both communicating agent is represented in figure 1. The condition is composed of two distinct parts of two bits: the first two bits are the word read from the other agent's post. The next two bit are the real local environment of agent. The action is also composed of two parts: the first two bits are the word to post and the next two bits are the guessed local environment. A classifier is thus a 8 bits long ternary string. Each individual of an agent is a set of four classifiers, one for each possible local environment. The

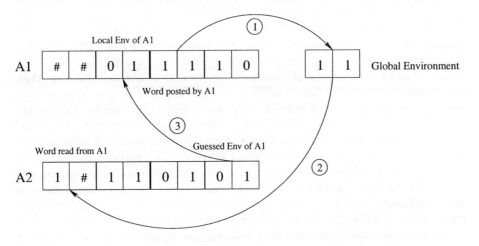

Fig. 1. A step by step communication example

basic cycle of a Pitt-style classifier system has only two steps: (1) the evaluation of the population, (2) the evolution of the population thanks to a genetic algorithm. Individuals are paired for evaluation, simply by taking the corresponding member from each agent, in other words the first individual from A1 is paired with the first individual from A2 etc. Individuals in the populations are not ordered in any way. Thus the coupling is randomly performed. Communication is performed in both directions: A1 tries to guess the local environment of A2 and vice-versa. This step is realised several times, i.e. trials, in order to test different classifiers within the individuals. Whenever the communication is done, both communicating individuals are given a shared reward if the local environment has been successfully guessed.

To communicate, agents post and read words via a global environment. Figure 1 describes a step by step example illustrating the evaluation mechanism and a successful communication: A1 chooses one of the four classifiers of the individual being evaluated and then posts the corresponding word 11 in the global environment. In its lexicon, 11 means that its local environment is 01. A2 reads the word from the global environment, and chooses in the individual which is being evaluated, the classifier to activate. If several rules match, the first of the more specialised ones will be chosen. Depending on this classifier, A2 deduces that when A1 "says" 11, this means that its local environment is 01.

3.3   Measurements

In our application, the fitness of individuals is a direct measure since it is computed from the number of times that two agents understand each other. However, we used results of the theory of communication [18] to analyse the establishment of a common referent between both agents.

MacLennan [19] studied simulated organisms called *simorg*. Each simorg consists in a deterministic automata which is able to communicate and to learn. They live in a synthetic world. The aim was to study how communication and learning influence communication rate. MacLennan constructs during the last 50 generations of the simulation a so-called denotation matrix [20] . This data structure has an entry for each read word/guessed local environment pair, that is incremented whenever the situation corresponding to this pair appears. We assume that the number of possible read words equals the number of possible guessed local environments. MacLennan underlines two noteworthy denotation matrixes. The uniform matrix translates that the pairs occurred in a haphazard fashion, that is to say with an equal frequency i.e. agents are not able to communicate. The ideal matrix represents the case where agents are able to understand each other: whatever the word read, the local environment is guessed in the right way. In such a matrix each row and each column has a single nonzero entry. There is a bijection between the set of the possible read words and the set of the possible local environments. Measuring the dispersion of the denotation matrix should be a good evaluation of the amount of information transmitted between agents. MacLennan chooses the entropy as a measure of the dispersion of the denotation matrix :

$$H = -\sum_{i,j} p_{ij} \; log_2(p_{ij}) \tag{1}$$

We choosed to modify the measure[1] as follow :

Old	New
$p_{ij} = \frac{M_{ij}}{\sum_{k,l} M_{kl}}$	$p_{ij} = \frac{M_{ij}}{\sum_k M_{kj} + \sum_l M_{il} - M_{ij}}$
$H_U = 2log_2(N)$	$H_U^* = \frac{N^2}{2N-1} log_2(2N-1)$
$H_I = log_2(N)$	$H_I^* = 0$

Where M_{ij} is the element of row i and column j in the denotation matrix. The new measure takes only into account the pairs of the denotation matrix

---

[1] We note H^* our measure of entropy and H the original MacLennan's measure.

belonging to the same row and the same column. With previous measure the following matrix will be considered as ideal :

Local Environment

		00	01	10	11
W	00	3	0	0	0
o	01	3	0	0	0
r	10	3	0	0	0
d	11	3	0	0	0

It is obvious that this resulting denotation matrix cannot distinct one local environment with a word. New measure will not consider such a matrix ideal but noisy. The following formula will give the communication success rate :

$$Comm\_S = (1 - \frac{H - H_I}{H_U - H_I}) \times 100 \qquad (2)$$

The following table compares communication success rates obtained in each of MacLennan and Burghardt first experiments :

Experimentation	$Comm\_S$	$Comm\_S^*$
No com. nor learning	8.50%	10.50%
Com. and no learning	51.25%	48.89%
Com. and learning	63.25%	50.75%

Both measure have the same behaviour. The new one only detects better false communication.

4   Experiments

Agents initial population is randomly generated and evolves thanks to a genetic algorithm. The first experiment we made is the direct implementation of the minimal model of communication thus communicating agent rule will be chosen randomly in order to maximise communication. In the second one we apply the model to robots which have to communicate each other their position in order to meet and stay together thus communicating agent rule will be chosen using the current robot position, bounding communication.

4.1   Implementation of the Minimal Model

An agent has to guess the local environment of the other one from a posted word. There are four possible words and four possible local environments. Entropy will be computed from 4x4 denotation matrixes. The population of each classifier system has 14 individuals which are composed of four classifiers. The evaluation of an individual is computed over 10 trials in order to give all the rules the opportunity to be activated. The first of the more specific rules is always taken to communicate i.e. with less wildcards. The whole system is run for 1000 generations. The genetic algorithm used is the most standard one: individual selection is made using roulette wheel, the single point crossover operator is applied with a 60% probability and the allelic mutation operator has a 0.05% probability. There is also a 14.30% of elitism.

Results are averaged over 100 experiments differing in random seed. Figure 2 plots the evolution of fitness and communication through generations. At the end of experimentation communication success is 93.77% and fitness is about 0.99. In less than 200 generations both fitness and communication success has attained such a level that we can state that agents are able to understand each other. If we look closer at the last populations of each agent, one can notice

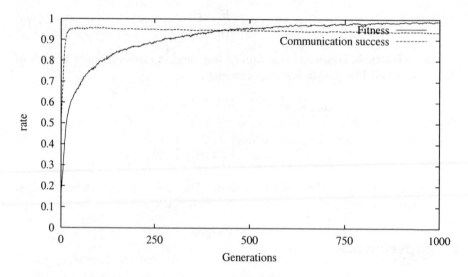

Fig. 2. Evolution of fitness and communication success for the minimal model

that they are homogeneous: they contain 14 almost identical individuals. As an example, here are those individuals for one of the performed experiments:

	Agent 1		Agent 2
C_1	*1 01 : 01 00	C_1'	10 00 : 01 11
C_2	0* 11 : 00 10	C_2'	*0 10 : 10 11
C_3	*0 01 : 01 10	C_3'	01 10 : 10 01
C_4	0* 11 : 10 11	C_4'	1* 00 : 01 01

Here are the resulting communication possibilities:

	Word sent	Guessed env.	Real env.
	00	11 (C_2')	11
A1	01	01 (C_3')	01
	10	11 (C_1',C_2') 01 (C_4')	11
	01	00 (C_1) 11 (C_2,C_4)	00
A2	10	10 (C_3)	10

Agents have learnt the meaning of three words: 00, 01 and 10. When A1 posts the word 10 in the global environment, A2 can thus activate classifiers C_1', C_2' and C_4'. The two last will not be chosen because of their low specificity. C_1' supposes that the environment of A1 is 11, which is true. Both individuals of each agent will be rewarded for this communication success.

Taking into consideration these two individuals and the fact that we always choose the first of the more specific rules, whatever the word an agent posts, the other agent is able to guess the right local environment.

These results are encouraging and lead us to make an other experiment applying the minimal model to two Khepera robots.

4.2 Adaptation of the Minimal Communication Model to a Khepera Robots Simulator

Khepera is a five centimetres diameter robot. It has height infrared sensors, two motors. We tested our minimal communication model with the Khepera Simulator [21].

To simplify the problem, we define a four positions circle-shaped world 3. Robots can go to any other spot in a single move. These positions are defined as the cardinal points on the circle and are the two bits local environment of the agents. A robot guesses where is the other one. This guess is based on the word placed in the global environment by the neighbour. The first robot moves to the guessed position and will be rewarded at the level of the accuracy of its guess. The difference between both experimentations lies on the fact that there is no randomly chosen rules, rules selection is directly linked with real position of the robot. A robot chooses the word it sends among the rules that have their local environment part matching its real position. Then, the rules that can be activated by the neighbour robot depends not only on the read word but also on real position, which is harder to happen. As an example, let us have a look at Figure 3 representing the current position of both robots. Their respective individuals are:

	K 1		K 2
C_1	11 00 : 01 00	C_1'	01 10 : 01 00
C_2	11 01 : 10 00	C_2'	10 00 : 10 01
C_3	10 01 : 10 00	C_3'	10 10 : 11 11
C_4	01 10 : 11 10	C_4'	11 01 : 10 10

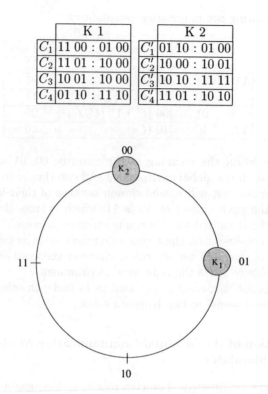

Fig. 3. The simulated world of Kheperas

Assuming it is K_1's turn to post a word: its position is 01, it thus chooses classifier C_2 and posts 10 in the global environment. K_2 reads the posted word and as its position is 00, K_2 chooses the rule C_2'. It thus supposes that K_1 is in position 01 and moves to this point. K_2 and K_1 are both rewarded because K_2 has well guessed K_1's position. Then it is K_2's turn to post a word: from the new position, K_2 posts 10 using C_4'. The reading of K_2's word 10 and K_1's position 01 make rule C_3 to be activated. As a result, K_1 moves to the guessed position: 00. Unfortunately, K_2 is not here but it is near, so K_1 and K_2 will be half rewarded due to the reward function which is distance dependant:

$$Reward = 1 - \frac{|Pos(TestedRobot) - Pos(OtherRobot)|}{Dist_{Max}} \qquad (3)$$

Each robot is evaluated 20 times per generation on a total of 200 generations. We average our results upon 20 experiments. Mutation rate is 0.1%. The other parameters are the same we used. Figure 4 plots the evolution of communication success through the generations. At the end of the experimentation, the averaged communication is about: 83.60%. This result is encouraging with only a ten point rate difference with previous experimentation at the same generation. The way the rules that put the word in the global environment are selected explains this difference. This high level of communication success let us conclude that there is communication established between the two robots i.e. they are able in most cases to "know" where is the other robot by using their own glossary.

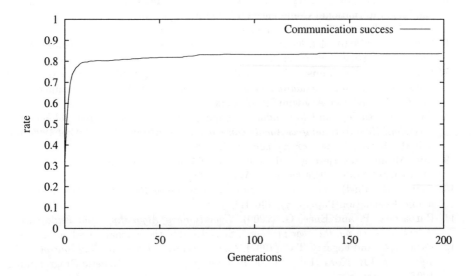

Fig. 4. Evolution of communication success for the communicating Kheperas

5   Conclusion

In this paper, we have shown that a *as simple as possible* model of communication successfully evolves in a Pittsburgh-style classifier multi-agents system. Our evolution of communication success measure, i.e. entropy, behave well and seems to be robust. This model can be easily extended by increasing agents / words number or local environment states for example. We have just applied with success [22] this model to another kind of classifier system described above : the XCS. We are currently working on three agents based extension. In this framework, we are studying communication parameters influence on communication success.

References

1. Bull, L., Carse, B., and Fogarty, T.C. (1995). *Evolving Multi-Agent Systems*. In Genetic Algorithms in Engineering and Computer Science, Periaux J. and Winter G., editors.
2. Holland, J.H. (1986). *Escaping the brittleness: The possibilities of general purpose learning algorithms applied to parallel rule-based systems*. In Mitchell, Michalski, and Carbonell (Ed.): Machine learning, an artificial intelligence approach, vol. II, chapter 20, pp. 593-623. Morgan Kaufmann.

3. Goldberg, D.E. (1989). *Genetic algorithms in search, optimisation, and machine learning*. Reading, MA: Addison-Wesley.
4. Wilson, S.W. (1995). *Classifier fitness based on accuracy*. Evolutionary Computation, 3(2), pp. 149-175.
5. Holland, J.H. (1985). *Properties of the bucket brigade algorithm*. Proceedings of the First International Conference on Genetic Algorithms and their Applications, pp. 1-7, Hillsdale, New Jersey: Lawrence Erlbaum Associates.
6. Smith, S.F. (1980). *A learning system based on genetic adaptive algorithms*. PhD. thesis. University of Pittsburgh.
7. Grefenstette, J.J. Ramsey, C. L., and Schultz, A. C. (1990). *Learning sequential decision rules using simulation models and competition*. Machine Learning, 5(4), pp. 357-381. Kluwer Academic Publishers.
8. Sudhir K. Rustogi and Munindar P. Singh (1999). *Be Patient and Tolerate Imprecision: How Autonomous Agents can Coordinate Effectively*. In IJCAI 1999, pp. 512-519. http://citeseer.nj.nec.com/237985.html
9. Luis Miramontes Hercog and Terence C. Fogarty (2000). *XCS-based Inductive Multi-Agent System*. Presented to IWLCS2000.
10. Arthur, B. (1994). *Inductive Reasoning and Bounded Rationality*. American Economic Association Papers, 84, 406-411.
11. Barbaroux, P. and Énée, G. (2000). *Evolutionary Algorithms and Endogeneous Adaptive Learning: the "bar problem"*. Submitted to the journal: Mind and Society.
12. Escazut, C. and Fogarty, T.C. (1997). *Coevolving classifier systems to control traffic signals*. In J.R. Koza (Ed.): "Late breaking papers book", Genetic Programming 1997 Conference.
13. Burghardt, G.M. (1970). *Defining "Communication"*. In J.W. Johnston, Jr., D.G. Moulton, and A. Turk (Ed.): Communication by Chemical Signals, pp. 5-18. New York, NY: Appleton-Century-Crofts.
14. De Jong, K.A. (1975). *An analysis of the behaviour of a class of genetic adaptive systems*. PhD Thesis. University of Michigan.
15. Énée, G. and Escazut, C. (1999). *Classifier Systems: Evolving multi-agent system with distributed elitism*. Proceedings of the 1999 Congress on Evolutionary Computation, pp. 1740-1746, IEEE Press, Washington D.C.
16. Steels, L. (1997). *The synthetic modeling of language origins*. Evolution of Communication Journal, 1(1), pp. 1-34.
17. Hinton, G. and Nowlan, S. (1987). *How learning can guide evolution*. Complex Systems, Vol. 1, pp. 495-502.
18. Shannon, C.E. and Weaver, W. (1949). *The mathematical theory of communication*. University of Illinois Press, Urbana, Ill.
19. MacLennan, B.J. and Burghardt, G.M. (1994). *Synthetic ethology and the evolution of cooperative communication*. Adaptive Behavior, 2(2), Fall 1993, pp. 161-188. MIT Press.
20. MacLennan, B. (1999). *The emergence of communication through synthetic evolution*. To appear in Honavar, V. Patel, M., and Balakrishnan K. (Ed.): Advances in evolutionary synthesis of neural systems. MIT Press.
21. Michel, O. (1995). Khepera simulator homepage: http://diwww.epfl.ch/lami/team/michel/khep-sim/
22. Énée, G. and Escazut, C. (2001). *A Minimal Model of Communication for Multi-Agent Systems*. To appear in the proceedings of the 8th IEEE International Conference on Emerging Technologies and Factory Automation, Antibes France.

A Representation for Accuracy-Based Assessment of Classifier System Prediction Performance

John H. Holmes

Center for Clinical Epidemiology and Biostatistics
University of Pennsylvania School of Medicine
Philadelphia, PA 19104 USA
jholmes@cceb.med.upenn.edu

Abstract. The increasing use of learning classifier systems (LCS) in data mining necessitates a methodology for improving the assessment of predictive accuracy at both the individual classifier and system levels. A metric, predictive value, is used extensively in clinical diagnosis and medical decision making, and is easily adapted to the LCS to facilitate assessing the ability of individual classifiers used as rules to predict class membership. This metric can also be used to assess the ability of a trained LCS to predict the class of unseen cases. Positive and predictive values were incorporated into an existing LCS model, EpiCS, and applied to 6-Multiplexer data and a sample data set drawn from a large hospitalization survey. The predictive performance of EpiCS on the hospitalization data was shown to be comparable to that of logistic regression and decision tree induction.

1 Introduction

As Learning Classifier Systems (LCS) are used more frequently in data mining, it is important to consider ways in which the information represented by the classifier population can be visualized and subsequently used for such purposes as decision making and modeling. Up to now, the classifier population has been considered primarily to be an internal feature of LCS. Rather than a source of information about the environment modeled by the LCS, the population has been viewed as a necessary means to make accurate predictions or decisions. This is an incomplete way of using the population, however, as many users want to examine one or more classifiers as IF..THEN rules, with associated metrics that describe the accuracy of these rules in explanation and prediction, two common tasks in data mining. This work describes an extension to an existing LCS design, EpiCS, that allows the assessment of the performance of each classifier in the population by incorporating two metrics traditionally associated with the evaluation of clinical diagnostic tests [2]. These metrics are the positive and negative *predictive values*. The rationale for this approach is found in the untapped potential use of classifiers as rule-based knowledge structures that can be visualized and assessed by naïve users.

P.L. Lanzi, W. Stolzmann, and S.W. Wilson (Eds.): IWLCS 2001, LNAI 2321, pp. 43-56, 2002.
© Springer-Verlag Berlin Heidelberg 2002

1.1   Predictive Value

In any two-class classification problem evaluated by a single test, there are four possible classifications, as shown in the confusion matrix in Figure 1.

Classification decision made by the test system	Classification decision known to be true ("gold standard")	
	Positive	Negative
Positive	*True positives*	*False positives*
Negative	*False negatives*	*True negatives*

Fig. 1. Confusion matrix for a two-class problem evaluated with a single test. The columns represent the number of classifications that are known to be true. The rows represent the number of classifications that have been made by a system that is under evaluation

In this matrix, classifications made by a test system (such as a diagnostic test, or an LCS) are compared with those made by another system or procedure taken as the "gold standard." The gold standard is known to be optimally accurate; an autopsy might be an example of a gold standard in certain diseases.

True positive classifications are those in which the system has classified a case as positive, and the case is a known positive according to the gold standard. Likewise, a known-negative case classified as a negative by the test system is a true negative. The discordant cells in the matrix represent false positive or false negative classifications. In these, cases have been classified as positive or negative, respectively, in direct opposition to their known classification.

A number of accuracy metrics, commonly used in clinical diagnosis, can be calculated from the matrix shown in Figure 1, and several of these have been discussed in detail elsewhere [4]. Two other metrics that are of particular interest are the *predictive values*. A predictive value is a metric that indicates the probability of the presence or absence of a disease (or other outcome), given a specific test result; for this reason, it is generally referred to as the *posttest*, or *posterior, probability* of disease. There are two predictive values, positive and negative, each expressed as a proportion or probability, with a range of 0 to 1. *Positive predictive value* (PPV) is the probability of a true classification, given a positive classification made by a test system. In clinical terms, the positive predictive value tells a physician the probability that a disease or other outcome is actually present, given a positive test result. The positive predictive value is calculated as:

$$\text{Positive Predictive Value} = \frac{\text{True Positives}}{\text{True Positives} + \text{False Positives}} \tag{1}$$

Similarly, the *negative predictive value* (NPV) is calculated as:

$$\text{Negative Predictive Value} = \frac{\text{True Negatives}}{\text{True Negatives} + \text{False Negatives}} \qquad (2)$$

It is important to note that the predictive values are influenced by the prevalence of an outcome. For example, if the outcome of interest is rare, then even if all positive cases were detected, the positive predictive value would be very low. Conversely, the negative predictive value will be very low in situations where the positive class is more prevalent than the negative.

A confusion matrix with the cells populated with counts of classification decisions is shown in Figure 2. These results will yield a positive predictive value of 0.95 (or 81/81+4) and a negative predictive value of 0.63 (92/55+92).

Classification decision made by the test system	Classification decision known to be true ("gold standard")	
	Positive	Negative
Positive	81	4
Negative	55	92

Fig. 2. Confusion matrix for evaluating a new test to detect a disease

These values can be interpreted as follows: using the test shown in Figure 2, if one has obtained a positive test result, then the probability that the test has accurately predicted a positive result is 0.95. In clinical terms, if the test returns positive, there is a 95% probability that the patient actually has the disease or outcome that the test is supposed to detect. The converse applies to a negative test result: there is a 63% probability that the patient does not have the disease. These results indicate that this test is very predictive of a positive outcome and therefore very useful in assessing the presence of disease, but is a poor predictor of the absence of disease. See [2] for more complete details on the predictive values.

1.2   Applying the Predictive Values to LCS

While the predictive values have been used extensively in medical diagnosis and signal detection, they offer a natural approach to assessing the ability of a classifier to predict class membership. Each classifier in the population after training represents a miniature diagnostic test, in that it can be applied to an unknown case to determine its class. Like any diagnostic test, a classifier has an implicit predictive accuracy, which is made explicit in the predictive values. With a population of classifiers in hand, the predictive values might serve the user with a metric for determining which to consider as accurate decision rules. While it would be interesting to use predictive values as a proxy for strength, similar to the way accuracy is used in XCS [10], the focus of this investigation is on using the predictive values as a means to evaluating the accuracy of classifiers extant in the population after training.

The first consideration is where the predictive values fit into the representation of the classifier. The most appropriate structure would include both the positive and the negative predictive values as separate metrics, attached to each classifier, just like any other "slot" like fitness, accuracy, or experience. The magnitude of the predictive values will depend upon how well the classifier predicts positive or negative cases, but one of the values will always be zero, depending on the value of the classifier's action bit. For example, the negative predictive value will always be 0 for a classifier with a positive that classifies positive, while the positive predictive value will always be 0 for one with an action that classifies negative. The reason for this is the way classifiers are admitted to the Action Set from the Match Set during training, which is based on matching classifier actions to the classification of a training case. The classifiers that advocate a positive action will cease to have any negative predictive value, for they will be penalized for doing so. Although not investigated here, a scheme that uses the predictive values for creating Action Sets is discussed below in Section 4.

Once installed on the classifier representation, the predictive values can be used in several domains of the LCS. These include determining membership in the Correct Set, identifying classifiers for selection or deletion under the genetic algorithm, and using the classifiers in the population after training as visual rule representations according to their predictive accuracy. However, the focus of this investigation is on the use of the predictive values to assess the predictive accuracy of individual classifiers in the population after training, and the overall predictive accuracy of the trained LCS when it is used as a rule-based classification system. The first is important in evaluating, with a specific classifier in hand, whether or not its prediction (positive or negative) is accurate. The second is important because it is essential to know whether or not a classification of an unseen case by a trained LCS is accurate, and the predictive values perform this function.

This work examines the use of such an approach to LCS design in a supervised learning environment using a two-class classification problem.

2   Methods

2.1   Data

Two data sources were used for this investigation. The first was a simple 6-Multiplexer (6MUX) dataset consisting of 64 unique instances, each representing a solution to the multiplexer problem. This data set was used to illustrate clearly the properties of the predictive values during and after training. Two copies of the data were used, one as a training set, the other for testing.

The source of the second dataset was the National Inpatient Sample (NIS) [9], a database of over 7 million United States hospital admissions occurring over a one-year period (1997) in 22 states. This database consists of several tables, addressing the admission event, diagnosis, therapeutic or diagnostic procedure, cost data, and weighting data. Only the admission and diagnosis data were used, as this study did not require a statistical analysis of weighted data.

The focus of this investigation is on the features of the admission that predicted death as an outcome. Specifically, these features were limited to 17 diagnosis categories, each coded dichotomously (0=Absent, 1=Present). The outcome, Death, was coded in the same way. In the NIS database , the diagnosis data are represented as the ICD-9-CM codes [6]. The diagnosis categories were created using the ICD-9-CM classification scheme. Each hospital admission record was linked via a unique identifier to one or more records in the diagnosis table, and the latter were scanned for ICD-9 codes that fell into one of the 16 categories. Upon finding codes that matched a given category, the appropriate diagnosis category indicator was set to 1 in the admission record. No attempt was made to quantify the number of times a diagnosis falling into a given category was found for a given admission, as the diagnostic category variables were intended to serve merely as indicators of the absence or presence of a disease for the admission. The diagnosis categories are shown in Figure 3, in the order in which they appear in the data.

1	Neoplasms	9	Genitourinary
2	Endocrine	10	Obstetrical
3	Blood	11	Dermatologic
4	Psychiatric	12	Musculoskeletal
5	Neurological	13	Congenital
6	Circulation	14	Other diseases
7	Pulmonary	15	Injuries or poisonings
8	Gastrointestinal	16	Medication errors

Fig. 3. The 16 diagnosis categories created from the NIS database and used as predictors in this investigation

After creating and updating the diagnosis categories, a total of 2,000 admission records were selected randomly from the main NIS database. Care was taken to ensure an equal number of outcome-positive and outcome-negative cases. The smaller database was then divided randomly into training and testing sets of 1,000 records, each of which contained 500 positive and 500 negative cases. Care was taken to ensure that the training and testing sets were mutually exclusive.

2.2   EpiCS

System Description. EpiCS [3] is a stimulus-response LCS employing the NEWBOOLE model [1]. It was developed to meet the unique demands of classification and knowledge discovery in epidemiologic data. The distinctive features of EpiCS include algorithms for controlling under- and over-generalization of data, a methodology for determining risk as a measure of classification [4], and the ability to use differential negative reinforcement of false positive and false negative errors in classification during training. EpiCS was further modified accommodate prevalence-based bootstrapping [5].

Developed to work in clinical data environments for explanatory and predictive rule discovery, EpiCS includes a variety of features such as risk assessment and metrics for system performance that derive from those used commonly in clinical decision making. These metrics, which quantify detection accuracy, include sensitivity and specificity, which are prior probabilities. They indicate the probability that a test is accurate in detecting positive and negative cases, respectively. The sensitivity and specificity can be combined into a single metric, the area under the receiver operating characteristic curve, which assists in determining the tradeoff between detection of positive versus negative cases. These metrics can be used to quantify the performance of individual classifiers in the population, thereby indicating to users how strong or weak each is in its role of classifying unknown cases. EpiCS was further enhanced to facilitate the assessment of the predictive accuracy of its classifiers and the system as a whole.

System Enhancement. Three enhancements were made to EpiCS for this investigation. First, the classifier population was restructured to handle the macroclassifier paradigm used in XCS. This has the effect of decreasing the number of distinct (but not unique, classifiers in the population, representing multiple instances using a numerosity parameter. As a result, search time is decreased in creating match sets, and updating of various classifier-related parameters is facilitated. Each macroclassifier, herewith called *classifier* for simplicity, contained a *numerosity* parameter, which holds the number of instances of that classifier in the population.

Second, the classifier structures were modified to include slots for positive and negative predictive values. These metrics supplemented the action in the traditional classifier representation; in practice, they were used to determine a classifier's predictive accuracy, while the action bit was used to determine the actual classification advocated by the classifier. The predictive accuracy was based on the value of the performance metrics vis a vis a predetermined threshold value. The threshold value would have to be met or exceeded for a predictive value in order for that value to be considered predictive. For example, if a classifier had a positive predictive value of 0.89, and the threshold was set at 0.75, then that classifier would be considered a good predictor of positives. If the threshold were set at 0.90, then the classifier's predictive accuracy would be weak, in terms of predicting positives. It is important to remember that there are two predictive values, one for negative, and one for positive, and that a classifier cannot have values greater than 0 for both. Given a dichotomous action, a classifier predicts either positively or negatively; the use of predictive values allows a gradient of positivity or negativity to be used in assessing the predictive accuracy of a classifier, rather than the single dichotomous action bit.

Third, an evaluation component was added to EpiCS so that the predictive values were updated regularly. This was accomplished by testing each classifier in the population against each case in the training set, but in a way that is the opposite of the way LCS are typically evaluated. Ordinarily, classifications are advocated by the LCS, and these are based on Match Sets that are culled from classifiers with taxa that match input cases. The metrics that are appropriate to this operation are *prior* probabilities, and quite useful for detection, as described above. However, in order to determine the predictive values, which are *posterior* probabilities, the matching operations must be used in the opposite manner. In this operation, all cases in the training set with taxa that match a given classifier are admitted to a special Match Set that is used only for determining the predictive values. The predictive values are then calculated from the tallies of the true positive, true negative, false positive, and false negative classifications.

2.3   Experimental Procedure

Training.   For the 6MUX experiments, EpiCS was trained over 5,000 iterations, while 20,000 iterations were used for training in the NIS data. At each iteration, the system was presented with a single training case. As training cases were drawn randomly from the training set with replacement, it could be assumed that the system would be exposed to all such cases with equal probability over the course of the 5,000 iterations of the training epoch. At the 0th and every 100th iteration thereafter, the learning ability of EpiCS was evaluated by presenting the taxon of every case in the training set, in sequence, to the system for classification. The decision advocated by EpiCS for a given testing case was compared to the known classification of the training case. The threshold was set at 0.95 for both positive and negative predictive values. The decision type was classified in one of four categories: true positive, true negative, false positive, and false negative, and tallied for each classifier. From the four decision classifications, classification accuracy metrics (sensitivity, specificity, and area under the receiver operating characteristic curve) were calculated and written to a file for analysis. In addition, the predictive values were calculated as described above in Section 2.2.

Testing.   After the completion of the designated number of iterations of the training epoch, EpiCS entered the *testing epoch*, in which the final learning state of the system was evaluated using every case in the testing set, each presented only once in sequence. As in the interim evaluation phase, the reinforcement component, and the genetic algorithm, were disabled during the testing phase. At the completion of the testing phase, the outcome measures were calculated and written to a file for analysis, as was done during the interim evaluations. The entire cycle of training and testing, over the 5,000 or 20,000 iterations, as appropriate to the experiments, comprised a single *trial*; a total of 20 trials were performed for this investigation for the 6MUX and the NIS experiments.

Parameterization.   The major EpiCS parameters used in this investigation were: crossover probability, 0.50; mutation probability, 0.001; invocations of the genetic algorithm at each iteration, 4; penalty factor, 0.95. The population sizes were fixed at 400 for the 6MUX experiments and 20,000 for the NIS experiments; the former is a commonly accepted population size for the 6MUX environment, while the latter was determined empirically to be optimal for the NIS data. All parameter settings were determined empirically to be the optimal settings for these data.

System Evaluation.   This investigation focused on two aspects of the LCS: the macrostate population (the population at the end of training), specifically the predictive accuracy of individual classifiers, and the predictive accuracy of the system overall at the completion of training (but prior to exposure to testing cases. After training, the macrostate populations were examined qualitatively for rules that seemed to make good intuitive sense, given the data.   This examination considered the composition of the classifier, such as the specificity of certain "key" features, as well as the values of the positive and negative predictive values. In the experiments using the HCUP data, stepwise logistic regression and decision tree induction were applied to the training set for rule discovery. The same data were used for these evaluation methods as well as the EpiCS trials.

In order to create the logistic model, all of the diagnostic category variables were considered as candidate terms in a forward stepwise model.   Interactions were assessed by means of bivariate analysis; no significant interactions were found. The p-value to enter the regression model was relaxed to 0.99 to ensure that all terms entered.   A final model was built, restricting the p-value to enter to 0.07.   The content and predictive accuracy of the rules discovered by these methods were compared with those evolved by EpiCS.

The See5 program [7] was used to induce decision trees and then rules from the HCUP training data. Boosting for 10 trials and 10-fold cross-validation were used to optimize the classification accuracy.

3   Results

3.1   6-Multiplexer Experiments

The results of the 6-Multiplexer experiments are shown below in Tables 1, 2, and 3.

Table 1.   Maximally general classifiers from the macrostate after training on 6-Multiplexer data for 5,000 iterations

Classifier	PPV	NPV
000***:0	0.00	1.00
001***:1	1.00	0.00
01*0**:0	0.00	1.00
01*1**:1	1.00	0.00
10**0*:1	0.00	1.00
10**1*:1	1.00	0.00
11***0:0	0.00	1.00
11***1:1	1.00	0.00

Table 1 shows the maximally general classifiers in the macrostate of one of the 20 trials chosen at random.   These classifiers all had high numerosity and comprised 95.8% of the population.   The remaining 4.2% was composed of "singleton" classifiers, or those with numerosity of 1. At the end of training over 5,000 iterations, all of the classifiers in the population were accurate. As can be seen in Table 1, the predictive values of these classifiers exceed the respective thresholds (0.95), indicating that, as rules, they predict class membership with maximal accuracy.

Several singleton classifiers are shown in Table 2. Note that the predictive values for these classifiers are 0.5, indicating that they predict class membership as accurately as a toss of a coin. Inspection of the classifiers themselves shows why this is so. For example, in the first classifier, the two address bits (01) indicate that the second data bit should be read. The value of this data bit is *, which can be interpreted as either 0 *or* 1. Regardless of the class associated with this classifier (in this case, 1), the predictive value would be 0.50. That is, if this classifier advocated an action of 0, its negative predictive value would likewise be 0. In this case, though, the class is 1, so this value is assigned to the positive predictive value.

Table 2. Sample singleton classifiers from the macrostate after training

Classifier	PPV	NPV
01**1*:1	0.50	0.00
101***:1	0.50	0.00
101**0:0	0.00	0.50
01***0:0	0.00	0.50

The predictive values calculated at the end of training, using the training set data, are consistent with the macrostate findings shown in Table 1. Both the negative and positive predictive values were 1.00 (1 S.D.=0.0) averaged over the 20 trials. These results indicate that the trained EpiCS macrostate population has maximal accuracy for predicting membership in either of the two classes.

3.2   National Inpatient Survey Data

The results of the experiments using the National Inpatient Survey (NIS) data are shown in Tables 3 and 4.

Table 3. Sample classifiers with high predictive accuracy, taken from the macrostate after training with NIS data

Classifier	PPV	NPV
11*00*10**0***0*:1	1.00	0.00
01**1**0*01*:1	1.00	0.00
1****0**000*00**:1	0.88	0.00
00**1*01*0*0****:0	0.00	1.00
00**1*01*0*0****:0	0.00	1.00
01*1*10*000*0***:0	0.00	0.85

The classifiers in Table 3 were of high numerosity (N>30) compared to the others in the population. As can be seen in the table, the predictive values were high for these classifiers, even though two of them failed to exceed the predictive value thresholds. However, a substantial number of classifiers (~200) with low numerosity (N<5) but with high predictive values were found in the population after training. Thus, numerosity alone may not be a good indicator of the importance of a classifier in terms of predictive value.

The classifiers in this table can be transcribed to IF..THEN rules, as shown in the following example for the first classifier. Refer to Figure 3 for the locations and names of the individual features.

IF	Neoplasm=Yes	AND
	Endocrine=Yes	AND
	Psychiatric=No	AND
	Neurologic=No	AND
	Pulmonary=Yes	AND
	Gastrointestinal=No	AND
	Dermatologic=No	AND
	Injury/Poison=No	
THEN	Death=Yes, Predictive value=1.00	

This rule is consistent with those produced by applying logistic regression and decision tree induction to the training set. In fact, the rules predicting death that were discovered by these methods included Neoplasm, Endocrine, Circulatory, and Pulmonary as antecedents more often than any other features. A similar pattern was persistent in the EpiCS population after training.

Now that a predictive value has been calculated for this rule, it informs the user as to how certain she can be that the rule accurately predicts class membership (in this case, death). Thus, this rule could be applied to an individual who is positive for the three diagnosis categories (Neoplasm, Endocrine, and Pulmonary), and the user would be confident that the rule is accurate in predicting the outcome, Death.

Table 4. Sample classifiers with poor predictive accuracy, taken from the macrostate after training with NIS data

Classifier	PPV	NPV
*1000110**0*000*:1	0.71	0.00
*10001*0**0**0**:1	0.64	0.00
1**00*010*:1	0.27	0.00
011*0*100*0***0*:0	0.00	0.75
0*0*1101**1***0*:0	0.00	0.50
011*01*1**0*000*:0	0.00	0.39

Table 4 shows six sample classifiers taken from the trained population that failed to meet the predictive value thresholds. Relative to other classifiers in the population after training, those shown in Table 4 were of low numerosity. No classifiers with low predictive values, either positive or negative, had a numerosity greater than 5.

The classifiers in Table 4 can be transcribed into IF..THEN rules, as was shown above:

IF	Psychiatric=Yes	AND
	Pulmonary=No	AND
	Gastrointestinal=No	AND
	Obstetric=No	AND
	Dermatologic=Yes	AND
	Injury/Poison=No	
THEN	Death=Yes, Positive predictive value=0.27	

In the third classifier, Psychiatric and Dermatologic diagnoses were considered predictive of death, yet the PPV was very low. This is not surprising, since bivariate and multivariate statistical analyses of these two features compared with the outcome showed that they were not predictive of death. In addition, none of the rules induced by See5 showed this relationship; rather, these two features were shown to be associated with a negative outcome. One would have decreased confidence in applying this rule predict a positive outcome in an individual who was positive for these two diagnoses.

The results obtained at the end of training with the NIS data, averaged over 20 trials indicated that the EpiCS system was mediocre in predicting membership in either of the two classes. However, EpiCS performed comparably to logistic regression and See5.

Table 5. Predictive accuracy of EpiCS after training, compared with logistic regression and decision tree induction. The predictive values for EpiCS are averaged over the 20 trials; standard deviation is shown in parentheses

	PPV	NPV
EpiCS	0.77 (0.06)	0.81 (0.07)
Logistic regression	0.75	0.77
Decision tree induction (See 5)	0.60	0.78

4   Discussion

This investigation demonstrated the incorporation of the predictive values into the LCS as metrics for assessing the ability of an individual classifier to predict class membership. In practice, these metrics are simple to calculate and use. For example, if a classifier advocates a positive class, and has a high predictive value, then one may conclude that the classifier is accurate in its prediction of the positive class. In other words, for all unseen cases that match the classifier's taxon, it is highly probable that they will be positive cases. If the positive predictive value of a classifier advocating a positive class is low, then one should assume that the classifier does not predict positive class membership well. This type of information is very useful to those who need to examine the population of classifiers as a rule base, weighing the relative value of each rule for use in another environment, such as a clinical prediction rule that would be used at the bedside.

Another use of the predictive values is in assessing the overall predictive accuracy of the LCS after training. After the classification of an unseen case or set of cases has been obtained, one needs to know if the classification is in fact accurate. This is the information conveyed by the predictive values, and they seem to be a natural adjunct to other metrics commonly used to assess LCS performance. One way in which this information would be used is in determining whether or not to use an LCS for a given classification task, especially when other methods might be available. For example, if one has a set of data or even an individual patient to be classified, one would want to know in advance how well a system actually predicts the correct classification once the results are in hand. No other accuracy metric provides this information. As intelligent systems, including LCS, are increasingly employed in the decision sciences, this information becomes increasingly important.

However, the predictive values should be applied with caution. One possible disadvantage of relying on the predictive values lies in the data being used for training or testing. If there is an unequal distribution of the classes, the predictive values are poor accuracy indicators, as they are sensitive to prevalence. Thus, if one wants to use the predictive values effectively, the data used for training and testing should have equal numbers of cases from each class. This is not insurmountable, even in extreme situations where outcomes might be very rare. Bootstrapping and boosting techniques [8] that create many training sets composed of equal class distribution can help to alleviate this problem.

While the approach used in this investigation employs metrics of predictive accuracy, there is a possible rationale for applying it to the components of the LCS, specifically the performance and discovery components, as well as extending even further the representation used for classifiers. As an example of the latter, the predictive values could be used to replace the action associated with each classifier. Rather than a single action bit, 0 or 1 in dichotomous decision environments, each classifier would have two phenotypic slots, one each for the positive and negative predictive values. As these slots could take on real values ranging from 0 to 1, they could be used to express fuzzy class membership, reflecting the overall predictive power of a given classifier.

In terms of the performance component, the predictive values can be used to assist the LCS with determining appropriate classifiers to select for inclusion in Correct Sets and for use by the genetic algorithm in selecting and deleting classifiers from the population. In the NEWBOOLE model, the Correct Set is analogous to the Action Set in the earlier BOOLE and later XCS models, although it is created in a different way. The Correct Set is the simply the classifiers in the Match Set that advocate the same action as a given training case; it is the classifiers in the Correct Set that will be reinforced via payoff, while the remaining (incorrect) classifiers in the Match Set will be penalized.

While this approach works well for simple problems, such as the 6-Multiplexer, more complex environments, such as clinical databases, may benefit from a less categorical approach that allows for fuzzy membership in the Correct Set as well as enhanced assessment of a given classifier's utility after training. Even in a two-class problem, this can be a rather coarse comparison, one that doesn't account for a classifier's past performance in classifying cases. An alternative approach could use the predictive values to determine if the action advocated by a given classifier compared (or not) with the classification of a training case. This approach would allow the use of a continuous, rather than a discrete metric on which to base membership in the Correct Set. As a consequence, one could tune the degree of membership in the Correct Set, much like a membership threshold in a fuzzy system. Whether or not there are certain data that would respond well to this approach will depend on gathering empirical evidence through applying it to data sets of varying complexity.

The discovery component is another subsystem of the LCS in which the predictive values might be used, specifically to benefit the learning process. For example, classifiers could be selected for reproduction based on their predictive values rather then their strength. The advantage of this approach is that the fitness of a classifier is directly tied to its predictive power, rather than a proxy measure for classification accuracy. Again, a threshold could be used (for either positive or predictive value, or both), this time to determine the probability of selection or deletion. Details such as inheritance of predictive values by an offspring from its parents would need to be worked out, of course, but it seems reasonable to assume that these would not be difficult to address.

5   Conclusion

This investigation demonstrated an approach to incorporating accuracy-based metrics into classifier representations that could be used to assist users in visualizing accuracy information associated with individual macroclassifiers. This information could assist LCS end-users in understanding the relative importance of specific classifiers in explanation and prediction. In addition, this representation could assist developers with the task of creating visualization tools for examining the population as it evolves during training and as it exists at the end of training. Finally, the predictive values could provide additional approaches to ascertaining correct decisions and to selecting classifiers for reproduction and deletion in the performance and discovery components, respectively.

References

1. Bonelli, P., Parodi, A., Sen, S., and Wilson, S.: NEWBOOLE: A fast GBML system, in: Porter, B. and Mooney, R. (eds.), Machine Learning: Proceedings of the Seventh International Conference. Morgan Kaufmann, San Mateo, CA (1990) 153-159.
2. Fletcher, R.W., Fletcher, S.W., and Wagner, E.H.: Clinical Epidemiology: The Essentials. Williams and Wilkins, Baltimore (1988).
3. Holmes, J.H.: A genetics-based machine learning approach to knowledge discovery in clinical data, Journal of the American Medical Informatics Association Supplement (1996) 883.
4. Holmes J.H.: Quantitative methods for evaluating learning classifier system performance In forced two-choice decision tasks. In: Wu, A. (ed.) Proceedings of the Second International Workshop on Learning Classifier Systems (IWLCS'99). Morgan Kaufmann, San Francisco (1999) 250-257.
5. Holmes J.H., Durbin DR, Winston F.K.: A new bootstrapping method to improve classification performance in learning classifier systems.   Schoenauer M., Deb K., Rudolph G., et al. (eds.): Parallel Problem Solving from Nature – PPSN VI, Proceedings of The Sixth International Conference (2000) 745-754, 2000.
6. International Classification of Diseases, Clinical Modification, 9th Edition.
7. RuleQuest Research Pty Ltd.: See 5 for Windows NT.
8. Schapire, R.E.: Theoretical views of boosting. In: Computational Learning Theory, 4th European Conference, EuroCOLT'99. Springer-Verlag, Berlin (1999) 1-10.
9. U.S. Agency for Healthcare Research and Quality: The Healthcare Cost and Utilization Project.
10. Wilson, S.W.: Classifier fitness based on accuracy, Evolutionary Computation (1995) 3:149-175.

A Self-Adaptive XCS

Jacob Hurst and Larry Bull

Intelligent Computer Systems Centre
University of the West of England
Bristol, United Kingdom
jacob.hurst@uwe.ac.uk

Abstract. Self-adaptation has been used extensively to control parameters in various forms of evolutionary computation. The concept was first introduced with evolutionary strategies and it is now often used to control genetic algorithms. This paper describes the addition of a self-adaptive mutation rate and learning rate to the XCS classifier system. Self-adaptation has been used before in the strength based learning classifier system ZCS. This self-adaptive ZCS demonstrated clear performance improvements in a dynamic Woods environment and stable adaptation of its reinforcement learning parameters. In this paper experiments with XCS are carried out in Woods 2, a truncated version of the Woods14 environment and a dynamic Woods environment. Performance of XCS in the dynamic Woods 14 environment is good with little loss of performance when the environment is perturbed. Use of an adaptive mutation rate does not help or improve on this behavior. XCS has already been shown to perform poorly in the Woods 14 environment, and other long rule chain environments. Use of an adaptive mutation rate is shown to increase performance significantly in these long rule chain environments. Attempts to also self-adapt the learning rate in Woods 14-12 fail to achieve satisfactory system performance.

1   Introduction

Within Genetic Algorithms (GAs) [Holland 1975] and Genetic Programming [Koza 1991] the parameters controlling the algorithm are traditionally global and remain constant over time. However this is not always the case; in Evolutionary Strategies [Rechenberg 1973], forms of Evolutionary Programming (Meta-EP) [Fogel 1992] and in some GAs [Bäck 1992], the mutation rate is a locally evolving entity in itself, i.e. it adapts during the search process. This "self-adaptive" form of mutation not only reduces the number of hand-tunable parameters of the evolutionary algorithm, it has also been shown to improve performance (e.g. [Bäck 1992]). This approach has been used to add adaptive parameters to the Michigan Style classifier system ZCS [Wilson 1994] by the authors [Hurst and Bull 2000]. In this previous work the mutation rate is adapted as are the parameters that control the reinforcement learning of the algorithm; the learning rate, tax rate and discount factor. The results presented demonstrated that adaptive parameters can provide improved performance in dynamic multi-step environments.

P.L. Lanzi, W. Stolzmann, and S.W. Wilson (Eds.): IWLCS 2001, LNAI 2321, pp. 57–73, 2002.
© Springer-Verlag Berlin Heidelberg 2002

ZCS [Wilson 1994] is a Michigan style classifier system where the reinforcement consists of redistributing strength between subsequent action sets on the basis of reward received from the environment. XCS [Wilson 1995] works in a different fashion. The strength of each classifier within the LCS is not determined by the payoff received from environment but by maintaining a prediction of the amount of payoff the classifier will receive from the environment. The accuracy of the prediction of each classifier determines the strength of the classifier. This should help the LCS to avoid problems caused by classifiers over generalizing. In particular it would be expected that XCS would avoid the dominance within the rule base of over general rules, i.e. rules that have the *correct* action in high payoff niches, but have *over* generalized and also match low payoff niches where they have the *incorrect* action. Such rules in XCS should become inaccurate and be removed from the rule base. This behavior of XCS has been most clearly shown and explained in single step mulitplexor experiments [e.g. Kovacs 2000]. Despite this basis "standard" XCS is not able to perform well in long chain multi-step tasks e.g. [Lanzi 1997]. This problem has also been studied in finite state world (FSW) environments [Barry 2001], there being attributed to over generalization caused by the small difference in payoff between niches at the end of the rule chain. The work presented here demonstrates how an adaptive mutation rate can alleviate some of the problems of over generalization in long chain multi-step problems.

The rest of the paper is laid out in the following manner. 2. Short description of XCS. 3. Self-Adaptation in Classifier Systems. 4. Self-Adaptive XCS in a multi-step environment. 5. Self-Adaptive XCS in a dynamic multi-step task. 6. Self-Adaptive XCS in a long chain multi-step task. 7. Conclusions.

2   The XCS Learning Classifier System

It is not intended to give an exhaustive description of the XCS classifier system here as this is carried out elsewhere [Wilson 1995, Butz and Wilson 2001]. The major distinctive trait of XCS compared to most other classifier systems (e.g. ZCS) is that rule fitness is not based on the rule predictions (strengths) but on the accuracy of these predictions (see also [Frey and Slate 1991]). By using accuracy instead of strength it should be possible to form efficient generalizations and a complete and accurate mapping of the search space (rather then focusing on the higher payoff niches in the environment). XCS also uses a niche GA rather then the traditional panmictic scheme.

Previously, work was carried with a self-adaptive mutation rate in XCS [Bull, Hurst, and Tomlinson 2000]. That work indicated that it was possible to self-adapt the mutation rate within the XCS classifier system. The current description differs from the one used then in the following ways:

1.GA is in the action set and not the match set.
2.A different accuracy function is used which is now based on a power law.
3.A different cover strategy is used, currently XCS completely fills the state action space if it detects that there are no classifiers of a given action for a match set.

4.Mutation is protected preventing the production of classifiers that do not match the environmental input.

5.Subsumption is used to remove specific classifiers in favour of more general classifiers.

The differences above indicate that the algorithm has changed greatly from its original description. It is therefore valid to repeat and present the results obtained with an adaptive mutation rate again. The full description of the version of XCS used is laid out in [Butz and Wilson 2000].

The default parameters presented for XCS and unless otherwise stated for this paper are: $N = 800$, $E_0 = 10$, $B = 0.2$, $\gamma = 0.71$, $\chi = 0.8$, $\mu = 0.02$, $\Phi = 0.5$, $p_0 = 10$, $\alpha = 0.1$, $P_\# = 0.5$, $\delta = 0.1$, $E_I = 0$, $F_I = 0.01$, $p_I = 10$. For a full description of these parameters the reader is referred to [Butz and Wilson 2000].

All results presented in this paper are the average of ten runs. Parameter settings, number of unique rules in the rule base and number of steps taken to reach food are sampled every exploit cycle and a window average of the last 50 values is recorded.

3   Self-Adaptation in Classifier Systems

Previously [Bull and Hurst 2000, Bull and Hurst, Tomlinson 2000], we have shown that it is possible to self-adapt the mutation rate within learning classifier systems using the same form as in Meta EP. That is, each rule has its own mutation rate μ, stored as a real number. This parameter is passed to its offspring either under recombination or directly. The offspring then applies its mutation rate to itself using a Gaussian distribution, i.e. $\mu_i' = \mu_i + N(0, \mu_i)$, before mutating the rest of the rule at the resulting rate. It is noted that this form of mutation is simpler than that typically used in Evolutionary Strategies, where a Lognormal is applied to μ. However, the simpler form was shown to be effective and has been suggested to work better in noisy environments [Angeline 1996].

Our previous work indicated that an adaptive mutation rate in ZCS responded well to environmental change. Experiments are carried out with XCS in the same dynamic environment in this paper.

Previous work with ZCS also used self-adaptation of the reinforcement learning parameters [Hurst and Bull 2001]. Three parameters were adapted, the learning rate, the discount factor and the tax rate. These parameters did not show any response to changes in the environment. However, the adaptive process was beneficial as it allowed the discovery of improved parameter settings that differ greatly from those described in the literature.

The adaptation of the learning rate and other reinforcement learning parameters was carried out in ZCS in a different manner from the adaptation of the mutation rate. As with adapting the mutation rates, each rule carries a real value for each parameter to be adapted. These values carried on the classifier are not applied to the carrier classifier, but are instead applied to classifiers belonging to different action sets. At each update the parameters required are obtained from the previous action set if the update is being carried in the current action set, or the parameter is obtained from the current action set if the update is being carried out in the previous action set. The selection method used is simple roulette wheel selection based on the fitness of the classifiers within the action set. This method of update is known as *enforced co-operation* and is used in the experiments detailed here for the adaptation of the learning rate. Enforced co-operation is needed to prevent classifiers selfishly adapting the learning rate, as explained in [Hurst and Bull 2001].

4   Self-Adaptive XCS in a Multi-step Environment

The Woods 2 environment was introduced [Wilson 1995] to examine the performance of XCS in multi-step tasks. Woods 2 is a two dimensional rectilinear toroidal grid, comprised of 30x15 cells. Each cell may be blank or may be occupied by four types of object; two classes of food (F,G) and two classes of rock exist (O,Q). The contents of the cells are coded using three bits. The code 000 represents a blank cell, 110 and 111 represent food objects, and 010 and 011 represent rocks. XCS is used to develop the controller of a robot/animat that must traverse the map in search of food. It is positioned randomly in one of the blank cells and can move into any one of the surrounding 8 cells on each discrete time step, unless occupied by a rock. If the animat moves into a food cell the system receives a reward from the environment (1000), and the task is reset, i.e. the food is replaced and the animat is randomly relocated. Performance is recorded from the results of the exploit trials only. Here 4000 exploit trials are displayed, the figures showing the average of ten runs. Optimal performance is 1.7 steps to food, with random performance around 27 steps.

```
. . . . . . . . . . . . . . . . . . . . . . . . . . . . . . . .
. QQ F . . QQ F . . OQF . . QQG . . OQG . . OQF .
. 000 . . Q00 . . 0Q0 . . 00Q . . QQ0 . . QQQ .
. 00Q . . 0QQ . . 0QQ . . QQ0 . . 000 . . QQ0 .
. . . . . . . . . . . . . . . . . . . . . . . . . . . . . . . .

. . . . . . . . . . . . . . . . . . . . . . . . . . . . . . . .
. QO F . . QO F . . OQF . . QQG . . 00G . . QOF .
. 000 . . Q00 . . 0Q0 . . 00Q . . QQ0 . . QQQ .
. 00Q . . 0QQ . . 0QQ . . QQ0 . . 000 . . QQ0 .
. . . . . . . . . . . . . . . . . . . . . . . . . . . . . . . .

. . . . . . . . . . . . . . . . . . . . . . . . . . . . . . . .
. QQ F . . QQ F . . OQF . . QQG . . OQG . . OQF .
. 000 . . Q00 . . 0Q0 . . 00Q . . QQ0 . . QQQ .
. 00Q . . 0QQ . . 0QQ . . QQ0 . . 000 . . QQ0 .
. . . . . . . . . . . . . . . . . . . . . . . . . . . . . . . .
```

Fig. 1. Woods 2 environment

4.1   XCS Results in Woods 2

XCS is run with an adaptive mutation rate that is initially randomly seeded between 0 and 1 as described above. Figure 2 indicates the results obtained.

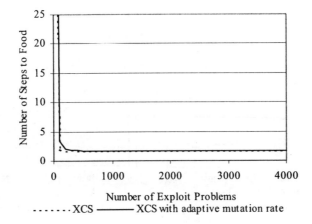

Fig. 2. XCS performance with adaptive and fixed mutation rates

Unlike in the previous work [Bull, Hurst, and Tomlinson 2000] the use of an initially high mutation rate does not demonstrate any degradation in performance. The figure indicates that the XCS system is able to produce the optimal performance as reported in [Wilson 1995], and the addition of an adaptive mutation rate does not adversely affect the system. It is unclear why there is a difference in performance from the previous work. This is probably due to one or more of the differences in software described previously. No improvement in performance is demonstrated in this environment, although this is unsurprising as the fixed parameter settings are as described in [Wilson 1995].

Figure 3a shows the average mutation rate. As the learning proceeds the mutation rate is gradually turned down. Figure 3b indicates the number of unique rules in the system. In both systems the number of rules increases at the start of the run and is gradually reduced at a similar rate by the subsumption and GA activity. It should be noted that including the mutation rate on each classifier does not result in a dramatic increase in population size.

4.2 Learning Rate

The next set of experiments shows the results of using self-adaptive learning along with a self-adaptive mutation rate, again as described in section 3. As with the adaptive mutation rate, the adaptive learning rate is initially seeded at a value very different from the value suggested in [Wilson 1995]. It is seeded randomly between 0 and 0.02. The normal parameter setting used for the learning rate is 0.2.

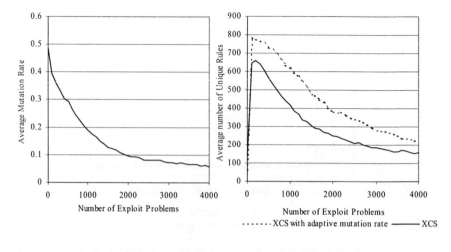

Fig. 3   (a)   (b)

a) Average Mutation Rate for XCS with adaptive mutation rate in Woods 2
b) Average Number of Unique Rules for XCS with and without adaptive mutation rate in Woods2

Figure 4a shows the performance of XCS with an adaptive learning rate as well as an adaptive mutation rate. The addition of the learning rate has no detrimental affect on performance. Figure 4b shows the movement of the adaptive learning rate, moving from its initial value to ~0.5. The rate of this movement is large considering its initial seeding value.

Figure 5a shows the number of unique rules needed in the system, again the addition of an extra adaptable parameter to each classifier does not result in a massive increase in the number of unique rules needed to solve the problem. Figure 5b indicates the mutation rate changes. It can be clearly seen how the addition of an extra self-adapting parameter changes the response of the adaptive mutation rate. Experiments are now carried out to determine if this change is due to the mutation rate trying to reach two different optima.

Figure 6 shows a series of experiments with the adaptive mutation rate and the adaptive learning rate seeded at two different levels. In both cases the average mutation rate drops more slowly when the learning rate is adapting. When XCS is run in Woods 2 with both the adaptive mutation rate and the adaptive learning rate seeded between 0-1, the learning rate remains at its initial seeding value (not shown). The initial implication is that the high level of the learning rate determines the level of the mutation rate and not the additional adaptation pressure. The other traces on the graph indicate that this is not the case. An experiment is run with the learning rate fixed at the high level of 0.5. As the graph indicates the level of the adaptive mutation rate stays close to the level when the learning rate is fixed low. Therefore having to self-adapt the learning rate causes a slow fall off.

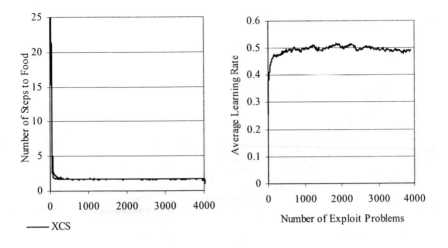

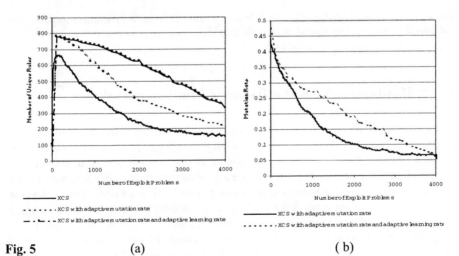

Fig. 4   (a)   (b)

a)   XCS performance in Woods 2 with adaptive learning rate and adaptive mutation rate.
b)   XCS learning rate in Woods 2 with adaptive learning rate and adaptive mutation rate.

Fig. 5   (a)   (b)

a) XCS average number of unique rules in Woods 2 for systems run with no adaptation, adaptive mutation rate and both adaptive mutation rate and adaptive learning rate
b) XCS average mutation rate in Woods 2 for systems with an adaptive mutation rate and both an adaptive mutation rate and an adaptive learning rate

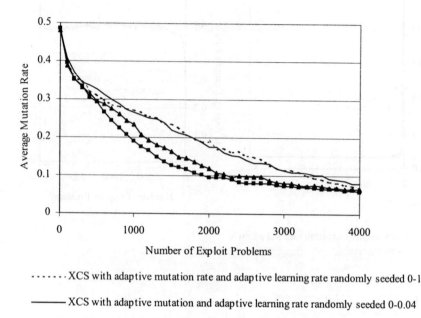

······ XCS with adaptive mutation rate and adaptive learning rate randomly seeded 0-1

───── XCS with adaptive mutation and adaptive learning rate randomly seeded 0-0.04

──▲── XCS adaptive mutation rate with learning rate fixed at 0.5

──■── XCS with adaptive mutation rate with learning rate fixed at 0.2

Fig. 6. Average Mutation Rate of XCS in Woods 2 with XCS run with adaptive mutation rate and adaptive learning rate seeded at two different levels and XCS with adaptive mutation rate with learning rate fixed at two different levels

5   Self-Adaptive XCS in a Dynamic Multi-step Task

The experiments above all used the Woods 2 environment. This environment was originally used when XCS was first described. As XCS can produce the optimal rules in this environment fairly easily, a more testing environment is needed to determine if the use of adaptive parameters can produce any advantage in system performance. The Woods 14 environment was originally introduced by Cliff and Ross [1995] to test the ability of LCS to chain rules. Like the Woods 2 environment it is a two dimensional rectilinear toroidal grid which is explored by an animat. Unlike Woods 2 which contains two types of food and two types of rock, Woods 14 only contains one type of food and one type of rock. So, instead of a three bit encoding for each environmental feature there is a two bit encoding, 01 for rock and 10 for food and 00 for space. This means that at each time step the animat receives a 16 bit binary string to process. It consists of a tunnel along which the animat learns to navigate. Cliff and Ross [1995] first introduced the environment to test the ZCS [Wilson 1994] algorithm. Experiments have been carried out using self-adaptive parameters using ZCS in the Woods

14-06 environment [Hurst and Bull 2001]. This is a truncated version of the Woods 14 environment. In our dynamic version of the task, half way through the run the position of the food is changed from one end of the tunnel to the other. This changes the environment by destroying one niche, creating a new one and altering the two neighbouring niches. The experiments in ZCS [Hurst & Bull 2001] indicated that a self-adaptive mutation rate provided performance benefit in a dynamic environment. The parameter settings used here for XCS in the Woods 14-06 environment are the same as those described for the Woods 2 experiments except that N=2000.

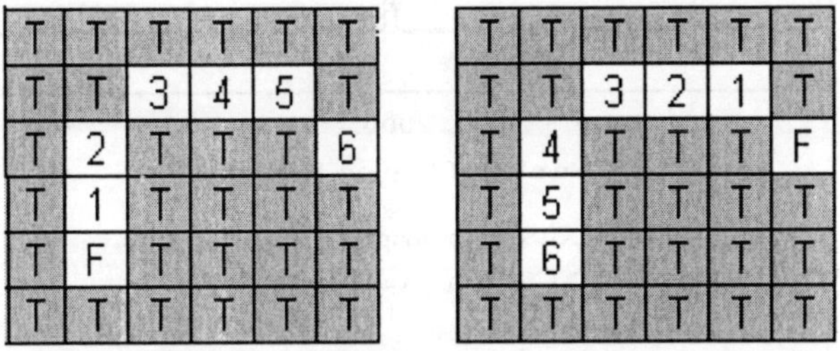

Fig. 7. The Woods 14-06 changing environment, the numbers represent the minimum number of steps to food, T represents the Trees and F represents the food

5.1   Adaptive Mutation Results in Woods 14-06

Figure 8 shows the performance of XCS with and without an adaptive mutation rate in the Woods 14-06 environment. The figure indicates that XCS performs well in this environment. The level of disruption that the system undergoes when the environment is changed is much smaller than in the ZCS work [Hurst and Bull 2001]. This could be attributed to the manner in which XCS forms a complete state-action map and not solely maintaining high payoff rules as in the case of ZCS. Figure 8 also illustrates that there is little difference in performance between XCS performance with or without an adaptive mutation rate. See [Hartley 1999] for related work in a single-step environment.

Figure 9a indicates there is a considerable loss in performance at the point of environment change when adapting the learning rate as well as the mutation rate. In Figure 9b XCS is run with the learning rate fixed at 0.5 (the level the adaptive learning rate moves to) and the mutation rate set at the default value of 0.02.

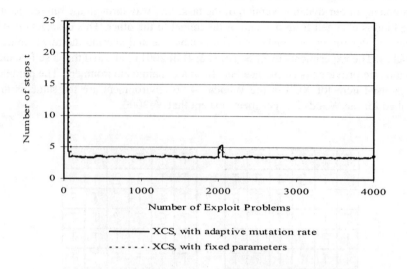

Fig. 8. Self-Adaptive XCS performance in the Woods 14-06 environment

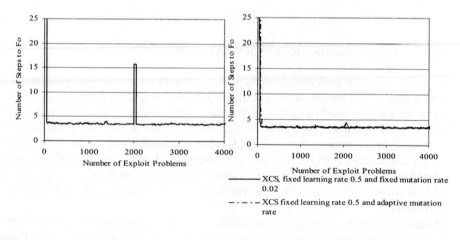

Fig. 9.   (a)   (b)

(a) XCS with adaptive mutation rate and adaptive learning rate in Woods 14-06c
(b) XCS run with fixed learning rate at 0.5 and run with fixed learning rate 0.5 and adaptive mutation rate

This line has excellent performance and displays no degradation when the environment is perturbed. When the mutation rate is allowed to adapt and the learning rate is fixed to 0.5 performance is better than before, although there is a slight loss of performance. From these series of experiments it can be seen that when adapting system parameters there is an additional load on the system. This prevents the system from reacting as quickly to changes in the environment. Another explanation is that the self-adaptation is trying to find the best learning rate or mutation rate for a classifier in a specific niche or action set. As the environment changes a new search has to be made for these correct values. These experiments also indicate that in this environment 0.5 is a better learning rate then the default value of 0.2. Hence, in this environment, no benefit is shown from self-adapting the system parameters.

6   Self-Adaptive XCS in a Long Chain Multi-step Task

T	T	T	T	T	T	T	T	T
T	T	3	4	5	T	T	T	T
T	2	T	T	T	6	T	T	T
T	1	T	T	T	7	T	12	T
T	F	T	T	T	8	T	T	11
T	T	T	T	T	T	9	10	T

Fig. 10. The Woods 14-12 grid environment, the numbers represent the minimum number of steps to food, T represents the Trees and F represents the food

This Woods 14 environment was introduced in [Ross and Cliff 1994] to examine the ability of ZCS to cope with long rule chains. They found that ZCS failed to perform well. The environment has also been used with XCS [Lanzi 1997] and results indicated that XCS was also unable to learn long rule chains. Other work on long rule chains [Barry 2001] also indicated that XCS fails to produce the optimal solution. Both authors explain that this failure is due to over generalisation of the classifiers. The use of adaptive parameters may alleviate this problem. As the explore policy of standard XCS is simply the choice of random actions a truncated version of the full Woods 14 environment is used mainly because of computer time and the suggested problems XCS has in dealing with multi-step tasks. Woods 14-12 has optimal performance at 6.5 steps to food. N is set to 2000; all other fixed rate parameters use the same values as those for the Woods 2 experiment.

6.1   XCS Adaptive Mutation Rate Results in Woods 14-12

The results from the use of an adaptive mutation rate are displayed in Figure 11. The figure clearly shows that XCS performs rather poorly in the Woods 14-12 environment. This is not surprising as results presented in [Lanzi 1997] demonstrate that XCS fails to learn the complete Woods14 environment (18 spaces to food). Other work in FSW [Barry 2001] has indicated that there is a limit of 14 steps before XCS starts to over generalise. Figure 11 shows a dramatic improvement in performance when using an adaptive mutation rate. This performance is still sub-optimal but is a considerable improvement over the fixed rate XCS.

Wilson (personal communication) has obtained optimal performance in the full Woods 14 environment by a variety of methods including control of the degree of generalization and limitation of exploration in the environment.

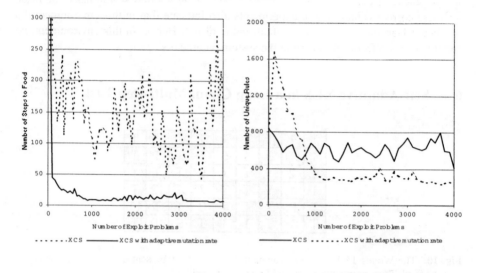

Fig. 11   (a)   (b)

a)   XCS performance in Woods14-12 with and without adaptive mutation rate
b)   XCS, number of unique rules in Woods14-12 with and without adaptive mutation rate

Figure 11b indicates the number of unique rules needed. The normal XCS system's rule base contracts quickly while the XCS with the adaptive mutation rate maintains a large number of rules, presumably preventing the worst excesses of over generalization. Eventually XCS with the adaptive mutation rate is able to form a smaller rule base than the fixed rate version. It may be possible to obtain better multi-step performance in XCS if the parameters are set differently, but these settings have not been identified. The use of adaptive parameters is a possible methodology for identifying such values. It should also be noted that the performance of XCS in Figure 11a is highly unstable, the poor performance is not maintained at a constant level but changes dramatically and never comes close to optimal performance. This is interesting as it raises questions about how the over generalization in the LCS occurs. If the over generalization occurs mainly at the end of the rule chain, should the performance loss in the system be relatively constant? This type of over generalization may be taking place, but we suggest that it is not the only factor explaining the loss of performance in multi-step tasks. The erratic loss of performance may well be caused by over generalizations occurring earlier in the rule chain. This has implications for the general use of XCS in long chain tasks.

Figure 12a shows the movement of the mutation rate in the Woods 14-12.

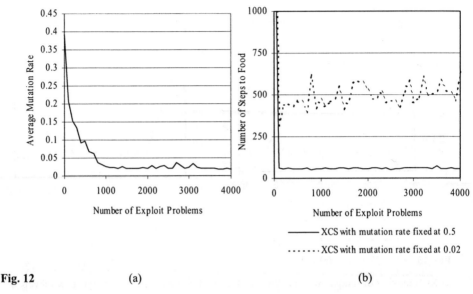

Fig. 12   (a)   (b)

a) XCS, average mutation in Woods-1412 using an adaptive mutation rate
b) XCS performance in Woods 14-12 using, fixed mutation rate at 0.5 and fixed mutation rate
   at 0.02

The change in mutation rate is not as smooth as the Woods 2 experiments, raising the possibility that the mutation rate is responding to over generalizations that occur sporadically in the run. Note also that the mutation rate falls to a lower value than that obtained for the Woods 2 experiments. This could be due to a difference in susceptibility of the two environments to the effects of over generalization. Clearly, the tunnel of Woods 14 is going to be very sensitive to over generalizations and therefore a greater pressure to turn the mutation rate down exists. Figure 12b shows the performance of XCS with the mutation rate fixed at two levels compared to the adaptive mutation rate performance. When XCS is run with the mutation rate fixed at 0.5 (the average initial seeding level of XCS) and 0.02 (the level the adaptive rate falls to when the parameter is allowed to self adapt) the performance in both cases is worse. When fixed at 0.02 it is worse, but when fixed at 0.5 it settles around 50 steps to food (compare with Figure 11a). These experiments do not discount the possibility of there being an optimal fixed setting for the mutation rate in Woods14-12, but it does indicate the difficulty in finding one and strongly suggests that it is the dynamic adaptation of the mutation rate to over generalization events that is responsible for the more impressive performance of the system.

Figure 13a indicates the number of unique rules needed in the experiments with the fixed mutation rates. These traces indicate that at higher mutation rates a higher number of unique rules are present in the population. Comparing Figure 13b it can be seen how with a self adaptive mutation rate the size of the number of unique rules can be minimized as well as ensuring reasonable performance in the environment.

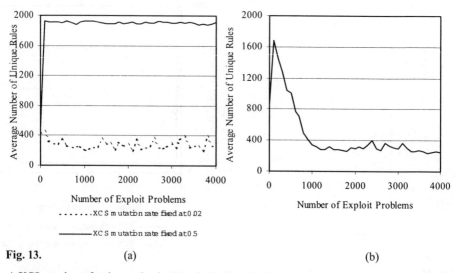

Fig. 13.   (a)   (b)

a) XCS number of unique rules in Woods 14-12 with the mutation rate fixed at two levels 0.5 and 0.02

b) XCS number of unique rules with XCS self adapts the mutation rate

6.2   XCS Learning Rate Results in Woods 14-12

Enforced co-operation has also been used in the adaptation of the learning rate for the long chain task. Figure 14a shows the performance of the adaptive XCS and compares its performance with XCS with no adaptation. The performance does not show an improvement over the fixed rate system. So when XCS adapts the mutation rate it has improved performance but the system produces worse performance when adapting the learning rate and the mutation rate in Woods 14-12 (in contrast to Woods 2). The conclusion to draw from this is it may not be possible to adapt reinforcement learning parameters using the current technique in long chain environments where the system is particularly sensitive to over generalizations.

Figure 15a shows the average mutation rate when XCS adapts both the learning rate and the mutation rate. When the system has to adapt both parameters it has to be at a higher rate than if it needs to only adapt one parameter, as is the case in Woods 2. Figure 15b again indicates the low "over head" in parameter adaptation, i.e. there is not a large increase in rule base size when adapting parameters.

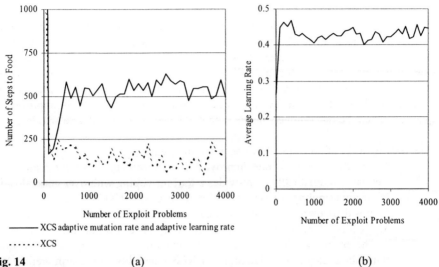

Fig. 14   (a)   (b)

a) XCS performance in Woods14-12 with both adaptive learning rate and an adaptive mutation and no adaptation
b) XCS average learning rate in Woods14-12 with the system adapting both learning rate and
   mutation rate

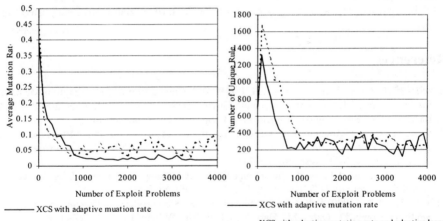

Fig. 15   (a)   (b)
a) XCS average mutation rate in Woods 14-12 with system adapting just the mutation rate and
   a system adapting both the mutation and the learning rate
b) XCS average number of unique rules in Woods 14-12; with system adapting just the mutation rate and a system adapting both the mutation rate and the learning rate

7   Conclusion

The results presented here indicate the potential of parameter adaptation in XCS and classifier systems in general. The use of an adaptive mutation rate in multi-step problems is shown to alleviate some of the problems of over generalization in long rule chain problems. However, the instability of XCS in these environments makes it difficult to truly assess the utility of self-adaptation in LCS that use accuracy as their fitness metric. When the basic learning process in these environments is improved the question should be re-examined, as the potential benefits described here are clear.

The contributions of this paper have been the following:
1. Adaptive mutation rate improves XCS performance in long chain multistep tasks dramatically. It provides a tool for coping with over generalization while not crippling the generalization mechanism of XCS.
2. It is difficult to adapt the learning rate in XCS.
3. XCS performs well in simple dynamic woods environments.
4. The erratic performance of XCS in long chain multi-step tasks asks questions about existing explanations of XCS's inability to perform well in long chain multi-step tasks. In particular it questions the explanation that performance degradation in XCS is solely due to over generalizations that occur at the end of the rule chain due to small difference in prediction [Barry 2000].

Acknowlegements
BT labs, Ipswich, UK and the University of the West of England, have supported this work.

References

Angeline, P.J., Fogel, D.B., and Fogel, L.J. (1996) A Comparison of Self-Adaption Methods for Finite State Machines in a Dynamic Environment. In Fogel, L.J, Angeline, P.J, and Back, T. (eds.) *Evolutionary Programming V,* Springer Press, pp 441-449

Bäck, T. (1992) Self-Adaptation in Genetic Algorithms. In F.J.Varela and P.Bourgine (eds.) *Toward a Practice of Autonomous Systems: Proceedings of the First European Conference on Artificial Life,* MIT Press, pp. 263-271.

Barry, A. (2001) The stability of long action chins in XCS to appear in *Special Issue Journal of Soft Computing on LCS* (eds.) Bull, L and Lanzi, P.L Springer

Bull, L., Hurst, L. (2000) Self Adaptive Mutation in ZCS controllers. In Cagnoni, S., Poli, R., Smith, G. Corne, D., Oates, M., Hart, E., Lanzi, P-L, Willem, Li, Y., Paecther, B., and Fogarty, T. (eds.) *Real-World Applications of Evolutionary Computing: Proceedings of the Fifth IEEE Conference on Evolutionary Computation,* Springer Press pp446-451

Bull, L., Hurst, J., and Tomlinson, A. (2000) Self-Adaptive Mutation in Classifier System Controllers. In J.-A. Meyer, A. Berthoz, D. Floreano, H. Roitblatt and S.W. Wilson (eds.) *From Animals to Animats 6 - The Sixth International Conference on the Simulation of Adaptive Behaviour,* MIT Press.

Butz, M.V. and Wilson, S.W. 2001 to appear in (eds.) Lanzi, P.L, Stolzmann, W. and Wilson, S.W., *Advances in Learning Classifier Systems. Third International Workshop (IWLCS 2000)*

Cliff, D. and Ross, S. (1995) Adding Temporary memory to ZCS, *Adaptive Behavior*, 3(2):101-150.

Fogel, D.B. (1992) *Evolving Artificial Intelligence.* PhD dissertation, University of California.

Frey, P.W and Slate, D.J (1991) Letter Recognition using Holland-style Adaptive Classifiers. *Machine Learning* 6:161-182

Hartley, A (1999) Accuracy-based fitness allows similar performance to humans in static and dynamic classification Environments. In Banzhurf, W., Daidu, J., Eiben, A., Garzon, M., Honavar, V., and Jakiela, M, Simth, R., (eds.) *Proceedings of the Genetic and Evolutionary Computation Conference 1999.* Morgan Kauffmann pp. 266-274

Holland, J.H. (1975) *Adaptation in Natural and Artificial Systems.* University of Michigan Press.

Hurst, J. and Bull, L. (2001) A Self-Adaptive Classifier System. In P.-L. Lanzi, W. Stolzmann and S. Wilson (eds.) *Proceedings of the Third International Workshop on Learning Classifier Systems.*

Kovacs, T. (2000) Strength or Accuracy? Fitness Calculation in learning classifier systems. In P-L. Lanzi, W. Stolzmann, and S. Wilson (eds.) *Learning Classifier Systems: From Foundations to Applications,* Springer pp. 143-160

Koza, J.R. (1991) *Genetic Programming.* MIT Press

Lanzi, P.L. (1997) A Model of the Environment to Avoid Local Learning. *Technical Report N.97.46*, Dipartimento di Elettronica E Informazione, Politecnio di Milano, Italia

Rechenberg, I (1973) *Evolutionsstrategie; Optimierung technischer Systeme nach Prinzipen der biologischen Evolution.* Frommann-Holzboog Verlag.

Wilson, S.W. (1994) ZCS: A Zeroth-level Classifier System. *Evolutionary Computation* 2(1):1-18

Wilson, S.W. (1995) Classifier fitness based on Accuracy. *Evolutionary Computation* 3(2):149-177

Two Views of Classifier Systems

Tim Kovacs

Department of Computer Science
University of Bristol, Bristol BS8 1UB, England
kovacs@cs.bris.ac.uk
http://www.cs.bris.ac.uk/~kovacs

Abstract. This work suggests two ways of looking at classifier systems; as Genetic Algorithm-based systems, and as Reinforcement Learning-based systems, and argues that the former is more suitable for traditional strength-based systems while the latter is more suitable for accuracy-based XCS. The dissociation of the Genetic Algorithm from policy determination in XCS is noted.

1 What Is a Learning Classifier System?

What a Learning Classifier System (LCS) is seems contentious, to the extent that discussion of this issue dominated the the First International Workshop on Learning Classifier Systems (IWLCS-92). In his report on the workshop Robert Smith paraphrased Lashon Booker as follows:

> "The LCS is usually described as a *method*: a set of algorithmic details that define a way to solve a class of problems. However, in many ways the LCS is more of an *approach*: a set of conceptual details that define a certain direction for developing methods. Therefore, the defining issues for the LCS are not necessarily algorithmic, but conceptual. The central problem addressed by the workshop's discussions was to clarify these defining, conceptual issues." [21] p. 2.

That conceptual issues remained a concern for classifier systems in 2000 is indicated by the inclusion of a series of 11 short essays under the title "What is a Learning Classifier System?" in a recent publication [13].

One conceptual issue addressed here is whether classifier systems are best characterised as evolutionary systems or Q-learning-like systems. Of course classifier systems traditionally incorporate both evolutionary and Reinforcement Learning (RL) algorithms. Given their hybrid nature it seems inappropriate to attempt to cast them strictly as one or the other, and this is not the aim of this work. There are, however, conflicting views of the relationship and relative importance of the classifier system's components, as the following quotes should suggest.

In Holland and Reitman's discussion of the two learning subsystems in the first classifier system, CS-1 [14], it is clear that they consider the Genetic Algorithm (GA) the primary learning system and the credit assignment system decidedly secondary:

P.L. Lanzi, W. Stolzmann, and S.W. Wilson (Eds.): IWLCS 2001, LNAI 2321, pp. 74–87, 2002.

"The second process [credit assignment] is a form of simple learning; after a series of actions, it stores in memory information about the consequences of these actions. The third process [the GA] is a more complex learning process ... the novelty of the model [the LCS] is not so much in the performance or simple learning processes [credit assignment], but rather in the process that changes memory [the GA]." [14] p. 470.

Although the quote above is from 1978, this view is not confined to early work on classifier system, as the following quote from 1998 suggests:

"The learning classifier system (LCS) is an application of the genetic algorithm (GA) to machine learning." [9] p. 299.

However, the classifier systems literature also contains contrasting views, in which the role of the GA is not emphasised so much. For instance:

"In many ways, the LCS can be thought of as a GA-based technique for grouping state-action pairs." [22] B1.5:8.

Although classifier systems are still "GA-based" in the above, the GA is clearly not the whole story. Grouping state-action pairs is not the ultimate goal of a classifier system; something must be done with these groups. Finally, a quote which appears to minimise the role of the GA, at least in XCS:

"In XCS, the 'discovery component' does not actually discover new classifiers, if one means classifiers that 'do the right thing' in the situations they match, i.e., correctly connect conditions with actions.

Instead, the discovery component searches along the specificity-generality axis for classifiers that are maximally general while still accurate." [41].

These quotes are meant to suggest a diversity of opinion in the literature, and that the issue of how to characterise classifier systems is worthy of further examination. In the following section the difference between classifier systems and genetic algorithms is briefly examined, following which different types of classifier systems and different views of them are considered.

2   Two Views of Classifier Systems

Although I was unaware of the diversity of opinion regarding the nature of classifier systems when I first began working with them in 1996, I soon became concerned that I was unsure of the difference between a genetic algorithm and a classifier system. I had seen the LCS described as a combination of a production system, rule discovery system and credit assignment system. I reasoned that since the rule discovery system typically *is* a genetic algorithm, the LCS must be something more, since it has two additional components. However, I decided the credit assignment system was just what we call the fitness function of a genetic algorithm. Granted, credit assignment in an LCS was more complex than the examples of function optimisation with a GA which I had seen, but it was still a kind of fitness function. This left the production system as the real difference between the LCS and GA. But since the production system is conceptually straightforward – its task is simply to apply the rules when appropriate – a classifier system seemed to be just a way of applying a GA to certain kinds of problems. Certainly we need to wrap the GA up with a little machinery (the production system and a special kind of fitness function) to interface it with the problem, and perhaps the GA needs a little help in the form of operators like covering (see, e.g., [11, 4, 40]), but the LCS seemed to be essentially a GA.[1]

This is a view which I still think is consistent with Holland's intentions, and those of many others. Classifier systems have, after all, been described as *Genetics-Based* Machine Learning (GBML) systems [10].

Less-Genetic Classifier Systems. The view of a classifier system as essentially a GA is somewhat extreme, and other less extreme views exist. In addition to the GA, a classifier system may contain rule discovery mechanisms such as covering, triggered chaining [19], bridging [12, 18], and corporate linkage [42, 36]. In such systems the GA is just one component of the rule discovery system, although perhaps an important one. However, some LCS emphasise the use of non-genetic operators more heavily than others, and in some cases the GA is even considered a 'background' operator [3].

Non-genetic Classifier Systems. That a classifier system is essentially a GA is flatly contradicted by the considerable recent work on LCS which use alternative rule discovery systems. In hindsight, there seems no justification for insisting on the use of GAs as opposed to other evolutionary algorithms. Alternatives were suggested some time ago [39, 37, 38, 22] and some recent work has indeed used Genetic Programming rather than Genetic Algorithms [16, 1]. What's more, a significant amount of recent work has been on systems which contain no evolutionary algorithms [27, 29, 28, 30, 31, 5, 6, 32–34, 7]. If we accept such systems as classifier systems (as is the norm, e.g., work on such systems has appeared at the IWLCS workshops), we are dealing with a much broader concept than that of a GA and some wrapping. Unfortunately, discussion of this trend lies outside the scope of this work.

Linking Classifier Systems and Mainstream RL. A second trend which breaks from the view of classifier systems as GA-based systems is that which seeks to link classifier systems and mainstream reinforcement learning. RL has made great strides since the introduction of classifier systems, and it is clear that most classifier systems are RL systems, that they address many of the same issues addressed by other RL systems, and that there is much to be gained from integrating classifier systems with mainstream RL. The need to bridge classifier

---

[1] A more detailed account of the differences between the two would be desirable, but must be deferred to another work.

systems and mainstream RL appeared to be the consensus during the discussion at IWLCS-99.

The GA-View and RL-View. This leaves us with two contradictory views of what a classifier system really is, what we might call the *GA-view* – that the LCS is essentially the application of a GA to a problem – and the *RL-view*, that the LCS is a kind of RL system, i.e., a Q-learning-like system in which the GA is (or may be) a component, but in which many of the interesting issues are to do with credit assignment. The two views place different emphasis on different subsystems: according to the GA-view, the GA, and issues relating to it, are of primary importance, while the RL-view places greater importance on credit assignment. The existence of two alternative views begs an important question: does a classifier system solve problems using evolutionary means, or does it solve them in the way non-evolutionary RL systems do?

One aim of this work is to recognise and publicise the existence of these alternative views, since they seem under-recognised, particularly in the literature. Another aim is to clarify these views, and to justify the RL-view of (some) LCS. Significantly, the RL-view focuses on XCS, which I have argued differs fundamentally from Holland's LCS, to the extent that it more closely resembles mainstream RL systems such as tabular or neural network-based Q-learners [15].[2]

Without a good, basic understanding of RL, the distinction between the GA and RL views of LCS is likely to be unclear. Unfortunately a review of RL algorithms is impossible here, but readers interested in the subject are encouraged to consult [35], which should be required reading for anyone wishing to apply LCS to RL problems. I believe the future of LCS research (for sequential tasks) is heavily grounded in the RL-view; the most important issues to be addressed in LCS research are those which are and will be addressed in RL. This is not to marginalise evolutionary approaches to RL, but to say that they too will benefit from understanding of non-evolutionary approaches.

3 Two Classifier Systems

To make matters more concrete we will consider two particular classifier systems: XCS and SBXCS (Strength-Based XCS). XCS, introduced by Wilson in 1995 [40], is the most popular classifier system to date, and is well-documented elsewhere (e.g., [40, 8]). Its primary distinguishing feature is its *accuracy-based fitness*; in the GA, it bases the fitness of a rule on the accuracy with which it predicts environmental reward. This contrasts with traditional *strength-based fitness*, in which the fitness of a rule depends on the magnitude of the reward it receives. This difference has a surprising number of consequences [15].

---

[2] Despite this, XCS originated and has been studied exclusively within the LCS community, and is by far most strongly integrated with the LCS literature. Much better integration with mainstream RL awaits.

SBXCS [15] is XCS's strength-based twin; that is, it is a version of XCS to which the minimal changes have been made in order to make it a strength-based system. SBXCS is a functional classifier system, quite capable of tasks such as the 6 multiplexer [15], and generally similar to ZCS [39]. SBXCS's value lies in the fact that while it is algorithmically very similar to XCS, it has rather different capacities. This combination of traits allows us to attribute the difference in capacity to the responsible mechanisms more easily.

Estimating Strength/Prediction. A classifier system contains two major processes which require estimates of the value of rules: action selection and rule discovery. Both XCS and SBXCS base their value estimates on the rewards they receive, though they differ in how they do so. To begin, both calculate the *strength* (called *prediction* in XCS) of a rule using the Q-learning update, adapted for classifier systems [40]. In non-sequential tasks the update is:

$$p_j \leftarrow p_j + \beta(P - p_j) \tag{1}$$

where p_j is the prediction of rule j, β is the learning rate and P is the payoff (reward) from the environment [40]. The update is applied to the set of rules which match the current input and advocate the action taken by the system, called the *action set* [A]. XCS and SBXCS differ in what follows the prediction update, as illustrated in figure 1, and explained in the following sections. Full specifications of XCS and SBXCS appear in [15].

3.1   SBXCS

In order to estimate the value of taking a given action in response to the current input, SBXCS consults all the rules which match the current input and advocate that action. $S(a_i)$, the strength of action a_i, is defined as:

$$S(a_i) = \sum_{c \in [\mathrm{M}]_{a_i}} \mathrm{p}_c \cdot numerosity(c) \tag{2}$$

where $[\mathrm{M}]_{a_i}$ is the set of matching rules advocating action a_i, and $numerosity(c)$ is the number of copies of rule c in the population [40]. In short, the strength of action a_i is the total of the strengths of all the rules which advocate it. Significantly, if $[\mathrm{M}]_{a_i}$ is empty action a_i cannot be selected.

Once SBXCS has calculated the strength of each action $S(a_i)$, any of a great number of methods can be used to select an action, e.g., random selection (pure exploration mode [40]), deterministic greedy selection (pure exploitation mode [40]), or ϵ-greedy selection [35], to name but a few.

3.2   XCS

In XCS, calculation of the advocacy for an action is more complicated than in SBXCS, in that we must initially calculate rule fitnesses using the following

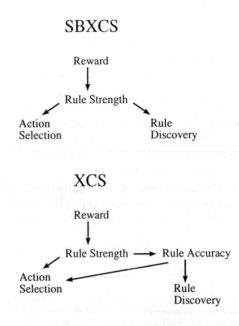

Fig. 1. How XCS and SBXCS use rewards to weight rules in action selection and rule discovery. The arrows indicate the flow of information.

series of updates. First we update the prediction error ε_j of each rule j in the action set:

$$\varepsilon_j \leftarrow \varepsilon_j + \beta(|P - p_j| - \varepsilon_j) \tag{3}$$

Next we calculate the *accuracy* κ_j of each rule:

$$\kappa_j = \begin{cases} 1 & \text{if } \varepsilon_j < \varepsilon_o \\ \alpha(\varepsilon_j/\varepsilon_o)^{-v} & \text{otherwise} \end{cases} \tag{4}$$

where $0 < \varepsilon_o$ is the *accuracy criterion*, a constant controlling the tolerance for prediction error. Any rules with $\varepsilon < \varepsilon_o$ are considered to be equally (and fully) accurate. The *accuracy falloff rate* $0 < \alpha < 1$ and *accuracy exponent* $0 < v$ are constants controlling the rate of decline in accuracy when ε_o is exceeded.

Once the accuracy of each rule in [A] has been calculated, we calculate the relative accuracy κ' of each rule:

$$\kappa'_j = \frac{\kappa_j \cdot numerosity(j)}{\displaystyle\sum_{x \in [A]} \kappa_x \cdot numerosity(x)} \tag{5}$$

Finally, we update each rule's fitness F_j towards its relative accuracy:

$$F_j \leftarrow F_j + \beta(\kappa'_j - F_j) \tag{6}$$

In summary, the XCS updates treat the strength of a rule as a prediction of the reward to be received, and maintain an estimate of the error ε_j in each rule's prediction. An accuracy score κ_j is calculated based on the error as follows. If error is below the accuracy criterion threshold ε_o the rule is fully accurate (has an accuracy of 1), otherwise its accuracy drops off quickly. The accuracy values in the action set [A] are then converted to relative accuracies (the κ'_j update), and finally each rule's fitness F_j is updated towards its relative accuracy. To simplify, in XCS fitness is inversely related to the error in reward prediction, with errors below ε_o being ignored entirely.

When it comes to selecting actions, XCS weights the predictions of the matching rules by their fitnesses in order to obtain the system prediction $P(a_i)$ for each action a_i:

$$P(a_i) = \frac{\sum_{c \in [M]_{a_i}} F_c \cdot p_c}{\sum_{c \in [M]_{a_i}} F_c} \tag{7}$$

Then, as in SBXCS, any action selection method may be used on the $P(a_i)$ values.

3.3   Representation in XCS and SBXCS

XCS tends to find rules which form *complete maps* of the input/action/reward space because 1) the fitness of a rule does not depend on the magnitude of the reward it receives, so no region is neglected simply because it does not generate high rewards, and 2) pressure towards diversity in the rule population drives it towards covering the entire space [40, 15].

In contrast, SBXCS (and other strength-based LCS) tend towards *best action maps*, in which only the most highly rewarded action for each state is represented. This is a form of *partial map*, since not all actions are advocated. In practice, SBXCS does not actually represent only the best action for each state, but it does tend to represent only a subset of the available actions. This occurs simply because the fitness of a rule *is* proportional to the magnitude of the reward it receives [15].

The difference between best action and complete maps is illustrated in figure 2 which shows the 3-bit multiplexer function represented using two sets of rules; in the centre a partial map, and on the right a complete map.

4   The Policy's the Thing

Section 1 outlined two views of classifier systems: the GA-view – that the LCS is essentially the application of a GA to a problem – and the RL-view, that the LCS is some kind of RL system, that is, something like Q-learning, perhaps with

A B C	Output
0 0 0	0
0 0 1	0
0 1 0	1
0 1 1	1
1 0 0	0
1 0 1	1
1 1 0	0
1 1 1	1

```
00# → 0
01# → 1
1#0 → 0
1#1 → 1
```

```
00# → 0
00# → 1
01# → 0
01# → 1
1#0 → 0
1#0 → 1
1#1 → 0
1#1 → 1
```

Fig. 2. Truth table (left), best action map (centre) and complete map (right) for the 3 multiplexer

some kind of evolutionary component. Which view is correct? Or, more likely, which view is most appropriate? Perhaps it depends on the classifier system in question. Are the two views compatible? The following sections suggest some answers.

Classifier systems for reinforcement learning have the same goal as any RL system: to maximise return. To do so, an RL agent must find an optimal policy.[3] However, an important feature of classifier systems – many would say the whole point of using them, rather than, say, tabular Q-learning – is their in-built capacity to exploit environmental regularities. We could say the primary tasks an LCS faces are finding good policies and finding useful generalisations while doing so. Consequently, we can address the GA- and RL-view question by considering how an LCS finds (selects, determines) policies, and how it finds generalisations. In fact, the issue of finding generalisations is not in doubt: they are expressed by #s in rule conditions, and rule conditions are evolved using the GA. In other words, it is up to the GA to find useful generalisations. But what about finding policies? Two broad approaches have been mentioned: evolution and Q-learning-like RL. Which approach does an LCS use? Let's consider SBXCS and XCS in turn.

4.1 How SBXCS Determines Policies

We know that, to a first approximation, SBXCS's rule population determines its policy, and that SBXCS's GA evolves its rules, so we could say that SBXCS's GA determines its policy. But this is a superficial analysis, and in fact we could apply the same reasoning to XCS. Let's consider SBXCS's operation in more detail.

A policy is a mapping of states to actions. A rule population may not specify a unique policy – often conflicting rules occur, and some states may have no matching rules. Given this, how can we tell what a classifier system's policy is?

---

[3] Return is a generalisation of the notion of environmental reward. A policy is a mapping from each state to an action; an optimal policy is one which maximises return. See [35].

Deriving a Policy from a Value Function: Tabular Q-Learning. Let's consider a tabular Q-learning system. It maintains a value function, and just as a set of rules is not a policy, neither is a value function.[4] (A set of rules can represent a value function, but it can also represent conflicting actions for the same state; it is more general than a policy.) From its value function, a tabular Q-learner derives a policy *as needed.* That is, each time the system must select an action it consults its value function for the current state, and applies some action selection method (e.g., ϵ-greedy selection). Since the value function is constantly being updated, so is the policy. The point here is that there is no explicitly represented policy; it is generated as needed.

Deriving a Policy from a Value Function: SBXCS. A classifier system selects actions based on the currently matching rules (see equations (7) and (2)), using some action selection method, in the same way a tabular Q-learning system does based on its value function. From this description an LCS operates just like a tabular Q-learner. But in some cases there's a difference. Recall from section 3.3 that SBXCS maintains partial map representations, and that consequently sometimes (in fact, usually) some of the actions available in a state have no value estimate. SBXCS (following XCS) cannot select actions whose values are not estimated (i.e., which are not advocated by a matching rule).

In contrast, in a tabular Q-learning system, all actions are represented and can be selected. Is this significant? Yes, because the presence or absence of rules is determined by the GA. By determining which actions are represented, the GA influences action selection.

4.2   How XCS Determines Policies

XCS and SBXCS can be configured to select actions using the same method (e.g., ϵ-greedy selection), and, just like SBXCS, cannot select actions which no matching rule advocates. However, XCS's strong tendency towards complete maps means that, typically, all actions *are* represented by some rule. The significance is that in XCS the GA *does not* influence action selection by preventing some actions from being selected. In XCS, all actions are eligible for selection, just as in tabular Q-learning.[5]

This point is somewhat subtle, since the same action selection method can be used with both systems. The behaviour of the chosen method differs in the two systems because of the form of representation upon which it operates (partial versus complete maps). In complex systems like classifier systems, this sort of interaction between components can easily occur by chance, although in this case XCS's designer, Stewart Wilson, intended action selection to operate on complete

---

[4] A value function is a mapping from each state (or state-action pair) to an estimate of its value. See [35].

[5] More carefully, initialising XCS with an empty population results in a temporarily partial map, allowing the GA and covering some influence on action selection.

maps [40]. What Wilson may not have intended was the resulting decoupling of the GA and action selection, i.e., of the GA and policy determination.

That XCS's GA is detached from action selection seems highly significant to the issue of how it determines policies. It is also relevant to the issue of the GA and RL-views, as we'll see shortly.

4.3   Three Approaches to Determining a Policy

We can distinguish three ways to determine a policy. The first is to evolve and evaluate complete policies, in which case policies are completely determined by the evolutionary algorithm. This is the approach used in Pittsburgh LCS (e.g., LS-1 [24–26]). A second approach is to derive a policy from a (complete) value function, as we do in tabular Q-learning. In this case the policy is completely determined by the Q-learning process. This is the approach used with XCS, where the value function is stored by the rule population.

Finally, the third approach, that used by SBXCS, lies somewhere between the first two. In SBXCS, the policy is derived from the incomplete representation of the value function SBXCS's partial map provides. Significantly, the policies which can be derived depend on which actions are advocated, which in turn depends on which rules the GA maintains in the population. Thus, the policy is determined by a combination of Q-learning and evolution (and any additional rule discovery mechanisms, such as covering).[6]

4.4   The GA-View and the RL-View

In this section we relate the two learning subsystems to the two primary tasks (policy learning and generalisation) of the classifier system, consider the emphasis to be placed on the role of the GA, and finally propose an answer to the question of whether classifier systems are GA-based or RL-based.

Which Subsystem Does What? Although all classifier systems contain a rule discovery and credit assignment system, we can now see that different classifier systems operate on very different principles. Although XCS and SBXCS are very similar algorithmically, XCS relies entirely on Q-learning to obtain policies, while SBXCS combines Q-learning with evolution. Pittsburgh classifier systems rely on the GA to address both issues. Figure 3 summarises the differences in the three approaches.

The Importance of the GA. The two approaches place different emphasis on the role of the GA; in SBXCS the GA is more significant as it directly affects the policy. This emphasis on the role of the GA is part of the rationale for traditional (strength-based) classifier systems. In case there is any doubt concerning the

---

[6] The fighter aircraft LCS [23] is an interesting case in which a default policy is applied in the absence of any matching rule.

	XCS	SBXCS	Pitt LCS
Policy	QL	QL & GA	GA
Generalisation	GA	GA	GA

Fig. 3. The method (Genetic Algorithm or Q-Learning) employed by each system for finding policies and generalisation

emphasis to be placed on the role of Q-learning in accuracy-based XCS, [15] shows how XCS reduces to tabular Q-learning when generalisation is disabled. The quotations at the start of this work seem entirely consistent with these conclusions regarding the importance of the GA.

Which View for Which System? The RL-view seems entirely appropriate for XCS, since it derives its policy solely from a value function, just as tabular Q-learning does. In contrast, the GA-view seems entirely appropriate for Pittsburgh LCS, which rely on the GA for both policy learning and generalisation. Somewhere in between the two extremes lies SBXCS, in which the GA and Q-learning both contribute to determining the policy.

5   Conclusion

I have tried to convey two somewhat imprecise points of view on what a classifier system is, and how it solves problems (adapts its policy). The GA-view holds that classifier systems solve problems using a GA, while the RL-view holds that they solve them as tabular Q-learning does.

An attempt was made to make these views more concrete by considering the goals of a classifier system, and how two particular systems operate to achieve these goals. We have considered how XCS and its strength-based twin SBXCS differ in how they determine their policies, and seen that XCS's GA has far less influence on the policy that SBXCS's. This suggests the GA-view is more appropriate for SBXCS (and other strength-based LCS like it). In contrast, the RL-view seems entirely appropriate for XCS. Indeed, it has been shown elsewhere that XCS is a proper generalisation of tabular Q-learning [15]. These differences indicate that XCS differs greatly from other classifier systems, even its twin SBXCS.

Acknowledgements

I am grateful to Stewart Wilson and Alwyn Barry for our our many discussions of XCS, and to Robert Smith for his comments.

References

1. Manu Ahluwalia and Larry Bull. A Genetic Programming-based Classifier System. In Banzhaf et al. [2], pages 11–18.

2. W. Banzhaf, J. Daida, A.E. Eiben, M.H. Garzon, V. Honavar, M. Jakiela, and R.E. Smith, editors. *GECCO-99: Proceedings of the Genetic and Evolutionary Computation Conference*. Morgan Kaufmann, 1999.

3. Alwyn Barry. *XCS Performance and Population Structure within Multiple-Step Environments*. PhD thesis, Queens University Belfast, 2000.

4. Lashon B. Booker. Improving the performance of genetic algorithms in classifier systems. In John J. Grefenstette, editor, *Proceedings of the 1st International Conference on Genetic Algorithms and their Applications (ICGA-85)*, pages 80–92, Pittsburgh, PA, July 1985. Lawrence Erlbaum Associates.

5. Martin Butz, David E. Goldberg, and Wolfgang Stolzmann. New challenges for an ACS: Hard problems and possible solutions. Technical Report 99019, University of Illinois at Urbana-Champaign, Urbana, IL, October 1999.

6. Martin Butz and Wolfgang Stolzmann. Action-Planning in Anticipatory Classifier Systems. In Wu [43], pages 242–249.

7. Martin V. Butz, David E. Goldberg, and Wolfgang Stolzmann. Probability-enhanced predictions in the anticipatory classifier system. In *Proceedings of the International Workshop on Learning Classifier Systems (IWLCS-2000), in the Joint Workshops of SAB 2000 and PPSN 2000*, 2000.

8. Martin V. Butz and Stewart W. Wilson. An Algorithmic Description of XCS. In Pier Luca Lanzi, Wolfgang Stolzmann, and Stewart W. Wilson, editors, *Advances in Learning Classifier Systems*, number 1996 in LNAI, pages 253–272. Springer–Verlag, 2001.

9. Henry Brown Cribbs III and Robert E. Smith. What Can I do with a Learning Classifier System? In C. Karr and L.M. Freeman, editors, *Industrial Applications of Genetic Algorithms*, pages 299–320. CRC Press, 1998.

10. David E. Goldberg. *Genetic Algorithms in Search, Optimization, and Machine Learning*. Addison-Wesley, Reading, MA, 1989.

11. John H. Holland. Adaptation. In R. Rosen and F.M. Snell, editors, *Progress in theoretical biology*. New York: Plenum, 1976.

12. John H. Holland. Properties of the bucket brigade. In John J. Grefenstette, editor, *Proceedings of the 1st International Conference on Genetic Algorithms and their Applications*, pages 1–7, Pittsburgh, PA, July 1985. Lawrence Erlbaum Associates.

13. John H. Holland, Lashon B. Booker, Marco Colombetti, Marco Dorigo, David E. Goldberg, Stephanie Forrest, Rick L. Riolo, Robert E. Smith, Pier Luca Lanzi, Wolfgang Stolzmann, and Stewart W. Wilson. What is a Learning Classifier System? In Lanzi et al. [17], pages 3–32.

14. John H. Holland and J.S. Reitman. Cognitive systems based on adaptive algorithms. In D.A. Waterman and F. Hayes-Roth, editors, *Pattern-directed inference systems*. New York: Academic Press, 1978. Reprinted in: Evolutionary Computation. The Fossil Record. David B. Fogel (Ed.) IEEE Press, 1998. ISBN: 0-7803-3481-7.

15. Tim Kovacs. *A Comparison of Strength and Accuracy-Based Fitness in Learning Classifier Systems*. PhD thesis, School of Computer Science, University of Birmingham, 2001.

16. Pier Luca Lanzi. Extending the Representation of Classifier Conditions Part II: From Messy Coding to S-Expressions. In Banzhaf et al. [2], pages 345–352.

17. Pier Luca Lanzi, Wolfgang Stolzmann, and Stewart W. Wilson, editors. *Learning Classifier Systems. From Foundations to Applications*, volume 1813 of *LNAI*. Springer-Verlag, Berlin, 2000.

18. Rick L. Riolo. Bucket Brigade Performance: I. Long Sequences of Classifiers. In *Proceedings Second International Conference on Genetic Algorithms (ICGA-87)*, pages 184–195. Lawrence Erlbaum Associates, 1987.

19. Rick L. Riolo. The emergence of coupled sequences of classifiers. In Schaffer [20], pages 256–264.

20. J. David Schaffer, editor. *Proceedings of the 3rd International Conference on Genetic Algorithms (ICGA-89)*, George Mason University, June 1989. Morgan Kaufmann.

21. Robert E. Smith. A Report on The First International Workshop on Learning Classifier Systems (IWLCS-92). NASA Johnson Space Center, Houston, Texas, Oct. 6-9, 1992.

22. Robert E. Smith. Derivative Methods: Learning Classifier Systems. In Thomas Bäck, David B. Fogel, and Zbigniew Michalewicz, editors, *Handbook of Evolutionary Computation*, pages B1.2:6–B1.5:11. Institute of Physics Publishing and Oxford University Press, 1997. http://www.iop.org/Books/Catalogue/

23. Robert E. Smith, B.A. Dike, B. Ravichandran, A. El-Fallah, and R.K. Mehra. The Fighter Aircraft LCS: A Case of Different LCS Goals and Techniques. In Lanzi et al. [17], pages 283–300.

24. S.F. Smith. *A Learning System Based on Genetic Adaptive Algorithms*. PhD thesis, University of Pittsburgh, 1980.

25. S.F. Smith. Flexible Learning of Problem Solving Heuristics through Adaptive Search. In *Proceedings Eight International Joint Conference on Artificial Intelligence*, pages 422–425, 1983.

26. S.F. Smith. Adaptive learning systems. In R. Forsyth, editor, *Expert systems: Principles and case studies*, pages 169–189. Chapman and Hall, 1984.

27. Wolfgang Stolzmann. Learning classifier systems using the cognitive mechanism of anticipatory behavioral control, detailed version. In *Proceedings of the First European Workshop on Cognitive Modelling*, pages 82–89. Berlin: TU, 1996.

28. Wolfgang Stolzmann. *Antizipative Classifier Systeme*. PhD thesis, Fachbereich Mathematik/Informatik, University of Osnabrück, 1997.

29. Wolfgang Stolzmann. Two Applications of Anticipatory Classifier Systems (ACSs). In *Proceedings of the 2nd European Conference on Cognitive Science*, pages 68–73. Manchester, U.K., 1997.

30. Wolfgang Stolzmann. Anticipatory classifier systems. In *Proceedings of the Third Annual Genetic Programming Conference*, pages 658–664. Morgan Kaufmann, 1998.

31. Wolfgang Stolzmann. Latent Learning in Khepera Robots with Anticipatory Classifier Systems. In Wu [43], pages 290–297.

32. Wolfgang Stolzmann. An Introduction to Anticipatory Classifier Systems. In Lanzi et al. [17], pages 175–194.

33. Wolfgang Stolzmann and Martin Butz. Latent Learning and Action-Planning in Robots with Anticipatory Classifier Systems. In Lanzi et al. [17], pages 301–317.

34. Wolfgang Stolzmann, Martin Butz, J. Hoffmann, and D. E. Goldberg. First cognitive capabilities in the anticipatory classifier system. In J. A. Meyer et al., editor, *From Animals to Animats 6: Proceedings of the Sixth International Conference on Simulation of Adaptive Behavior*, pages 287–296, 2000. Also Technical Report 2000008 of the Illinois Genetic Algorithms Laboratory.

35. Richard S. Sutton and Andrew G. Barto. *Reinforcement Learning: An Introduction.* MIT Press, Cambridge, MA, 1998.
36. Andy Tomlinson and Larry Bull. A Corporate Classifier System. In A. E. Eiben, T. Bäck, M. Shoenauer, and H.-P. Schwefel, editors, *Proceedings of the Fifth International Conference on Parallel Problem Solving From Nature – PPSN V*, volume 1498 of *Lecture Notes in Computer Science*, pages 550–559. Springer Verlag, 1998.
37. Patrick Tufts. Evolution of a Clustering Scheme for Classifier Systems: Beyond the Bucket Brigade. PhD Thesis proposal, 1994.
38. Patrick Tufts. Dynamic Classifiers: Genetic Programming and Classifier Systems. In E. V. Siegel and J. R. Koza, editors, *Working Notes for the AAAI Symposium on Genetic Programming*, pages 114–119, MIT, Cambridge, MA, USA, 1995. AAAI.
39. Stewart W. Wilson. ZCS: A Zeroth Level Classifier System. *Evolutionary Computation*, 2(1):1–18, 1994.
40. Stewart W. Wilson. Classifier Fitness Based on Accuracy. *Evolutionary Computation*, 3(2):149–175, 1995.
41. Stewart W. Wilson. Personal communication to Alwyn Barry and Tim Kovacs. June 12, 1998.
42. Stewart W. Wilson and David E. Goldberg. A Critical Review of Classifier Systems. In Schaffer [20], pages 244–255.
43. Annie S. Wu, editor. *Proceedings of the 1999 Genetic and Evolutionary Computation Conference Workshop Program*, 1999.

Social Simulation Using a Multi-agent Model Based on Classifier Systems: The Emergence of Vacillating Behaviour in the "El Farol" Bar Problem

Luis Miramontes Hercog and Terence C. Fogarty

School of Computing, South Bank University
103 Borough Rd., London SE1 0AA, U.K.
Telephone: +44-20-78157008, Fax: +44-20-78157499
{miramol,fogarttc}@sbu.ac.uk

Abstract. In this paper, MAXCS – a Multi-agent system that learns using XCS – is used for social modelling on the "El Farol" Bar problem. A *cooperative* reward distribution technique is used and compared with the original *selfish* "El Farol" Bar problem reward distribution technique. When using selfish reward distribution a vacillating agent emerges which, although obtaining no reward itself, enables the other agents to benefit in the best way possible from the system.

Experiments with 10 agents and different parameter settings for the problem show that MAXCS is always able to solve it. Furthermore, emergent behaviour can be observed by analysing the actions of the agents and explained by analysing the rules utilised by the agents. The use of a learning classifier system has been essential for the detailed analysis of each agent's decision, as well as for the detection of the emergent behaviour in the system.

The results are divided into three categories: those obtained using cooperative reward, those obtained using selfish reward and those which show emergent behaviour.

Analysis of the values of the rules' performance show that it is the amount of reward received by each XCS combined with its reinforcement mechanism which cause the emergent behaviour.

MAXCS has proved to be a good modelling tool for social simulation, both because of its performance and providing the explanation for the actions.

Keywords: Multi-agent Systems, emergent behaviour, XCS, Learning Classifier Systems, "El Farol" Bar problem.

1 Introduction

In this paper, MAXCS – a Multi-agent system (MAS) [15,31] that learns using XCS [38] – is used for social modelling on the"El Farol" Bar problem [2]. The aim of this paper is to analyse the usefulness of a LCS as the learning agent for a MAS in social modelling.

P.L. Lanzi, W. Stolzmann, and S.W. Wilson (Eds.): IWLCS 2001, LNAI 2321, pp. 88–111, 2002.
© Springer-Verlag Berlin Heidelberg 2002

A Multi-agent System is a set of individual entities that can partially perceive their environment and interact autonomously with it. The agents learn from the rewards obtained from the environment. The resources and skills available to each agent, its perception and representation of the environment and, in some cases, communication with other agents, direct the behaviour of the agent toward satisfying its objectives either individually or in association with others. Multi-agent simulation is based on the idea of a computerised representation of entities' behaviour in the world. This computerised representation gives the possibility of representing a phenomenon, which emerges from the interactions of a set of agents with their own operational autonomy [35]. The operational autonomy, in this particular case of study, is provided by a learning classifier system: XCS. The agents base their decisions on evolving rule sets, which are improved against the performance of the agent on the desired problem.

Experiments with 10 agents and different parameter settings for the problem show that MAXCS is always able to solve it. Furthermore, emergent behaviour[1] can be observed by analysing the actions of the agents and explained by analysing the rules utilised by the agents. The use of a learning classifier system has been essential for the detailed analysis of each agent's decision, as well as for the detection of the emergent behaviour in the system.

The "El Farol" Bar problem is explained in the following section. There is then a brief description of XCS. After that, the use of XCS as the learning engine for the Multi-agent system MAXCS is explained and the results are presented and discussed. The results are divided into three categories: those obtained using cooperative reward, those obtained using selfish reward and those which show emergent behaviour.

2   The "El Farol" Bar Problem (EFBP)

A good benchmark for multi-agent systems is the "El Farol" Bar Problem (EFBP), invented by B. Arthur[2]. The problem is based on a bar in Santa Fe which offers entertainment each week. The place is small and uncomfortable if overcrowded but boring if not full.

A comfort **threshold** (Λ_{cm}) is defined then, as the number of people which makes the place an enjoyable one. The original problem assumes 100 agents and 60 seats in the bar. The agents have to decide, based on their strategies, whether or not to go the bar each week. The agents are rewarded in two different ways: if the agent decides to go to the bar and the comfort threshold is not exceeded then the agent is rewarded, if the agent decides to stay at home and the threshold is exceeded then it gets rewarded, otherwise they are not rewarded. In other words, if they make the correct choice they are rewarded.

Each agent takes one of a number of fixed strategies to predict the number of agents who will go, based on past data, e.g. the same as two weeks ago, the

---

[1] Emergent behaviour is considered as any computation that achieves predictable global effects, formally or stochastically, by communicating directly with only a bounded number of neighbours and without the use of global visibility[16].

average of the last 3 weeks, etc. Each week, each agent evaluates its strategies against past data and chooses the strategy with the best predictor. The predictor is updated according to its reliability. The agent predicts the number of agents that will attend the bar and then decides to go if this prediction is below the value of Λ_{cm}.

After the EFBP was stated, many approaches have followed – most of them used for economics - due to its formalisation, as an evolutionary game: the Minority Game [12, 11, 13]. The Minority Game(MG) is an abstraction, it considers Λ_{cm}=0.5 and the agents are rewarded if they are on the side with less agents. The agents base their decisions in rules that state whether it was good to attend (1), or to stay at home (0). The agents are initialised with a random number of rules and they only update a value that estimates how good the rule is. The GA works periodically every several rounds(100). The fittest agent is cloned and its rules mutated and the measure initialised to 0 to replace the worst performing agent in the system.

The results reported for EFBP and the MG are oscillating lines around the comfort threshold, with an average close or equal to the threshold selected. However, there are no reports of what the strategies used by each agent (for the MG), nor reports for different thresholds.

There have also been some MAS approaches but, unfortunately, little can be taken from them, since they over-simplify the problem by allowing the agents to choose a particular night out of seven to go to the bar [30, 40]. The most interesting approach used genetic programming [26] to solve the problem by letting 16 agents communicate with each other [14]. The fact that communication is allowed destroys the very nature of the problem itself.

2.1   Why Is this Problem Difficult to Learn?

Unlike other games, the EFBP has no Nash equilibrium, i.e. there is no ideal situation or answer that the agents can choose, the solution must arise from the interaction between the agents.

The EFBP can be considered a coordinated collaboration task which the agents have insufficient resources and skills to achieve. Coordinated collaboration is the most complex of cooperation situations, since it combines task allocation problems with aspects of coordination shaped by limited resources. It is a very difficult problem to learn, since the agents are not endowed with any notion of their previous actions – they must base their current action on the overall statistics of attendance at the bar in previous weeks. All of them have access to the same information, therefore this problem goes beyond deductive rationality. The agents can "think" that "if the attendance was 80 last week and 40 the previous week then it's good to go this week"; if all the agents think this they will overcrowd the bar. This is the reason that the problem is called a bounded rationality problem; rationality takes the agents to solve the problem partially.

EFBP is a single-step problem, because the answers of the agents are taken, the attendance is computed and the reward is distributed immediately. The problem is non-Markovian, i.e. the environmental perception of the agent is not sufficient to solve the problem. It is also non-stationary, because it is a very dynamic environment. The complexity of the problem lays in accomplishing the correct number of agents in the bar, that depends in the action taken by each of the agents. For this problem the same state perceived by the agents does not have the same correct answer.

In the minority game, the abstraction is extreme: the agents cannot see the attendance figure, but can only see one bit 0 or 1; the former if it was good and the latter not good to go to the bar in previous weeks. The abstraction level has been kept for this research.

2.2   Reward Distribution Schemes

In this paper two reward distribution schemes are used. The traditional "El Farol" Bar reward, called from now on the **selfish** reward scheme, and a **cooperative** reward scheme. The cooperative reward scheme was introduced in [20]: if the bar is overcrowded none of the agents are rewarded, otherwise every agent is rewarded with a scalar value proportional to the attendance with a maximum of 1000.

3   Extended Classifier System

The extended classifier system (XCS) is a Michigan style learning classifier system (LCS) [22, 17], invented by Wilson in 1995 [38]. XCS has a simple architecture for the study of LCSs. The knowledge in XCS is encoded in rules called classifiers. The rules are generally formed by a **condition** and an **action** part, represented as *condition→action*. The rule syntax is very simple, representing very fine-grained knowledge. This simple representation allows the LCS to use the evolutionary algorithm for rule discovery. Each rule has a performance indicator (fitness) associated. The fitness is used for conflict resolution by the LCS when many rules are active. The reinforcement mechanism updates the fitness value generating a competitive scheme. This scheme ensures that good rules survive and bad rules die off when applying the genetic algorithm, improving the population performance [2].

The rule representation depends on the problem being solved: ternary (most common) {0,1,#} (the # is known as the don't care symbol), integers, integer intervals [36], real intervals, fuzzy rules [3, 5, 4] and even S-expressions [1](LISP expressions which may resemble genetic programming[26]).

XCS incorporates accuracy based fitness, considered to be a breakthrough in the LCS field. XCS learns to maximise the reward obtained from the environment, this reward is what drives the search and the self-improvement of the system.

---

[2] There is a LCS that does not use a performance indicator, based on Holland's ECHO systems [22], questioning whether there should be a performance indicator or not [6].

One of the innovations in XCS is that each classifier has three parameters to measure its fitness:

- Prediction (p): Is the value for the reward expected if this rule was selected
- Prediction error (ϵ): Estimates the error of the prediction
- Fitness (F): Evaluates the quality of the prediction, based on the error

Each of these three parameters is updated every time that the reward is obtained by the system. A reinforcement learning algorithm is used to update the three parameters mentioned above (see Table 1 for the formulae).

XCS also adds a concept called macro-classifiers. A macro-classifier is the fusion of identical classifiers into a single one. This is done for practical reasons, instead of having n classifiers that have the same condition and action, there will be only one with numerosity n.

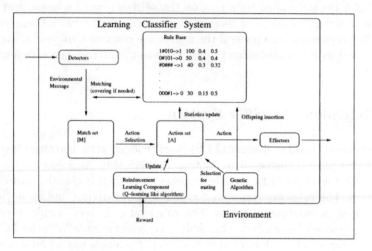

Fig. 1. Functional diagram of XCS

3.1   XCS Functionality

XCS (see Fig.1) perceives the environment through its sensors and encodes this into an environmental message. The classifiers in the rule base that satisfy the environmental message form the match set [M]. If there are no classifiers that match the environmental message, a new one is generated using covering.

The classifiers that have the action with the best prediction in [M] form the action set [A], when exploiting. If XCS is exploring, the action is chosen randomly.

XCS selects the action [39] by computing $\frac{\Sigma F_j p_j}{\Sigma F_j}$ for all the classifiers in the match set, where j are the classifiers with the same action, this is done for each different action in [M].

Then, the selected action is put into the effectors and posted to the environment.

The environment evaluates the action and, for a single-step problem, gives the reward to XCS. As explained before, XCS uses a reinforcement learning algorithm [33] to update the p, ϵ and F values for all the classifiers in [A] in single-step problems and $[A]_{-1}$ in multiple-step problems ($[A]_{-1}$ is the action set at the previous time step).

The reinforcement mechanism updates are calculated as shown in Table 1 for each $classifier_j$ in [A], first p_j and ϵ_j are updated; then the accuracy (κ) for each classifier is computed. A relative accuracy (κ'_j) is calculated for each classifier, and finally the fitness is updated.

Table 1. XCS Formulae for classifier update used by the reinforcement learning algorithm; where p'_j, ϵ'_j, F'_j are the current values and F_j, ϵ_j, p_j are the new values

Prediction update $\qquad p_j \leftarrow p'_j + \beta(R - p'_j)$

Prediction error update $\quad \epsilon_j \leftarrow \epsilon'_j + \beta(|R - p_j| - \epsilon'_j)$

Accuracy
$$\kappa_j = \exp(\ln(\alpha)\tfrac{\epsilon_j - \epsilon_0}{\epsilon_0}) \qquad \text{or}$$
$$\kappa_j = \alpha(\tfrac{\epsilon_j}{\epsilon_0})^{-n}; n = 5 \qquad \text{if } \epsilon_j > \epsilon_0;$$
$$\kappa_j = 1.0 \qquad \text{otherwise}$$

Relative accuracy $\qquad \kappa'_j = \dfrac{\kappa_j}{\sum \kappa_j}$

Fitness $\qquad F_j \leftarrow F'_j + \beta(\kappa'_j - F'_j)$

Therefore the fitness is based on how accurate the prediction of the reward is. After the updates are done, a new environmental message is encoded and the process continues.

3.2 Discovery Mechanisms

There are two discovery mechanisms in XCS, one, the genetic algorithm(GA), is evolutionary and the other, covering, is not.

Covering happens when [M] is null, then a new classifier is created: the condition is produced by taking the environmental message and performing a mutation to introduce don't care(#) symbols and the action is generated randomly (a similar mechanism is used in [19]). A new effector covering operator has been introduced, it inserts a new classifier for every possible action that is not covered by the classifiers in the match set.

The GA is applied only in [A], instead of the whole population [7], so it imposes a selection pressure as well as an implicit niching technique [18, 23]. Each classifier records when was the last time that the GA was applied, and if the average of this value in the classifiers in [A] is greater than θ_{GA}, then the GA is applied.

The GA selects 2 classifiers (parents) using a roulette wheel algorithm based on the fitness. The parents are cloned producing children. The children are recombined, with a χ probability using a two-point crossover. Then, mutation takes place with a μ probability. When there is only one classifier in [A], cloning and mutation take place. The children are inserted in the population. If the maximum population size is reached, some classifiers are deleted based on their experience and fitness (see [24] for deletion techniques).

3.3   Motivation

Experiments have shown that XCS evolves accurate, complete, and minimal representations for Boolean functions [24]. The GA provides accurate generalisation and helped by a deletion technique, its application will get rid of the overgeneral classifiers [3] [24, 28].

XCS has been tried in several test problems: the multiplexer[17], "woods" environments [37], some mazes [27], the monk's problems [32] and lately it has been used for data mining as a real world problem [36], though more research has to be done in complex environments. Markovian and non-Markovian test problems have been tried and XCS has proved to be quite effective. Though due to the lack of an internal memory, XCS cannot cope with aliasing sates. The bit register memory introduced by Lanzi [29] is not a feasible solution for this particular problem, as it is discussed in the results section.

A non-Markovian, non-stationary problem as a multi-agent system, where the answer to the problem does not depend uniquely on the actions by the agent itself, but by all the agents, is a great challenge for LCS and XCS in particular.

4   MAXCS: A Multi-agent System that Learns Using XCS

The idea of representing an agent as a LCS [9, 8, 41] – such as XCS – is based on the following reasoning: if the characteristics of an agent and XCS are put together, XCS covers the features needed by an agent[15].

Each agent in the system is represented as an XCS (see Figure 2).

By this analysis it can be seen that the classifier system engine brings a category where cognitive and reactive agent types [21] are interlaced and complementary: XCS gives a reliable internal representation (encoded individually in each classifier) and an inference mechanism (GA and covering)– complying with the cognitive agent definition. It can memorise the situations in a very simple way. Using the accuracy measure XCS can foresee the possible reaction (taken as the reward from the environment) to its actions, therefore it can decide which action to take, and why.

---

[3] An overgeneral classifier is a classifier which has many # symbols and it will interact in too many action sets, but is not accurate.

Table 2. Comparison of the agent and XCS characteristics

XCS	Agent
Detectors	Perception of the environment
Classifier database	Partial representation of the environment
Accuracy measure	Skill (to evaluate its own performance)
Reinforcement component	Behaviour toward satisfying its objectives
Environmental interaction	Autonomy, not directed by commands
Action posting	Capacity to alter its environment

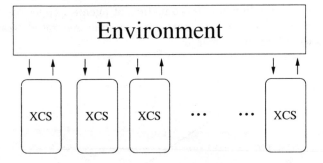

Fig. 2. Diagram of MAXCS

On the other hand, the classifier system can be seen also as a reactive agent. XCS shows a specific behaviour depending on the environmental state sensed, selecting the rules and triggering an action.

XCS evolves readable sets of rules which help in understanding how the system is adapting to a specific problem or to a variable environment [4, 9].

5 Experiments

Ten agents have been used for all the experiments. This number of agents eases the task of keeping track of both the populations and the decisions taken by each agent. To simplify the control of the system as a whole, all the agents explore or exploit at the same time. Interestingly, setting the explore or exploit at the same time and at different time for each agent yielded the same results.

For the experiments reported here, each XCS can only see whether it was good (1) or not (0) to attend the bar the previous 5 weeks (M=5). The system can only see the correct answer for each of those weeks, i.e. a 0 if the bar was overcrowded and a 1 if it was good to attend. The rule conditions represent what was good to do last week with the leftmost bit and what was good to do 5 weeks ago with the rightmost bit.

The maximum population size for all the agents is 64 classifiers. This value is set to allow the system to keep all the possible states visible for both actions if no generalisation would happen at all.

The system has been extensively tested using both reward schemes –selfish and cooperative (see subsection 2.2)– with the whole range of possible comfort thresholds for 10 agents (Λ_{cm}= 0, 0.1, 0.2, 0.3, 0.4, 0.5, 0.6, 0.7, 0.8, 0.9, 1).

The following parameters have been used for all the experiments: # probability = 0.333, explore/exploit rate = 0.5, crossover rate(χ)= 0.8, mutation rate(μ) = 0.02, θ_{GA} = 25, minimum error(ϵ_0)=0.01 and learning rate (β) =0.2.

Subsumption deletion is used only at GA level. The effector covering is enabled(see section 3.2).

Unlike in the EFBP and MG, all the agents are preserved throughout the experiment, no elimination nor reproduction of agents happens in the experiments here reported. The agents start with random generated strategies, that they evolve, according to their needs.

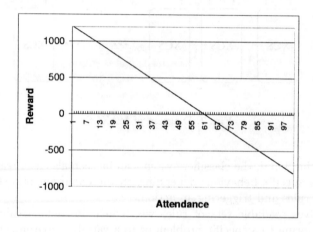

Fig. 3. The Minority Game reward function for Λ_{cm}=0.6

The original minority game reward function $R = -a_i*(\sum a_i - A_0)$ e.g. A_0=20 for Λ_{cm}=0.6, A_0=0 for Λ_{cm}=0.5 ; a_i is the action of *classifier*$_i$ (actions are considered 1 ,-1 instead of 1,0 for this function), plotted in Fig. 3. This function based on the attendance rate has been found misleading for MAXCS, producing random behaviour. This might be explained because the MG function does not give any reward to the system when the attendance equals Λ_{cm}.

Then, based on the assumption that a LCS works similarly to a neural network(NN) [34], a different reward function has been used. The new reward function, referred as "peak function" from now on, was inspired by the NN backpropagation error update function:

$R = 1000/(e^{(attendance-\Lambda_{cm})^2} * 1000)^2$; plotting this function (see Fig. 4) it can be seen that it has only one maximum, corresponding to the comfort threshold. The NN inspiration refers to squaring and escalating the error, represented in this equation by *attendance* $- \Lambda_{cm}$.

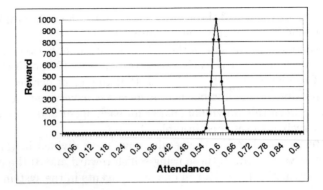

Fig. 4. The "peak" reward function for $\Lambda_{cm}=0.6$

The peak function lets the system converge faster when it approaches the desired Λ_{cm} value. The function has been biased intentionally and if the attendance is very low or very high the system will get no reward. This bias resembles the original EFBP, in the sense that it will keep the attendance to an enjoyable level [2].

An important remark that has to be made is, that when using 10 agents, the peak function would give only 1000 or 0 as rewards. In order not to lose the idea of the layered payoff of the peak function, a 679 reward is introduced for $attendance = \Lambda_{cm} + 1$ and $attendance = \Lambda_{cm} - 1$.

6   Results and Discussion

Each set of results is presented as a single run of 5000 time steps. The graphics are not plotted as lines, since the values are scattered and discontinuous. Each figure presented shows results for one run and the scattered points represent the attendance as a percentage of the total number of agents.

It has been found that the behaviour of the agents is exact when the Λ_{cm} values are close to 0 and 1. Due to the threshold value, they either go or not go. A more interesting behaviour of the population as a whole can be observed for the thresholds in the central interval($\Lambda_{cm}=[0.1, 0.9]$).

All the possible Λ_{cm} values were tested in 10 different experiments for each type of reward. MAXCS solved all the problems correctly. After analysing all the results, those obtained for the $\Lambda_{cm}=0.0, 0.3, 0.6, 1.0$ values have been chosen. The behaviour observed for these Λ_{cm} values are representative of the system's performance.

In order to analyse what happens once the agents have explored and exploited their rules for 2500 time steps, the exploration and the GA was switched off(this leaves the LCS without any rule discovery means). The $\Lambda_{cm}=0.0, 0.3, 0.6, 1.0$ values were tested in 10 different experiments for each type of reward.

The results are displayed throughout Figs. 7 - 10, the right graphic is filtered from the left one, to show only the exploitation trials.

Tables 3 and 5 show the sum of the individual attendance every 100 steps only for exploitation trials, that is, each row corresponds to 100 possible exploitation trials; e.g. if the number in the table is 2, that the agent decided to go 2 times out of 100 possible, if the number is 0, it means it never went. A sample of the correlation between the individual answer for each agent and the environmental state they perceive is presented in tables 4 and 6.

For better comprehension the results have been divided in three: 1) those using cooperative reward, 2) those using selfish reward and 3) the emergence of vacillating "altruistic" behaviour in one of the agents in the system using selfish reward.

6.1 Cooperative Reward

The results show that the optimal percentage of the population= Λ_{cm} learns to go and the rest refrain from attending, in the case of the cooperative reward. Therefore MAXCS solves the problem.

It can be seen from the figures 7-8, when the cooperative reward is used, the system performs an exploitation trial, the performance converges very fast. Random behaviour can be observed when all the trials (exploration and exploitation) are taken, i.e. the left side graphics. The reason for this behaviour is that the system is exploring, i.e. all the agents are taking random decisions at the same time.

It has been observed after the experiments with Λ_{cm}=0.0, 0.3, 0.6 and 1.0 using the cooperative reward scheme, that some agents tend to go more than others (see Table 3) and there are agents which definitely do not attend the bar.

MAXCS adapts properly for all the values of Λ_{cm} tested. Certain Λ_{cm} values are difficult for the system to learn. It takes longer for the system, to adapt to Λ_{cm}=[0.3, 0.7] values, though. Looking at Fig. 5, after 1000 weeks, the system has almost converged to the desired Λ_{cm}=0.3.

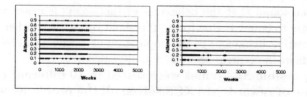

Fig. 5. All (left) and exploitation (right) trials for cooperative reward Λ_{cm}=0.3

The analysis of the results for Λ_{cm}=0.6 (Fig. 6)have been chosen, based in the performance of the system for both reward schemes. The system showed, for this specific value very interesting behaviour using the selfish reward. The results obtained using the cooperative reward are shown to establish a comparison.

Table 3. Individual attendance sum only for exploitation trials, cooperative reward and Λ_{cm}=0.6

Row	Agent 1	Agent 2	Agent 3	Agent 4	Agent 5	Agent 6	Agent 7	Agent 8	Agent 9	Agent 10
1	15	22	25	11	37	18	17	16	30	37
2	13	36	36	26	44	15	35	15	7	49
3	28	15	16	39	12	34	45	16	30	45
4	39	10	14	20	31	41	16	9	33	41
5	32	6	11	34	11	33	30	34	15	38
6	30	25	13	19	29	33	33	32	21	45
7	21	40	10	9	24	35	20	32	18	39
8	53	57	19	7	57	54	4	21	2	56
9	9	8	44	8	47	35	46	13	28	43
10	40	0	54	2	56	57	57	20	53	2
11	0	1	45	0	46	46	46	46	46	1
12	0	0	55	0	55	55	55	55	55	0
13	0	0	53	0	53	53	53	53	53	0
14	0	2	53	29	53	21	53	53	53	1
15	19	32	36	36	34	6	19	49	45	4
16	35	50	50	35	22	20	2	35	52	21
17	2	47	50	8	51	49	5	2	47	51
18	25	2	17	48	1	2	32	49	46	48
19	1	53	50	3	1	54	2	50	54	55
20	5	51	51	4	5	48	4	49	52	51
21	24	5	43	37	44	40	26	27	25	3
22	33	47	0	6	46	38	53	42	2	54
23	51	26	0	24	51	25	51	51	1	27
24	49	0	1	49	49	49	49	29	20	0
25	59	2	33	26	4	59	59	1	59	55
26	100	0	100	0	0	100	100	0	100	100
27	100	0	100	0	0	100	100	0	100	100
28	100	0	100	0	0	100	100	0	100	100
29	100	0	100	0	0	100	100	0	100	100
30	100	0	100	0	0	100	100	0	100	100
31	100	0	100	0	0	100	100	0	100	100
32	100	0	100	0	0	100	100	0	100	100
33	100	0	100	0	0	100	100	0	100	100
34	100	0	100	0	0	100	100	0	100	100
35	100	0	100	0	0	100	100	0	100	100
36	100	0	100	0	0	100	100	0	100	100
37	100	0	100	0	0	100	100	0	100	100
38	100	0	100	0	0	100	100	0	100	100
39-49	100	0	100	0	0	100	100	0	100	100

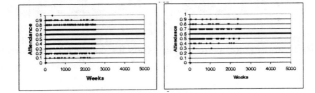

Fig. 6. All (left) and exploitation (right) trials for cooperative reward Λ_{cm}=0.6

For $\Lambda_{cm} > 0.5$ the system shows a more static behaviour, only the percentage that satisfies Λ_{cm} attends the bar and the rest stay at home. This can be explained by analysing the reward function. The reward function for any Λ_{cm} value, the cooperative reward will give to all the agents: 679 for attendance = Λ_{cm}-0.1, 1000 for attendance = Λ_{cm} and 0 otherwise. That is, all the agents are rewarded only when the attendance equals Λ_{cm} or $\Lambda_{cm} - 0.1$.

Once the exact number of agents attend the bar several times, their rules are reinforced strongly and their behaviour remains static.

The agents that tend to go all the time can be seen clearer in Table 3, where the sum of the attendance is always 100 for these six agents. At row 25, when exploration is turned off, it is clear that there are only 6 agents going and the

Table 4. Agent's individual decisions from step 2900 to step 2930 cooperative reward and $\Lambda_{cm}=0.6$

Step	Ag. 1	Ag. 2	Ag. 3	Ag. 4	Ag. 5	Ag. 6	Ag. 7	Ag. 8	Ag. 9	Ag. 10	State	Reward	Att.
2900	1	0	1	0	0	1	1	0	1	1	11111	1000.0	0.6
2901	1	0	1	0	0	1	1	0	1	1	11111	1000.0	0.6
2902	1	0	1	0	0	1	1	0	1	1	11111	1000.0	0.6
2903	1	0	1	0	0	1	1	0	1	1	11111	1000.0	0.6
2904	1	0	1	0	0	1	1	0	1	1	11111	1000.0	0.6
2905	1	0	1	0	0	1	1	0	1	1	11111	1000.0	0.6
2906	1	0	1	0	0	1	1	0	1	1	11111	1000.0	0.6
2907	1	0	1	0	0	1	1	0	1	1	11111	1000.0	0.6
2908	1	0	1	0	0	1	1	0	1	1	11111	1000.0	0.6
2909	1	0	1	0	0	1	1	0	1	1	11111	1000.0	0.6
2910	1	0	1	0	0	1	1	0	1	1	11111	1000.0	0.6
2911	1	0	1	0	0	1	1	0	1	1	11111	1000.0	0.6
...	...	...	...	...	...	...	...	...	...	...	...	1000.0	0.6
2930	1	0	1	0	0	1	1	0	1	1	11111	1000.0	0.6

rest stay at home. It is always only the exact number of agents that attend the bar for every experiment, though the agents are different; for experiment 1 the agents that go are 1, 3, 4, 5, 7 and 8; for experiment 2 the agents that go are 3, 4, 6, 7, 8 and 9, etc. This is due to the independent learning. The system converges very fast when exploiting, as it can be observed in the right graphic of Fig. 5, after step 1000 the system has reached optimum performance, being the last time the bar is overcrowded at step 700.

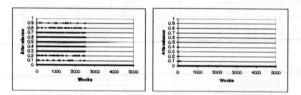

Fig. 7. All (left) and exploitation (right) trials for cooperative reward $\Lambda_{cm}=0.0$

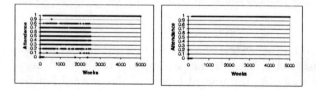

Fig. 8. All (left) and exploitation (right) trials for cooperative reward $\Lambda_{cm}=1.0$

6.2   Selfish Reward

As stated before, the results analysed are representative of the behaviour observed for all the Λ_{cm} values tested.

In the case of the selfish reward the system adapts very well to the $\Lambda_{cm}=0.0$ and $\Lambda_{cm}=1.0$ (see Figs. 9 and 10), though the behaviour is not so straight forward for other Λ_{cm} values. It can be seen in Fig. 11, the attendance oscillates between 0.6 and 0.7, when $\Lambda_{cm}=0.6$.

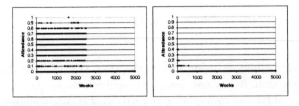

Fig. 9. All (left) and exploitation (right) trials for selfish reward $\Lambda_{cm}=0.0$

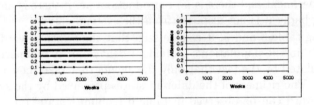

Fig. 10. All (left) and exploitation (right) trials for selfish reward $\Lambda_{cm}=1.0$

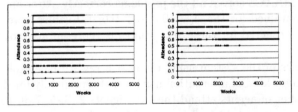

Fig. 11. All (left) and exploitation (right) trials for selfish reward $\Lambda_{cm}=0.6$

Similar oscillations have been found when analysing $\Lambda_{cm}=0.3$ (see Fig. 12), the interesting point is that MAXCS oscillates 10% above the Λ_{cm} value.

This behaviour is not really understandable until the reward function is analysed. The peak function for any Λ_{cm} value and using the selfish reward, will give to the attendees: 679 for attendance = Λ_{cm}-0.1, 1000 for an attendance of Λ_{cm} and 0 for an attendance greater than Λ_{cm}; on the other hand it will give to those staying at homes: 679 for attendance=Λ_{cm}+0.1 and 0 otherwise. The peak function used for reward has a double effect depending on the reward scheme used:

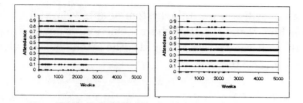

Fig. 12. All (left) and exploitation (right) trials for selfish reward $\Lambda_{cm}=0.3$

stimulating static behaviour using the cooperative reward, and stimulating attendance and dynamic behaviour using the selfish reward. Let us suppose the same example used for the cooperative reward. In this case the exact percentage that attend the bar would be getting 1000, while the rest get 0 as a reward. The reward $= 0$ could lead all the agents that are not going to go seeking reward, overcrowding the bar.

It must be emphasised that all the agents are kept in the system throughout the whole experiment and there is no reproduction, i.e. if there is an agent that is performing badly it is not disposed from the system.

Comparing table 3 and 5, it can be seen that the selfish reward stimulates dynamism within the population's individual behaviour. A real need for exploration is simulated by the fact that only the agents that take the correct action are rewarded. The richness of the different states perceived by the system using the selfish reward can be observed in table 6 (column "state") and cannot be compared to the monotonous states that the cooperative reward generates (table 4). Thus, is this richness what makes more difficult for MAXCS using the selfish reward.

As stated before, all the possible Λ_{cm} values were tested in 10 different experiments and MAXCS solved all the problems correctly. After analysing all the results, those obtained for the $\Lambda_{cm}=0.0$, 0.3, 0.6, 1.0 values have been chosen. The behaviour observed for these Λ_{cm} values is representative of the system's performance.

The dynamics of the system using the selfish reward (see table 5) are interesting: a particular kind of alternation has been observed only for $\Lambda_{cm}=[0.1,0.9]$. The exact number of agents attend the bar (agents 2, 3, 5, 7, 9, 10 in Table 5), the other agents stay at home except agent 4, which starts going and not going. After some steps agent 4 keeps going to the bar and "alters" one of the previous agents that was not going (agent 2). Agent 2 balances the system, so the agents that go and those staying at home are always rewarded. This behaviour is analysed in detail in the next subsection.

It seems that once that MAXCS has found a combination that solves the problem, it keeps repeating it, generating loops in the states perceived. This behaviour is also favoured by the way the reinforcement is given.

As it can be seen from Figs. 12 and 11 this need is reflected in the general attendance. Especially in the case of $\Lambda_{cm}=0.6$ (Fig. 11) the attendance does not fall below 0.5, but 4 out of 5000 possible trials. In all of the possible Λ_{cm}

values tested, the overall behaviour of MAXCS is successful: either the agents overcrowd the bar only by 0.1 – so the agents that do not go are rewarded with 679– or the exact number of agents attend, so the agents attending obtain 1000.

Comparing the cooperative and selfish rewards performance (tables 3 and 5) –just after exploration is switched off (row 25)– a more even distribution can be observed in the selfish reward case, converging slowly toward the emergent behaviour, reflected in the attendance of each agent. In the case of the cooperative reward, it can be clearly seen that is only six agents that are going while the rest stay at home.

Table 5. Individual attendance sum for exploitation trials, selfish reward and Λ_{cm}=0.6, exploration finishes at row 25

Row	Agent 1	Agent 2	Agent 3	Agent 4	Agent 5	Agent 6	Agent 7	Agent 8	Agent 9	Agent 10
1	57	40	58	31	46	30	53	50	46	23
2	54	34	45	31	50	34	53	53	50	22
3	51	30	49	19	51	27	51	49	51	21
4	53	54	32	54	49	23	31	51	54	53
5	31	46	38	29	44	43	39	42	32	43
6	48	46	45	48	47	48	48	46	42	48
7	30	54	42	30	49	27	51	33	48	55
8	32	40	44	40	41	37	41	37	43	35
9	39	46	40	45	31	39	46	46	46	36
10	47	50	34	49	46	33	47	50	50	31
11	35	50	50	44	50	50	45	50	50	45
12	39	44	39	37	39	44	37	43	41	42
13	51	38	54	54	49	38	34	52	34	51
14	34	39	33	44	51	38	36	49	48	48
15	43	42	42	48	45	47	32	48	30	24
16	47	52	52	46	52	47	40	51	37	41
17	54	55	51	34	52	32	52	47	30	55
18	47	44	48	48	47	44	47	47	48	44
19	47	44	50	50	47	46	50	46	49	50
20	40	49	49	46	48	47	49	38	39	44
21	55	55	55	47	50	55	55	46	53	46
22	46	46	47	37	37	47	46	39	45	36
23	32	46	39	46	42	46	46	36	45	34
24	42	45	45	44	49	30	42	24	34	43
25	43	58	63	65	38	34	65	34	66	65
26	1	100	100	100	65	0	100	0	100	97
27	0	100	100	100	100	0	100	0	100	53
28	0	100	100	92	100	0	100	0	100	65
29	4	100	100	45	100	1	100	0	100	100
30	62	100	100	0	100	0	100	0	100	100
31	67	100	100	0	100	0	100	0	100	100
32	67	100	100	0	100	0	100	0	100	100
33	66	100	100	0	100	0	100	0	100	100
34	67	100	100	0	100	0	100	0	100	100
35	67	100	100	0	100	0	100	0	100	100
36	66	100	100	0	100	0	100	0	100	100
37	67	100	100	0	100	0	100	0	100	100
38	66	100	100	0	100	0	100	0	100	100
39	67	100	100	0	100	0	100	0	100	100
40	67	100	100	0	100	0	100	0	100	100
41	67	100	100	0	100	0	100	0	100	100
42	66	100	100	0	100	0	100	0	100	100
43	67	100	100	0	100	0	100	0	100	100
44	67	100	100	0	100	0	100	0	100	100
45	66	100	100	0	100	0	100	0	100	100
46	67	100	100	0	100	0	100	0	100	100
47	66	100	100	0	100	0	100	0	100	100
48	67	100	100	0	100	0	100	0	100	100
49	67	100	100	0	100	0	100	0	100	100

Detailed analysis of the individual answers for the different experiments are discussed for Λ_{cm}=0.6 in the following subsections.

6.3   Emergent Behaviour in MAXCS

For all the experiments with selfish reward and $0 < \Lambda_{cm} < 1$: there is an agent – called the "vacillating" agent (shown as agents 1 and 4 in Tables 6 and 5)– that is always taking the wrong decision: it overcrowds the bar or it stays at home when the *attendance* $<= \Lambda_{cm}$. This phenomenon does not happen when the cooperative reward is used, as it can be seen in Table 4.

Considering that the agents are rewarded when they attend the bar and the attendance (att) $att <= \Lambda_{cm}$ or when they stay at home and $att >= \Lambda_{cm}$. From Table 6 can be seen clearly that agents 2,3,5,7,9 and 10 are going every week; while 1, 6 and 8 are not. This phenomenon would not arise if agent 4 was not overcrowding the bar from time to time. This behaviour can be observed also for $0 < \Lambda_{cm} < 1$ (see Fig. 11 for $\Lambda_{cm} = 0.6$). This behaviour will be referred as the "vacillating" agent(VA).

Analysis of the VA's rules revealed similarity with other agent's populations (Tables 9 8 7). Furthermore, no particular discernible structure directs the behaviour of the VA, but its behaviour is directed by reacting to the states in the environment.

There are two features about the VA: One is the result of its existence, the other how and why its behaviour arises.

The result of the existence of the VA is that the whole system is balanced. If the agent would not be vacillating, all the agents staying at home all the time would have to go to the bar to be rewarded. Moreover, the agents that are going all the time would not be rewarded if the vacillating agent was not staying at home, since the bar would always be overcrowded.

It can be observed (Fig. 11, Table 5), that the system converges in the late stages toward the vacillating behaviour. In the case of $\Lambda_{cm}=0.6$ the agents that attend receive 1000 each, while when $\Lambda_{cm}=0.7$, the agents that do not go receive 679 and the VA receives 0.

As none of these actions is preset or imposed on the agents, it can be concluded that the VA arises as an emergent property of the system. It has been found that there are three agents that vacillate throughout the experiment. The number of VAs does not vary by stopping the exploration later nor by running the experiment for 10,000 steps.

The patterns and behaviour observed in these experiments are not as stochastic, but more uniform and less complex than in the original work [2]. It can be argued that the reason for this behaviour could be the reward function used, since it is more smooth and encourages the attendance to the bar to the extent of making it enjoyable.

It could be argued that the agents should be encouraged to attend at least once a week, but in real life is not like that, there are people who decide to go to a certain bar and after a bad experience they decide not to go ever again.

6.4   Detailed Analysis of the Vacillating Agent for $\Lambda_{cm}=0.6$

The vacillating agents get as reward 0, they are always taking the wrong decision. The decrease in their predictions reflects correctly this fact, and sometimes, it makes the agents change their behaviour.

It can be seen also as an emergent property of the system to balance the resources and the reward that the agents are getting. It can be argued that if the agents were taking turns to go to the bar, it would be even more profitable. This is not possible considering the information perceived by the agents.

Different agents vacillate throughout the experiment. The last agent that vacillates and cannot change its behaviour again is the final vacillating agent. For this example the vacillating agent (1) appears, to be the same until the end at step 2917(see table 6). Agent 4 has been vacillating for several steps 2811-2907 –just the last part of the vacillation appears in the table to analyse the agent 1 behaviour change– until the system arrives to a state where the agents taking action 0 are not rewarded (steps 2908-2916). This has been found as a detonating factor for the agents to change behaviour and become the vacillating agent in all the experiments. Then agent 1 changes its behaviour and it becomes the vacillating agent until the end of the experiment.

Table 6. Agent's individual decisions from step 2900 to step 2930 selfish reward and $\Lambda_{cm}=0.6$

Step	Ag. 1	Ag. 2	Ag. 3	Ag. 4	Ag. 5	Ag. 6	Ag. 7	Ag. 8	Ag. 9	Ag. 10	State	Reward	Att.
2900	0	1	1	1	1	0	1	0	1	1	10101	679.0	0.7
2901	0	1	1	1	1	0	1	0	1	1	01010	1000.0	0.6
2902	0	1	1	1	1	0	1	0	1	1	10101	679.0	0.7
2903	0	1	1	0	1	0	1	0	1	1	01010	1000.0	0.6
2904	0	1	1	1	1	0	1	0	1	1	10101	679.0	0.7
2905	0	1	1	0	1	0	1	0	1	1	01010	1000.0	0.6
2906	0	1	1	1	1	0	1	0	1	1	10101	679.0	0.7
2907	0	1	1	0	1	1	1	0	1	1	01010	679.0	0.7
2908	0	1	1	0	1	0	1	0	1	1	00101	1000.0	0.6
2909	0	1	1	0	1	0	1	0	1	1	10010	1000.0	0.6
2910	0	1	1	0	1	0	1	0	1	1	11001	1000.0	0.6
2911	0	1	1	0	1	0	1	0	1	1	11100	1000.0	0.6
2912	0	1	1	0	1	0	1	0	1	1	11110	1000.0	0.6
2913	0	1	1	0	1	0	1	0	1	1	11111	1000.0	0.6
2914	0	1	1	0	1	0	1	0	1	1	11111	1000.0	0.6
2915	0	1	1	0	1	0	1	0	1	1	11111	1000.0	0.6
2916	0	1	1	0	1	0	1	0	1	1	11111	1000.0	0.6
2917	1	1	1	0	1	0	1	0	1	1	11111	679.0	0.7
2918	0	1	1	0	1	0	1	0	1	1	01111	1000.0	0.6
2919	1	1	1	0	1	0	1	0	1	1	10111	679.0	0.7
2920	0	1	1	0	1	0	1	0	1	1	01011	1000.0	0.6
2921	0	1	1	0	1	0	1	0	1	1	10101	1000.0	0.6
2922	1	1	1	0	1	0	1	0	1	1	11010	679.0	0.7
2923	0	1	1	0	1	0	1	0	1	1	01101	1000.0	0.6
2924	1	1	1	0	1	0	1	0	1	1	10110	679.0	0.7
2925	0	1	1	0	1	0	1	0	1	1	01011	1000.0	0.6
2926	0	1	1	0	1	0	1	0	1	1	10101	1000.0	0.6
2927	1	1	1	0	1	0	1	0	1	1	11010	679.0	0.7
2928	0	1	1	0	1	0	1	0	1	1	01101	1000.0	0.6
2929	1	1	1	0	1	0	1	0	1	1	10110	679.0	0.7
2930	1	1	1	0	1	0	1	0	1	1	01011	679.0	0.7

As shown in Table 6 Agent 1 is receiving 679 reward every time that agent 4 takes action 1, because the bar is overcrowded. Step 2908 is crucial, since at this point agent 4 stops going to the bar, taking from then on action 0. From step 2908 until step 2917, the agents taking action 0 receive 0 as reward, since the bar has the exact attendance.

Table 7. Rules of agent 7 at step 2916, prediction avg.=440.3188, fitness avg.= 0.0571

Rule no.	Classifier	P	ε	Fitness	Num.	Exp.	[A]Size	timeStamp
1	#####→1	913.2894	266.53976	0.7131391	21	1918	24.81754	2496
2	###0#→1	528.4965	482.1391	0.04860587	2	1039	26.919956	2496
3	###1#→1	921.4973	232.63841	0.082458295	1	849	24.432928	2468
4	#####→0	8.006927	35.460114	0.54073155	24	602	25.974117	2478
5	#01##→1	234.05333	322.5261	0.061474573	2	359	27.372623	2444
6	##000→1	562.779	519.4714	0.044096783	1	199	28.62868	2496
7	##1##→1	793.4511	377.15775	0.24452665	2	504	25.300354	2444
8	#00##→0	157.1317	250.40042	0.04259053	3	66	28.173223	2478
9	###00→1	459.8784	532.9017	0.03268224	1	195	28.762745	2496
10	1#11#→0	0.0	6.9350743	0.7107297	1	15	25.153269	2293
11	##00#→1	781.7744	416.60828	0.083382346	1	199	26.093882	2496
12	###0#→0	7.5382147	35.489113	0.20297545	1	41	26.513472	2478
13	####0→1	850.80255	330.6244	0.20356946	2	331	25.765448	2496
14	0####→1	790.68896	356.83777	0.1907639	1	303	25.732357	2496
15	##0##→0	0.0	14.914063	0.4540896	1	4	27.0	2478

By analysing the rules in Table 8 that match state 11111 before and after the vacillation starts, it can be seen that it is the update of the different values the classifiers have for tracking the performance that determines the change of behaviour. Because there is no covering and no GA applied to the rule set at this point.

Table 8. Rules of agent 1 at step 2916, prediction avg.=99.85586, fitness avg.=0.05727675

Rule no.	Classifier	P	ε	Fitness	Num.	Exp.	[A]Size	timeStamp
1	#####→1	79.594185	207.26578	0.46554962	11	1666	22.554201	248
2	#####→0	58.87646	180.9805	0.8118321	22	1177	24.53473	2480
3	1####→1	191.22229	356.85776	0.07090828	3	710	23.259945	2454
4	#1###→1	127.67248	276.75278	0.10058066	2	711	23.053572	2484
5	0####→1	26.972912	102.21316	0.4226791	2	770	21.523392	2484
6	##0##→1	39.979782	133.40735	0.23753978	3	754	21.582243	2468
7	#11##→0	172.57654	281.33066	0.25770864	2	134	24.858635	2480
8	#1#01→0	199.61969	334.89005	0.047840085	1	74	25.507643	2402
9	###1#→1	110.8296	271.1363	0.10387483	4	211	23.069704	2484
10	##1##→1	114.7772	280.54065	0.094019644	3	208	22.80423	2484
11	#11#1→0	219.78224	334.37183	0.046121255	1	36	25.595444	2402
12	###00→1	144.99974	258.79248	0.06815666	1	94	22.374504	2438
13	####0→1	131.8298	267.13098	0.11887836	3	157	23.024149	24841
14	###1→1	335.3514	477.07156	0.013172091	1	64	22.471684	2454
15	###0#→0	320.15088	327.37244	0.20033106	1	262	23.955145	2480
16	0##0#→0	91.64518	230.51915	0.13170789	1	124	24.789629	2480
17	#0###→1	56.2212	176.35359	0.019435128	1	44	21.388403	2468
18	##0##→0	106.08536	201.76761	0.44617447	1	250	23.498508	2429
19	#0##1→1	214.912	425.85266	0.009202877	1	7	21.616	2468

Rules 1,2,3,4,7,9,10,11,14 are the only rules that match the 11111 message. This message is the only message from step 2913 to 2917, therefore the only rules stated previously are the only rules that are updated. The estimate $\frac{\Sigma F_j p_j}{\Sigma F_j}$, i.e. the aggregate for selection for the rules with action 0, for these rules changes from 537.7766 at step 2908 to 91.792 at step 2916. On the other hand, the estimate for action 1 remains constant at 102.7141. This proves that it is the update that causes the vacillation.

Even though the previously mentioned rules are not fired at step 2908, since the state is 00101, the comparison is still valid, as it is done only for those rules matching 11111 at step 2908, i.e. if the state perceived by the agents at step 2908 was 11111 the action taken would be 0.

By step 2916, the rules in agent 4 (Table 9) that have action 0 have higher estimates, and it does not go anymore. So the reaction of agent 1 to stop going in the next step is wrong for state 01111, as it does not receive any reward.

Table 9. Rules of agent 4 at step 2916, prediction avg.=8.57109 fitness avg.= 0.04634809

Rule no.	Classifier	P	ϵ	Fitness	Num.	Exp.	[A]Size	timeStamp
1	#####→0	18.226933	59.23972	0.69201475	13	888	19.03696	2480
2	####0→1	0.106381565	1.1257594	0.05204487	1	1035	23.373425	2500
3	####1→1	0.2564734	2.3591378	0.2421	7	873	24.929897	2486
4	#####→1	1.305638E-4	0.0023387873	0.656811	15	1743	24.640448	2500
5	#1###→0	28.535048	78.836464	0.13354418	6	224	19.41842	2480
6	#1###→1	3.246411	21.889786	0.0018795894	6	614	26.667675	2500
7	###00→1	0.5926582	5.0136166	0.07152896	2	365	23.938295	2500
8	#0###→1	0.01489604	0.18779579	0.043282706	1	584	24.49761	2472
9	#1##0→1	9.619884	53.17525	8.4259675E-4	1	236	26.133728	2500
10	1###1→1	1.1823378	9.309471	0.00909294	1	192	25.218025	2486
11	#1#0#→1	27.947147	118.41909	0.007757831	2	176	30.30118	2500
12	0##00→1	12.650696	65.05056	0.007767346	2	105	27.33095	2423
13	#1#0#→0	3.8224301	19.117569	0.022192683	1	45	22.095205	2480
14	###0#→1	0.007780917	0.102105774	0.043223664	1	321	24.92096	2500
15	#11##→1	16.580875	81.37671	0.002010811	1	90	27.13542	2500
16	#00##→0	5.0619984	28.799244	0.19940239	1	27	15.189486	2429
17	###0#→0	0.16811226	1.4424431	0.5014252	2	35	20.041632	2480
18	#0#0#→0	0.0	0.0	0.2793562	1	15	16.544691	2429

It can be argued that the vacillating agent becomes such because of the strategies that it has followed during the period of exploration. Let us analyse the amount of accumulated reward for each agent, this is a direct representation of their performance. In Table 10 can be seen the evolution of the reward accumulated by each agent throughout the experiment.

Table 10. Accumulated reward for the agents throughout the experiment, sorted by performance

step 2500		step 2908		step 3500		step 5000	
agent 6	410885.0	agent 7	569256.0	agent 6	823717.0	agent 6	1502038.0
agent 7	397577.0	agent 3	566503.0	agent 8	796619.0	agent 8	1474940.0
agent 3	394824.0	agent 6	561623.0	agent 7	782256.0	agent 4	1456140.0
agent 5	389170.0	agent 9	559182.0	agent 3	779503.0	agent 2	1257775.0
agent 9	387503.0	agent 2	544775.0	agent 4	777819.0	agent 7	1282256.0
agent 8	387182.0	agent 1	533846.0	agent 9	772182.0	agent 3	1279503.0
agent 4	386404.0	agent 4	517083.0	agent 5	731244.0	agent 9	1272182.0
agent 10	376836.0	agent 5	518244.0	agent 2	757775.0	agent 5	1231244.0
agent 1	374713.0	agent 10	463836.0	agent 10	676836.0	agent 10	1176836.0
agent 2	373096.0			agent 1	528167.0	agent 1	528167.0

The most interesting aspect of this experiment, is that as an agent (in this case agent 1, which is a XCS) receives as reward 0 for 8 steps it changes so much a "mental" model to twist it in such a way that it stops operating properly.

It is not a very common behaviour from a learning algorithm to be so drastic toward reward, especially XCS which has been proved before to be very reliable (e.g.[29, 25]), though lately it has been discovered [10] that XCS cannot remap the environment if it changes drastically. Still, previous research has focused in simple problems, even if they were non-Markovian. To test XCS in a complex, dynamic, non-Markovian environment brings the LCS research a step forward.

These results confirm that the vacillating agent is an emergent phenomenon of the system, since it is not programmed, but arises from the interaction of the different components(the agents). The way the behaviour is obtained then, is a combination of the states perceived by the agent and the reward obtained from the environment. As the agents change their hypothesis, some become stronger, some become weaker, as seen in the example, despite the little difference between the best performing (agent 7, Table 7) and the vacillating agent.

In case of trying to coordinate the agents by using an internal bit memory. Let us think the extreme case of threshold 0.5, where the alternation of 5 and 5 different agents attending in each turn. How can the agents coordinate, if the only perception they have is 11111, in the case that only 5 of them have attended the pub the previous 5 weeks; it can be argued that this can be solved by an internal memory register, so for example agents 1,2,3,4,5 go at time 2n and agents 6,7,8,9,10 go at time 2n+1. This argument can be easily refuted by analysing the case of a very low threshold, as 0.1, now each agent should go once every 10 times, or once every 100 times in the case of 100 agents, the agents would need a memory size of 100! If thought from a global perspective, the vacillating agent is an "intelligent" (emergent) solution to this problem. In the case of having 100 agents, instead of having to coordinate 100 agents to go each time step, one agent "fixes" its behaviour to go all the time, getting 1000 when the bar is not overcrowded, then the vacillating agent appears, so in this way the 98,(or 8 agents in the case of 10 agents) which stay at home receive a reward. In this case the vacillating agent is left with no reward, to the benefit of the majority.

7   Conclusions

MAXCS is able to solve the EFBP. Experiments with 10 agents against all the possible values prove that MAXCS adapts properly to the threshold set. Furthermore, emergent behaviour has been detected by analysing the XCS population reports.

The ability to read a snapshot of the "mind" of the agents at a certain time step or moment of the problem has proved to be essential to understand the behaviour of the system. This feature stresses the advantage of using MAXCS for social modelling.

The cooperative reward allows MAXCS to perform better than the selfish reward, but this is due to the nature of the problem: MAXCS has to explore less number of possibilities to adapt. By getting the correct attendance several times, the rules are reinforced enough to keep a correct –though static– behaviour. From the behaviour observed, it is certain that MAXCS can adapt to all the thresholds that it was set to. The behaviour is quite extreme, either there are alcoholics or abstemious, and the vacillating agent, whose attendance is not as regular as the alcoholics'.

These experiments prove, to some extent, the feasibility of using XCS as the learning engine of a MAS adapting to a complex environment. And by analysing the behaviour, an interesting feature about XCS's internal mechanisms has been found. So far, the performance of MAXCS on the EFBP is encouraging.

Further work is planned with MAXCS and "El Farol" problem, experiments with other parameters: a bigger number of agents, different θ_{GA} values, varying Λ_{cm} etc. MAXCS will be tested in other benchmark problems.

Acknowledgements

The first author would like to thank the Consejo Nacional de Ciencia y Tecnología for their financial support.

The original code for XCS (Java version)[4] written by Martin Butz has been modified in several ways to suit the multi-agent learning engine.

The first author would like to thank the fruitful discussions held with the members of the University of the West of England LCS Group, Martin Butz and Tim Kovacs.

References

1. M. Ahluwalia and L. Bull. A genetic programming-based classifier system. In Wolfgang Banzhaf, Jason Daida, Agoston E. Eiben, Max H. Garzon, Vasant Honavar, Mark Jakiela, and Robert E. Smith, editors, *Proceedings of the Genetic and Evolutionary Computation Conference (GECCO-99)*, pages 11–18. Morgan Kaufmann: San Francisco, CA, 1999.
2. W. B. Arthur. Complexity in economic theory: Inductive reasoning and bounded rationality. *The American Economic Review*, 84(2):406–411, May 1994. http://www.santafe.edu/~wba/Papers/El_Farol.html.
3. B.Carse, T.C. Fogarty, and A.Munro. Evolving rule based controllers using genetic algorithms. In *Proceedings of the Sixth International Conference on Genetic Algorithms*, 1995.
4. A. Bonarini. Reinforcement distribution for fuzzy classifiers: a methodology to extend crisp algorithms. In *Proceedings of the IEEE Conference 1998*. IEEE, 1998.
5. A. Bonarini. *Learning Classifier Systems: From foundations to applications*, chapter An introduction to learning fuzzy classifier systems, pages 83–104. Lecture notes in computer science; Vol. 18113: Lecture notes in artificial intelligence. Springer-Verlag, 2000.
6. L. Booker. *Learning Classifier Systems: From foundations to applications*, chapter Do we really need to estimate rule utilities in classifier systems?, pages 125–141. Lecture notes in computer science; Vol. 18113: Lecture notes in artificial intelligence. Springer-Verlag, 2000.

---

[4] The code is available at:
ftp://ftp-illigal.ge.uiuc.edu/pub/src/XCSJava/XCSJava1.0.tar.Z.

7. L. B. Booker. Improving the performance of genetic algorithms in classifier systems. In D.Schaffer, editor, *Proceedings of the First International Conference on Genetic Algorithms*, pages 80–92, 1985.

8. L. Bull. On zcs in multi-agent environments. In A.E. Eiben, T. Baeck, M. Schoenauer, and H-P. Schwefel, editors, *Parallel Problem Solving from Nature V.* Springer-Verlag, 1998.

9. L. Bull and T.C. Fogarty and M. Snaith. Evolution in multi-agent systems: Evolving communicating classifier systems for gait in a quadrupedal robot. In *Proceedings of the Sixth International Conference on Genetic Algorithms*, 1995.

10. L. Bull and J. Hurst. Zcs redux. *Evolutionary Computation Journal*, 2002.

11. D. Challet, M. Marsili, and R. Zecchina. Statistical mechanics of systems with heterogeneous agents: Minority games. *Phys. Rev. Lett.*, (84), 2000. Available at http://www.unifr.ch/econophysics/.

12. D. Challet and Y. C. Zhang. Emergence of cooperation and organization in an evolutionary game. *Physica A*, 246, 1997. Available at http://www.unifr.ch/econophysics/.

13. D. Challet and Y. C. Zhang. On the minority game: Analytical and numerical studies. *Physica A*, 256:407, 1998. Available at http://www.unifr.ch/econophysics/.

14. B. Edmonds. Gossip, sexual recombination and the el farol bar: modelling the emergence of heterogeneity. *Journal of Artificial Societies and Social Simulation*, 2(3), 1999. http://www.soc.surrey.ac.uk/JASSS/2/3/2.html.

15. J. Ferber. *Multi-Agent Systems: An introduction to distributed artificial intelligence*. Adisson Wesley, 1999.

16. D.A. Fisher and H.F. Lipson. Emergent algorithms – a new method for enhancing survivability in unbounded systems. In *Proceedings of the 32th Hawaii International Conference on System Sciences*, 1999.

17. D.E. Goldberg. *Genetic algorithms in Search, optimization and Machine Learning*. Addison Wesley, 1989.

18. D.E. Goldberg, J. Horn, and K. Deb. What makes a problem hard for a classifier system? Technical Report 92007, Illinois Genetic Algorithms Laboratory, May 1992.

19. L. Miramontes Hercog. Hand-eye co-ordination: An evolutionary approach. Master's thesis, University of Edinburgh, 1998.

20. L. Miramontes Hercog and T.C. Fogarty. XCS-based inductive intelligent multi-agent systems. In *Late Breaking Papers*, pages 125-132. Genetic and Evolutionary Computation Conference, 2000.

21. L. Miramontes Hercog and T.C. Fogarty. *Proceedings of the Eurodays 2000 meeting dedicated to the memory of B. Mantel*, chapter Analysing Inductive Intelligence in a XCS-based Multi-agent System (MAXCS), Wiley, 2001.

22. J.H.Holland. *Hidden Order: How adaption builds complexity*. Perseus Books, 1996

23. J. Horn, D.E. Goldberg, and K. Deb. Implicit niching in a learning classifier system: Nature's way. *Evolutionary Computation*, 2(1):37–66, 1994.

24. T. Kovacs. XCS Classifier System Reliably Evolves Accurate, Complete, and Minimal Representations for Boolean Functions. In Roy, Chawdhry, and Pant, editors, *Soft Computing in Engineering Design and Manufacturing*, pages 59–68. Springer-Verlag, London, 1997.

25. T. Kovacs. Strength or accuracy? a comparison of two approaches to fitness calculation in learning classifier systems. In *2nd. International Workshop in Classifier Systems*, 1999.

26. J.R. Koza. *Genetic Programming*. MA: The MIT Press/Bradford Books, 1992.

27. P.L. Lanzi. Generalization in wilson's classifier system. In *Proceedings of the Seventh International Conference on Genetic Algorithms*, pages 501–509, 1997.
28. P.L. Lanzi. Adding memory to xcs. Technical report, Politecnico di Milano, 1998.
29. P.L. Lanzi and S.W. Wilson. Toward optimal classifier system performance in non-markov environments. *Evolutionary Computation Journal*, 8(4):393–418, 2000.
30. A. Pérez-Uribe and B. Hirsbrunner. The risk of exploration in multi-agent learning systems: A case study. In *Proceedings of the AGENTS-00/ECML-00 Joint Workshop on Learning Agents*, pages 33–37, 2000.
31. T. Sandholm and R. Crites. Multiagent reinforcement learning in the iterated prisoner's dilemma. *Biosystems*, (37):147–166, 1995. Special Issue on the Prisoner's Dilemma.
32. S. Saxon and A. Barry. *Learning Classifier Systems: From foundations to applications*, chapter XCS and the Monk's problem, pages 272–281. Lecture notes in computer science; Vol. 18113: Lecture notes in artificial intelligence. Springer-Verlag, 2000.
33. W. Shen. *Autonomous learning from the enviroment*. Computer Science Press, 1994.
34. R.E. Smith and H. Brown Cribbs. Is a learning classifier system a type of neural network? *Evolutionary Computation*, 2(1):19–36, 1994.
35. T.Eymann, B.Padovan, and D.Schoder. Artificial coordination- simulating organizational change with artificial life agents. Technical report, University of Freiburg, 1998.
36. S. W. Wilson. Mining oblique data with xcs. In P.L. Lanzi, W. Stolzmann, and S.W.Wilson, editors, *Proceedings of the 3rd International Workshop on Classifier Systems 2000*. Springer-Verlag, 2000.
37. S.W. Wilson. Zcs: A zeroth level classifier system. *Evolutionary Computation*, 2(1):1–18, 1994.
38. S.W. Wilson. Classifier fitness based on accuracy. *Evolutionary Computation*, 3(2):149–175, 1995.
39. S.W. Wilson and D.E. Goldberg. A critical review of classifier systems. In *Proceedings of the Third International Conference on Genetic Algorithms*, 1989.
40. D.H. Wolpert, K. R. Wheeler, and K. Tumer. Collective intelligence for control of distributed dynamical systems. Technical report, NASA Ames Research Centre, 1999.
41. S. Zhang, S. Franklin, and D. Dasgupta. Metacognition in software agents using classifier systems. Technical report, The University of Memphis, 1997.

Part II

Applications

XCS and GALE: A Comparative Study of Two Learning Classifier Systems on Data Mining

Ester Bernadó, Xavier Llorà, and Josep M. Garrell

Enginyeria i Arquitectura La Salle
Psg. Bonanova, 8, 08022 Barcelona, Spain
{esterb,xevil,josepmg}@salleURL.edu

Abstract. This paper compares the learning performance, in terms of prediction accuracy, of two genetic-based learning systems, XCS and GALE, with six well-known learning algorithms, coming from instance based learning, decision tree induction, rule-learning, statistical modeling and support vector machines. The experiments, performed on several datasets, show the suitability of the genetic-based learning classifier systems for classification tasks. Both XCS and GALE significantly achieved better results than IB1 and Naive Bayes. Besides, any method could not outperform XCS and GALE significantly.

1 Introduction

Data Mining, termed as the process of discovering patterns in large databases, can be addressed from different perspectives: clustering, dependence modeling, numerical prediction and classification [49]. Classification is the process of assigning a class label to an input example, based on the model built from a previous set of examples (database), properly classified. In this context, two main goals are often required: an accurate model, which can be used in the prediction of future incomes, and an explanation of the model itself, i.e., to provide a comprehensible explanation useful for the human experts.

Many classification methods have been proposed in the fields of machine learning, statistics, neural networks and evolutionary computation [18]. In particular, the application of genetic algorithms (GA) [20] to classification in data mining is receiving a growing interest [3, 48]. GAs can explore efficiently large search spaces due to their implicit parallel nature, being competitive with other schemes. They can also be applied to a wide range of domains because they can work with a minimum knowledge of the input domain [42]. Other methods, specially those based on statistics, often make assumptions on data that can bound their performance. Another interesting feature of GAs is their ability to explain the acquired knowledge in a way easily understandable by the human experts. In this sense, GAs can evolve rule sets which, besides offering a good performance, can also fulfil the *explanatory* goal. Another potential of GAs is their ability to develop other types of representations, as instance sets or decision trees, by exploiting the sub-symbolic knowledge manipulation [34].

In general, genetic-based machine learning algorithms (GBML) can be classified into the Michigan or the Pittsburgh approaches. The Michigan approach,

P.L. Lanzi, W. Stolzmann, and S.W. Wilson (Eds.): IWLCS 2001, LNAI 2321, pp. 115–132, 2002.

also known as classifier systems (CS), is based on the model introduced by Holland [20, 21]. A classifier system is an adaptive system that learns a set of rules by the interaction of the environment, from which it receives reward. Two main components can be distinguished: the credit assignment algorithm, which evaluates the efficiency of rules; and the discovery component, performed by a genetic algorithm, which acts on the rule level, seeking for new promising rules that can improve the system performance. The Pittsburgh approach, also known as learning systems (LS), resembles the traditional GA, because individuals represent complete solutions to the learning problem; thus, the credit assignment algorithm is not required and the GA acts on the rule set level. Both approaches have successfully been applied on a variety of classification problems, from artificial domains [19, 10, 44] and real-world domains such as medicine [24, 48, 10, 5], biology [15], letter recognition [14], etc.

The purpose of this paper is twofold: to evaluate the performance of two different GBML algorithms in their application to data mining, focusing on classification tasks, and their comparison with other non-evolutionary learning schemes. We chose one representative GBML algorithm for each of the two previously presented approaches. XCS [44] is a CS that represents the current state-of-the-art in the *Michigan* approach, whereas GALE [31] is a knowledge-independent parallel GA that summarizes the characteristics of LS, exploiting fine-grained parallelism. We compare these GBML systems with six non-evolutionary classifier schemes, coming from different disciplines like instance-based learning, rule and decision-tree induction, statistical modeling and support vector machines. The algorithms are compared on several datasets, from both artificial and real-world domains. The real-world domains used in this paper come from our own repository [37, 35] and from the UCI repository [4].

This paper is organized as follows. Section 2 presents an overview of GAs for Machine Learning. Next, sections 3 and 4 describe the two learning classifier systems (LCS) studied in this paper, XCS and GALE. Section 5 presents the experimental framework, and the results obtained with XCS and GALE compared to the other non-evolutionary learning schemes. Finally, section 6 summarizes the conclusions and further work.

2   Genetic-Based Machine Learning

The application of genetic algorithms to machine learning has been addressed from two different approaches: the *Michigan* approach, first exemplified by CS-1 [22], and the *Pittsburgh* approach, originally developed in LS-1 [43].

The *Michigan* approach evaluates the rules with a reinforcement learning scheme by means of a credit assignment algorithm. Holland proposed the *bucket brigade* algorithm [22], where the quality (strength) of rules is assigned according to the payoff prediction (that is, the payoff that the rule would receive from the environment if its action is selected). The GA task is to discover new promising rules, while ensuring the co-evolution of a diverse set of rules. The GA uses the strength calculated by the credit assignment algorithm as the fitness of each rule, thus biasing the search towards highly rewarded rules. The maintenance of different rules along the evolution is addressed by a non-generational scheme and the use of niching techniques [16]. Different systems have been developed under the *Michigan* framework: SCS [16], NewBoole [5], EpiCS [23], and applied successfully to different classification tasks. Nevertheless, some problems associated with *traditional* classifier systems are the achievement of accurate generalizations and the co-evolution and maintenance of different niches in the population. XCS [44] differs from traditional CSs on the definition of rule fitness, which is based on the accuracy of the payoff prediction rather than on the prediction itself, and the use of a niched GA. These aspects have resulted in a strong tendency to evolve accurate and maximally general rules, favouring the achievement of knowledge representations that, besides being complete and accurate, are minimal [27]. This makes XCS particularly suitable for the *data mining goals*, which are related to the accuracy and the explanatory capabilities.

In the *Pittsburgh* approach, each individual represents a whole rule set, instead of a single rule. This allows the evaluation of an individual as a complete solution to the learning problem, avoiding thus the use of a credit assignment algorithm. The fitness of each individual is evaluated as the performance of its rule set as a whole, considering different aspects as the classification accuracy, the number of required rules, etc. Some noticeable approaches for supervised learning are GABIL [10] and GIL [25], both designed for single-concept learning.

Some other approaches lay between the Michigan and the Pittsburgh schemes. An example is COGIN [17], designed to solve multi-class learning tasks. It evolves a population of rules under a competition model based on training set coverage. REGAL [15] uses a similar coverage-based scheme for multi-concept learning, by means of the universal suffrage selection operator, where different rules tend to cover different training examples that globally solve the complete solution. GA-MINER [12] is a system designed for pattern discovery in databases. Each individual in the population has a single rule (expressed in DNF form), but its evaluation is done independently from other rules in the population; so it does not need any credit assignment algorithm. The formation of rule sets is performed using an incremental update strategy based on heuristics. The main goal of GA-MINER is to find some interesting patterns in the dataset, instead of fully covering the database as expected in a classification task. Under this framework, the evolution of a complete rule set is not necessary and in fact, this is not guaranteed by the system.

Among others, REGAL and GA-MINER were applied to real-world databases. Usually, these databases contain a large number of instances, as well as other characteristics as noise, missing data, etc, which can difficult learning and imply large computational resources. In an effort to reduce the high computational learning time, these systems have exploited the inherent parallelism of the evolutionary processes. GA-MINER has used fine-grained parallelism as well as data parallelism [12, 3]. Another approach to the parallelization of GBML is proposed in GALE [31], a Pitt-style classifier system. GALE is based on fine-grained parallelism, exploiting locally-defined relations on a 2D grid. It also differs from other approaches on the evolved knowledge: it is not constrained to evolve sets of rules, it can also obtain decision-trees or instance sets, exploiting sub-symbolic manipulation of knowledge.

In this paper, we want to analyse in some detail the efficiency of the evolutionary approaches compared to other well known non-evolutionary schemes. Recently, XCS has been applied to different problems of data mining. Saxon and Barry [42] reported an experimental evaluation of the system in the monk's problem domain. Wilson [48] studied the performance of XCS in oblique data sets, and presented a cross-validation experiment in the Wisconsin database. Both results were encouraging. For example, the results obtained for the Wisconsin database were successful and competitive to other schemes. On the other hand, GALE has shown a good performance and robustness in different classification tasks [34]. We want to extend these results, both from XCS and GALE, by making a deeper experimentation on several datasets, comparing them to six other non-evolutionary machine learning schemes.

3   XCS

In this section, we present a brief description of XCS, focusing on its application to classification problems. More detailed descriptions of XCS can be found in [44, 45, 6].

3.1   Knowledge Representation

XCS evolves a population of classifiers, where each classifier has a rule and a set of associated parameters estimating the quality of the rule. Each rule $\mathbf{r}$ consists of a condition part and an action (predicted class): $condition \rightarrow action$. It was originally represented by a fixed length string, where $condition = \{0, 1, \#\}^n$, and $action = \{0, 1\}^k$ [44]. Besides its simplicity, this codification offers the advantage of a good fit with the traditional GA representation and consequently, the application of the traditional GA operators is straightforward. Nevertheless, if the instances have numeric attributes, the condition representation and its associated genetic operators can be adapted, as proposed in the XCSR approach. This modification codifies the condition as a set of interval predicates of type: (c_i, r_i), where c_i and r_i are real numbers, which represent the center and radius of the interval respectively [46]. In this way, a numeric attribute x_i is matched by its corresponding interval if: $c_i - r_i \leq x_i \leq c_i + r_i$.

We allow mixed attributes in the instances, by combining both representations in the same rule. Then, the condition part of a rule consists of a set of tests, where each test t_i is codified as $\{0, 1, \#\}$ if the corresponding attribute x_i is binary or as an interval if x_i is numeric. The action is represented as an integer, allowing binary classifications as well as n-ary classifications. The genetic operators are adapted accordingly. Two point crossover can occur anywhere in the rule, whereas mutation acts differently depending on the type of gene. If it is real, the gene is changed by a random increment $\pm[0, m)$. Otherwise, mutation is performed on the ternary alphabet. The mutation in the action changes it equiprobably to one of the other actions.

3.2 Performance Component

Each classifier has three main parameters: a) the payoff prediction p_j, a measure of the payoff that the classifier would receive if its action was selected, b) the prediction error ϵ_j, which estimates the error between the classifier's prediction and the payoff received and c) the fitness F_j, computed as an inverse function of the prediction error.

Each time step, a training instance is presented and a match set [M] is built, consisting of those rules whose conditions are satisfied by the instance. If the match set is empty, a new classifier matching the training instance (with a random action) is created through the *covering* operator. Covering can also occur when the number of predicted actions in [M] is less than a threshold θ_{mna}. In this case, a new classifier matching the current input (with an action randomly chosen from those not present in [M]) is created.

Once the match set is obtained, a prediction $\mathcal{P}(\mathbf{a_i})$ is computed for each action $\mathbf{a_i}$ available in [M]. This is performed as a fitness weighted average of the predictions of those classifiers voting $\mathbf{a_i}$. The winning action can be selected from a variety of regimes, ranging from the *pure-explore mode* (random action) to the *pure-exploit mode* (the best action). We used the explore mode in training and the exploit mode, with the update and discovery components disabled, in test. The chosen action specifies the action set [A], formed by all the classifiers in [M] proposing this action.

3.3 Update

Once the action is selected, the environment returns a reward R, which is used to adjust the parameters of the classifiers in [A]. First, the prediction p_j is adjusted using the Q-learning technique [44]: $p_j \leftarrow p_j + \beta(R - p_j)$, followed by the prediction error ϵ_j: $\epsilon_j \leftarrow \epsilon_j + \beta(|R - p_j|)$. Next the classifier's accuracy is computed: $k_j = \alpha * (\epsilon_j/\epsilon_0)^{-\nu}$ if $\epsilon_j > \epsilon_0$, else $k_j = 1$. Then, the relative accuracy over the action set: $k'_j = k_j / \sum_j k_j$ and finally, the fitness F_j is updated according to: $F_j \leftarrow F_j + \beta(k'_j - F_j)$.

In data mining problems, the reward is maximum when the predicted action is "correct" (the same as the input example) and minimum otherwise.

3.4 Discovery Component

The GA in XCS is applied to the action sets, rather than panmictically (i.e., over all the population). First, it selects two parents from the actual [A] with probabilities proportional to their fitnesses. Next, it performs the genetic recombination on them, by using the appropriate crossover and mutation operators with their corresponding probabilities [44, 46].

The resulting offspring are introduced into the population. First, each offspring is checked for subsumption [45] with its parents. If either of the parents is accurate and more general, then the offspring is not introduced and its parent's numerosity is increased. If subsumption is not possible with the parents, the offspring can also be checked for subsumption with the other classifiers in the action set. Subsumption was introduced by Wilson [45] in an effort to eliminate specific classifiers that are covered by more general versions, tending thus to condensate the population. If the offspring classifier can not be subsumed, it is inserted in the population, deleting another classifier if the population is full. The deleted classifier is selected probabilistically, according to the *t3* Kovacs' deletion algorithm [28]. The deletion method tries to bias the search towards highly fit rules, while trying to balance the classifier allocation in the different action sets (or niches).

XCS has shown a strong tendency to evolve consistent and complete knowledge representations that, moreover, tend to be minimal because of the generalization bias (see the generalization hypothesis [45]). In this paper, we only address the first two characteristics, analysing the classification accuracy of XCS over several datasets, and leaving the last aspect for further research.

4   GALE

GALE is a classification scheme based on fine-grained parallel genetic algorithms. GALE was introduced in [32], being designed for solving classification tasks. This section briefly describes GALE focusing on its parallel evolutionary model, and how it evolves different knowledge representations, providing an unified classification scheme for data mining. For more details, please see [31, 33, 34].

4.1   Knowledge Representation

The evolutionary model of GALE is independent of the evolved knowledge representation. In this paper, GALE evolves either of five available knowledge representations: rule sets, instance sets and decision trees (orthogonal, oblique and multi-variant). This goal can be achieved by exploiting the sub-symbolic manipulation of knowledge.

The first knowledge representation that GALE can deal with is based on rules. As a *Pittsburgh* learning system, individuals in GALE represent sets of rules that are complete solutions to the classification problem. Thus, an individual has a variable-length set of rules, whereas an individual in XCS represents a single rule. Rules in GALE use a binary encoding.

GALE can also evolve sets of instances. This kind of knowledge representation is based on instance-based learning algorithms [1] and nearest neighbor algorithms [9]. Each individual in GALE codifies an induced set of instances which tries to summarize the knowledge contained in the training set [33]. An input example is then classified according to the class of the nearest instance, using a pre-specified distance metric (usually, Euclidean distance).

The last three knowledge representations that GALE can evolve are related to decision trees. The simplest representation uses orthogonal decision trees, which were introduced by Quinlan [41]. The internal nodes of orthogonal trees perform a simple test on a single attribute, defining parallel axis classification boundaries. GALE can also evolve oblique decision trees [38], where non parallel axis classification borders are produced by the internal nodes using tests based on hyperplanes. Some related work on oblique decision trees and GAs can be found in [7]. Finally, another available knowledge representation is based on multi-variant decision trees. Non-linear tests can be introduced into the internal nodes, combining instance-based knowledge representation and oblique decision trees. This is achieved using each internal node as an instance and defining a *hierarchical nearest neighbor algorithm* [31].

4.2   Population Topology

GALE uses a 2D grid for spreading spatially the evolved population. Each cell of the grid contains either one or zero individuals: for instance, a 32×32 grid may contain up to 1024 individuals, each one placed on a different cell. An individual is a complete solution to the classification problem, codifying one of the previously mentioned representations (with the constraint that all individuals in a run have to share the same knowledge representation). The grid where individuals are placed also shapes the population dynamics. Each individual is a part of a small subpopulation (deme), where evolution takes place. The individual in a cell is restricted to the immediate neighborhood, whose size is limited by r. For example, given $r = 1$, the neighborhood of a certain cell c consists of its eight adjacent cells.

4.3   Fine-Grained Parallel GA

Every cell in GALE runs the same algorithm in parallel, without any sequential control. The algorithm run by GALE can be summarized as follows:

```
FOR-EACH cell C in Grid
PAR-DO
   initialize the cell C
   evaluate the accuracy of the individual in C
   REPEAT
     merge among neighborhood(C)
     split individual in C
     evaluate the accuracy of individual in C
     survival among neighborhood(C)
   UNTIL <end-criterion>
DONE
```

The initialization of each cell builds a random individual. Not all the cells contain individuals, thus they can be full (with one individual) or empty. An occupation rate of 70-80% has empirically been a good initialization value. An individual kept in a cell is evaluated by means of the fitness function, based on the classification accuracy in the training set: $fit(ind) = \left(\frac{c}{t}\right)^2$ [10], where c is the number of correctly classified instances and t the number of training instances. Next, the evolutionary cycle starts. *Merge* is applied to the individual in the cell with a certain probability p_m. It recombines the genetic material of the individual in the cell with an individual chosen randomly among its neighbors, using a knowledge-dependent crossover operator. One of the obtained offspring is then selected randomly to replace the individual in the cell. Next, *split* is applied with a given probability $p_s \cdot fit(ind)$. *Split* reproduces and mutates the individual in C, placing it in the empty neighbor cell with the highest number of neighbors (occupied cells), or if all cells in the neighborhood are full, in the cell that contains the worst individual. The last step in the evolutionary cycle, *survival*, decides whether the individual is kept for the next cycle or not, as explained in the following paragraph. The cell repeats this process until the individual classifies correctly all the training instances, or a certain amount of cycles are run.

The survival step decides if an individual is kept in the cell for the next cycle. This process uses the neighborhood information. If a cell C has up to one neighbor then the probability of survival of the individual is proportional to its fitness: $p_{sr}^{0,1}(ind_c) = fit(ind)$. Else if a cell has seven or eight neighbors $p_{sr}^{7,8}(ind_c) = 0$, and the individual is replaced by the best neighbor. In the remaining neighborhood configurations, an individual survives if and only if $fit(ind) \geq \overline{\mu}_{nei} + k_{sr} \times \sigma_{nei}$, being $\overline{\mu}_{nei}$ the average fitness value of the occupied neighbor cells, σ_{nei} their standard deviation and k_{sr} a parameter that controls the survival pressure applied to the individual in C. Summarizing, *split & survival* bias the evolution towards good individuals; poorly adapted individuals tend to die leaving room in the grid, whereas highly fit individuals tend to spread rapidly on the grid.

4.4 Genetic Operators

Each knowledge representation has its own sub-symbolic genetic operators: crossover (used in *merge*) and mutation (used in *split*). In order to choose the appropriate operators for each knowledge representation, some issues must be considered, according to the schema theorem and the Price's theorem. Among others, Altenberg [2] claims that: (1) the recombination operator determines which schemata are being combined; and (2) there must be a correlation between complementary schemata of high fitness and the fitness distribution of their recombinant offspring to increase the chance of sampling fitter individuals. The knowledge-independent model depends on those operators to perform a useful search across the hypothesis space.

Instead of building new genetic operators, GALE uses well-known crossover and mutation operators. These operators have proved their usefulness on several EAs, fulfilling the factors mentioned above. Rule sets and instance sets use the two point crossover defined in [10]. Crossover can occur anywhere (i.e., both on rule/instance boundaries as well as within rule/instances). The only requirement is that the corresponding crossover points on the two parents are valid. That is, if one parent is cut on a rule/instance boundary, then the other parent must be also cut on a rule/instance boundary. Similarly, if one parent is being cut within a rule/instance, then the other parent must be cut in a similar spot. Rule and instance representations also share the same mutation algorithm, which generates at random new gene values.

Tree-based knowledge representations use the same one point crossover operator as in Genetic Programming [29], where two parent trees are cut at a randomly generated point, and their subtrees are exchanged. The mutation operator visits all the nodes in the tree, randomly generating new gene values on some of them.

5   Experiments

We compare the performance, in terms of classification accuracy, of XCS and GALE with six traditional non-evolutionary classifier schemes. The comparison is performed with fifteen datasets, from both real-world and artificial domains.

5.1   Classifier Schemes

For these experiments, we use our own implementation of XCS in $C++$. Prior to the generation of these results, we tested our software with the results reported in previous papers and with those obtained using the XCSC code, provided by Barry in http://www.csm.uwe.ac.uk/~ambarry/LCSWEB/computer.htm. The implementation of GALE is a serial version coded in *Java*. Parallel implementations of GALE, and their analysis, are beyond the scope of this paper.

The non-evolutionary algorithms chosen for the comparison come from different learning schemes. The chosen algorithms are: *a, b)* **IB1** and **IBk**, *c)* **Naive Bayes**, *d)* **C4.5 revision 8**, *e)* **PART** and *f)* **SMO**. We also include **0-R**, a simple classifier scheme that predicts the majority class in the training data, introduced to establish a lower bound for the other learning schemes [49].

IB1 [1] is a nearest neighbor instance-based learner, where an input instance is classified according to the class of the nearest stored instance from the training set. **IBk** is a generalization of the IB1 algorithm, where the k nearest neighbors are located in the training set and their majority class used for the prediction. This algorithm was run with $k = 3$. **NaiveBayes** [26] uses the Baye's rule of conditional probabilities to estimate the predicted class. **C4.5 revision 8** [41] is based on tree induction. The actual version is the result of a set of improvements to ID3 [40] which includes methods for dealing with numeric attributes, missing values and noisy data. **PART** [13] is a rule-learning scheme that induces rules by combining the creation of rules from decision trees and the separate-and-conquer rule-learning technique. **SMO** [39] implements the *sequential minimal optimization algorithm* for training a support vector classifier. It only performs binary classifications.

All these algorithms are obtained from the *Weka* package developed at the University of Waikato in New Zealand. The code is available from the http address: http://www.cs.waikato.ac.nz/ml/weka. These algorithms are run with the default configuration provided by *Weka*.

5.2   Datasets

Our experiments are performed on fifteen datasets, belonging to a variety of domains, having numeric and nominal attributes, with different number of classes and ranging over different dataset sizes. Table 1 gives a summary of the characteristics of these datasets.

Table 1. Datasets used for the experiments

Dataset	Instances	Missing(%)	Numeric att.	Nominal att.	Classes
1 Biopsies (bps)	1027	0.0	24	-	2
2 Breast-w (bre)	699	0.3	9	-	2
3 Bupa (bpa)	345	0.0	6	-	2
4 Cmc (cmc)	1473	0.0	2	7	3
5 Glass (gls)	214	0.0	9	-	6
6 Heart-c-14 (h-c)	303	0.2	6	7	5
7 Heart-h-14 (h-h)	294	20.4	6	7	5
8 Iris (irs)	150	0.0	4	-	3
9 Led (led)	2000	0.0	-	7	10
10 Mammograms (mmg)	216	0.0	21	-	2
11 Mux11 (mux)	2048	0.0	-	11	2
12 Pima-indians (pmi)	768	0.0	8	-	2
13 TAO (tao)	1888	0.0	2	-	2
14 Vehicle (veh)	846	0.0	18	-	4
15 Wine (wne)	178	0.0	13	-	3

Three of the datasets are generated artificially: *led*, *mux11* and *tao*. *Led* is the classification of seven binary attributes, representing seven light-emitting diodes, into a decimal digit. The examples are obtained with the addition of noise: each attribute has a ten percent probability of having its value inverted (the C program is available in the UCI repository [4]). *Mux11* is the multiplexer problem with eleven binary inputs. *Tao* is a dataset obtained by sampling the TAO figure with 1888 instances equally spaced along the horizontal and vertical axis. The resulting instances have two real valued attributes corresponding to the $\langle x, y \rangle$ coordinates, and the associated class which is the colour of the figure on that point.

Twelve datasets belong to real-world domains. They come from the UCI repository, except for *biopsies* and *mammograms*. *Biopsies* is a dataset containing 1024 samples coming from cancerous biopsy images. The problem is to predict whether the cancer is low or high. The dataset contains two classes, and 24 real-valued features, which describe the characteristics of the cells' nucleus in a biopsy image, such as shape, size and grey level [37]. *Mammograms* is the prediction of mammography images in malignant or benign cancer, based on the characteristics of several microcalcifications present in the image. The samples are the result of a digital mammography image analysis, with 21 numeric features related mainly to the shape of the microcalcifications [35].

5.3   Experimental Setup

In order to compare the performance of the different algorithms in terms of classification accuracy, we use the following methodology. Classification accuracy is estimated in two different ways, depending on the dataset size. For large datasets, we use the holdout estimate. In fact, this is only applied to the *led* problem, where the led program was used to generate a training set of 2000 instances and a test set of 4000 instances. The remaining datasets are run on a stratified ten-fold cross-validation test. To estimate the difference in performance between the algorithms, we use a test for the difference of two proportions, based on the approximation of the binomial distribution by a normal distribution, if the runs are based on holdout, and a paired t-test if the experiments are based on cross-validation [11]. Additionally, a Wilcoxon signed rank test [8] is used on the average accuracies of each method.

In XCS, the parameters were set according to previous works on similar experiments. In particular, we basically obtained the parameter settings from Wilson's experiment on the Wisconsin dataset [48], where ϵ_0 was quite small in order to favour accuracy, and the experience parameters were increased. However, we also performed a previous experimental test over these parameters on all the datasets, and we adjusted some of them differently. For example, we did not use action set subsumption because the performance in terms of classification accuracy was sometimes degraded. Instead, we used GA subsumption, which was found more conservative. Action set subsumption causes a greater condensation in the population, but this can make the system more vulnerable [6]. This is an aspect that should be further analysed. From the previously mentioned experiment, we also adjusted the population size for each dataset. The maximum population size N must be large enough to ensure that covering is only applied in the early stages of learning [6]. Another criterion for setting N is to give a sufficient number of resources (microclassifiers) for each niche which is expected to be evolved. For example, Saxon and Barry [42] chose the population size limit as fifteen microclassifiers per niche. Since we do not know the necessary number of niches (i.e., the optimal population) in our databases, we tried different population sizes. We started by $N=6400$, which was used by Wilson in the Wisconsin database, and if the performance was poor we doubled this value to seek for better performance. The resulting sizes were: $N=6400$ for the majority of the datasets (bre, bpa, cmc, h-c, h-h, irs, pmi, tao, wne), $N=13000$ for bps, gls, led and mmg datasets and $N=800$ for mux. These differences in the required population sizes may be a measure of the complexity of the databases for XCS. For example, bps and mmg datasets have the highest number of features, with 24 and 21 real-valued features respectively. The led problem is also a difficult database for XCS, maybe due to the 10% of noise added in its examples. In the multiplexer problem, we set $N = 800$ according to previous experiments [44, 27]. The remaining parameters were the same for all the experiments: $R = 1000/0$, $\beta=0.2$, $\alpha=0.1$, $\epsilon_0=1$, $\nu = 5$, $\chi=0.8$, $\mu=.04$, $m=0.1$, $s_0=0.7$, $P_\#=0.33$, $\theta_{GA}=50$, $\theta_{del}=50$, $\delta=0.1$, $\theta_{mna}=\#$ available actions and 100000 explore iterations. Please, see [6, 46] for notation.

GALE has a reduced set of parameters, which was adjusted to the following values for all the datasets: $grid\_size=64 \times 64$, $r=1$, $iterations=150$, $p_m=.4$, $p_s=.01$ and $k_{sr}=-.25$. As mentioned before, GALE can evolve either of five different knowledge representations (based on rule sets, instance sets and induction trees). This gives us the possibility of testing which is the best suited knowledge representation for each dataset, thus minimizing the error due to the language limitations (language-intrinsic error [36]). Therefore, we conducted five different experiments on every dataset, each one with a different knowledge representation. From there, we can can analyse the performance of GALE as well as the most appropriate knowledge representation.

5.4 Results

The results of each algorithm on all the datasets are listed in table 2. They give the percentage of correct classifications, averaged over the ten-fold cross-validation runs, along with the standard deviation. The results on the *led* problem show the percentage of correct classifications, measured on the test set of a holdout experiment. The average of each method over all the datasets is also given in the last row of the table.

Statistical differences of XCS and GALE compared to the other non-evolutionary algorithms are shown in table 3. For each data set, we show the result of a one-tailed t-test, except for *led* where a test for the difference of two proportions based on the normal approximation is used. A significant improvement of XCS or GALE over the other learning schemes (in a particular dataset) is denoted by •, at a 95%•, 99%••, and 99.5%••• confidence levels. Similarly, a degradation is indicated using ∘ with the same confidence levels. Rows labeled as b-w summarize these results, by giving the number of improvements and degradations of XCS and GALE to each of the other schemes. Furthermore, the confidence level of a Wilcoxon signed rank test is shown in the last row of the table. Positive values indicate that XCS or GALE are "better" than the scheme being compared, while negative values indicate that XCS or GALE are "worse."

Table 2. Prediction accuracy on all the datasets (average and standard deviation). Each GALE result also marks the used knowledge representation. A $\star$ stands for rule sets, a $\dagger$ for instance sets, $\oplus$ for orthogonal decision trees, $\otimes$ for oblique decision trees, and $\odot$ for multivariant decision trees

DS	0-R	IB1	IBK	NaiveBayes	C4.5r8	PART	SMO	XCS	GALE
bps	51.6±0.6	83.2±3.2	82.8±4.3	78.6±5.5	80.1±4.8	79.0±3.3	86.4±3.0	83.2±3.1	83.7±3.8$^{\otimes}$
bre	65.5±1.1	96.0±1.5	96.7±1.4	96.0±2.3	95.4±1.6	95.3±2.2	96.7±1.7	96.4±2.5	95.7±2.2$^{\odot}$
bpa	58.0±1.4	63.5±6.6	60.6±6.6	54.3±2.8	65.8±6.9	65.8±10.0	58.0±1.4	65.4±6.9	68.4±6.7†
cmc	42.7±0.4	44.4±2.7	46.8±3.3	50.6±2.8	52.1±2.3	49.8±3.6	-	55.5±2.5	50.3±5.1†
gls	34.6±2.5	66.3±10.9	66.4±10.9	47.6±8.9	65.8±10.4	69.0±10.0	-	70.8±8.5	65.6±11.9$^{\oplus}$
h-c	54.5±2.2	77.4±7.6	83.2±5.2	83.6±6.0	73.6±8.8	77.9±6.4	-	80.3±7.8	79.9±5.2†
h-h	63.9±2.1	78.3±6.4	82.4±8.4	83.7±7.8	80.3±9.0	79.6±10.6	-	79.9±6.3	78.2±7.2†
irs	33.3±0.0	95.3±3.2	95.3±3.2	94.7±2.8	95.3±3.2	95.3±3.2	-	94.7±5.3	98.7±2.8$^{\otimes}$
led	10.5±0.0	62.4±0.0	75.0±0.0	74.9±0.0	74.9±0.0	75.1±0.0	-	74.5±0.0	75.0±0.0*
mmg	56.0±2.9	63.0±12.4	65.3±6.3	64.7±7.7	64.8±6.4	61.9±4.2	67.0±7.4	64.3±6.4	71.3±5.9$^{\oplus}$
mux	49.9±0.1	78.6±4.0	99.8±0.3	61.9±2.7	99.9±0.2	100.0±0.0	61.6±3.0	100.0±0.0	100.0±0.0*
pmi	65.1±1.0	70.3±3.4	73.9±5.3	75.4±6.8	73.1±5.2	72.6±5.0	76.7±4.6	75.4±4.7	75.8±4.0$^{\oplus}$
tao	49.8±0.2	96.1±1.2	96.0±1.4	80.8±1.8	95.1±2.0	93.6±2.8	83.6±2.3	89.9±1.3	95.5±1.0†
veh	25.1±0.5	69.4±5.3	69.7±5.9	46.2±5.7	73.6±5.3	72.6±4.6	-	73.0±4.4	68.8±3.8†
wne	39.8±4.5	95.6±5.0	96.8±4.5	97.8±2.9	94.6±6.6	92.9±6.1	-	95.1±6.8	97.2±2.9†
Avg	46.7	76.0	79.4	72.7	79.0	78.7	75.7	79.9	80.3

The results in table 2 show, under GALE learning scheme, that knowledge representations based on instances or decision trees were best suited for the

Table 3. Significant tests of XCS and GALE compared to non-evolutionary learning schemes. Differences in accuracies are significant using a one-tailed test at $p = .05^\bullet, .01^{\bullet\bullet}, .005^{\bullet\bullet\bullet}$. A $\bullet$ means that XCS or GALE outperform significantly the compared algorithm, while $\circ$ means a significant degradation. Rows labeled as b-w list the number of improvements and degradations of XCS and GALE to the column being compared, at a certain significant level. The last row shows the Wilcoxon test confidence level

	Comparison of XCS								Comparison of GALE							
DS	0-R	IB1	IBk	NBa	C4.5	PART	SMO	GALE	0-R	IB1	IBk	NBa	C4.5	PART	SMO	XCS
bps	•	•		• • •	• •	•		∘ ∘	•	•		• • •	•	• • •		∘ ∘ ∘
bre	•	•							•	•						
bpa	•	•		• • •		• • •			•	•	• •	• • •			• • •	
cmc	•	• • •	• • •	• • •	• • •	• • •		• •	•	• •	•		• • •			∘ ∘
gls	•	•		• • •					•	•		• • •				
h-c	•	•	∘		•				•	•						
h-h	•	•		∘					•	•		∘				
irs	•	•						∘ ∘ ∘	•	•	•	• • •	•	• •		• • •
led	•	• • •							•	• • •						
mmg	•	•						∘	•	•	•	•	•		• •	•
mux	•	• • •	•	• • •				• • •	•	• • •	•	• • •			• • •	
pmi	•	• • •							•	• • •			•	•		
tao	•	∘ ∘ ∘	∘ ∘ ∘	• • •	∘ ∘ ∘	∘ ∘ ∘	• • •	∘ ∘ ∘	•			• • •		•	• • •	• • •
veh	•	• •	•	• • •				•	•			• • •	∘	∘		∘
wne	•	•							•	•				•		
Average	46.7	76.0	79.4	72.7	79.0	78.7	75.7	80.3	46.7	76.0	79.4	72.7	79.0	78.7	75.7	79.9
b-w .05	15-0	5-1	3-2	7-1	3-1	2-1	3-1	2-3	15-0	6-0	5-0	8-1	3-1	6-1	3-1	3-2
b-w .01	15-0	5-1	1-1	7-0	2-1	1-1	3-1	1-2	15-0	4-0	1-0	7-0	1-0	3-0	3-1	2-1
b-w .005	15-0	4-1	1-1	7-0	1-1	1-1	3-0	0-2	15-0	3-0	0-0	7-0	0-0	2-0	3-1	2-0
Wilcoxon	99.5	99.0	54.0	96.5	81.2	96.9	75.0	-62.5	99.5	98.2	76.7	97.7	96.0	95.0	90.0	62.5

majority of the datasets (13 of 15). Rule sets were only used in two datasets, led and mux, both with binary attributes. This is possibly due to the binary encoding used by GALE in its rules, which performs worse in real-valued attributes than other representations, based on instances or trees. A rule encoding based on hyperrectangles, as XCS uses, could counterbalance this effect.

Some observations can be made from the results in table 3. In cmc and mux datasets, XCS outperforms significantly nearly all classifier schemes. XCS also shows a good performance on bpa and veh datasets, whereas the worst performance of XCS is obtained on tao. In this dataset, XCS is overcome by five methods, outperforming only three of them. On the contrary, GALE seems to be well suited for this particular dataset. Furthermore, GALE shows a significant outperformance in several datasets (e.g., bpa, irs, mux and tao), whereas there is not any dataset where it performs poorly.

In the multiplexer problem, XCS, GALE and PART reach the optimal prediction accuracy. These three approaches use rules as the knowledge representation. This representation fits the solution perfectly. On the other hand, the results of XCS and GALE on the tao dataset are significantly different. This dataset represents the TAO figure, where boundaries between classes are non-linear. It was generated artificially, as explained in section 5.2, and no noise was added. The results of XCS in tao dataset may be due to the knowledge representation: XCS evolves rules, while GALE was run using instances. This fact, together with the results achieved by IB1 and IBK in tao, suggest that a knowledge representation based on instances is more appropriate for the tao dataset. The representation with rules only can approximate the non-linear boundaries of the TAO figure. Besides, using the real hyperrectangles of XCSR tends to produce a high number of rules, which makes the learning harder. Further efforts on the reduction of the number of evolved rules should be done in order to achieve an efficient use of XCS in data mining.

From the summary rows of table 3, we can observe that both XCS and GALE have significantly higher prediction accuracy than IB1, Naive Bayes and SMO in several datasets, according to a t-test at 99% level. Besides, the results of the Wilcoxon test indicate that XCS and GALE algorithms have a significant improvement over IB1, Naive Bayes and PART, at a confidence level greater than 95%. These two statistical tests agree that the genetic-based approaches have higher accuracy than IB1 and Naive Bayes, for this kind of datasets. They also indicate these GBML approaches are not outperformed significantly by the other methods, in terms of classification accuracy. Other interesting performance criteria as training time, size of solution set, explanatory capabilities, etc, are left for future work.

In comparing the prediction accuracy of XCS with GALE, no significant differences were found (regarding both the t-test and the Wilcoxon signed rank test). In relation to the training times, XCS and GALE are implemented using different languages (C++ and Java respectively), so the comparison of the training times can not be done quantitatively. Usually, Pitt-style systems take longer training times than Michigan classifier systems. This also applies to GALE and XCS. For instance, in a ten-fold cross-validation run on the multiplexer problem, the serial implementation of GALE takes up to two orders of magnitude higher than XCS. Hovewer, parallel implementations of GALE [34] can theoretically achieve competitive training times in comparison to XCS. Further efforts should be done on this direction.

6   Conclusions and Future Work

This paper has compared two different GBML approaches, XCS and GALE, with six well-known learning algorithms, in terms of prediction accuracy, on fifteen datasets. The results obtained by both XCS and GALE reach or even improve the performance of the non-evolutionary learning schemes. In particular, statistical tests indicate a significant improvement of XCS and GALE over IB1 and Naive Bayes, whereas we did not obtain a significant degradation of XCS and GALE compared to the other methods. An advantage of using GAs for learning might be its robustness across different domains and its independence on the evolved knowledge representation. In these experiments, GALE was run with rule sets, instance sets and decision trees, while XCS evolved rule sets, although other representations can be considered in further work. Further research will also be focused on extending this comparison to other representative datasets, including other performance measures such as training time, complexity and comprehensibility of the obtained solution. These aspects are related to the data mining interests, where not only an accurate prediction is expected, but also an explanatory description of the learnt knowledge [49]. It is easy for a GBML approach to give such a description, because of the use of rule sets as its knowledge representation (in case of the induction trees and instance sets developed by GALE, some explanatory models can also be extracted). More insight should be done in the type and number of rules which are evolved. In case of XCS, it seems that the use of the XCSR representation tends to distribute a high number of rules in the population. Some techniques for reducing the number of final rules (see for example, [27]) as well as providing additional comprehensible visualization of them (like the graphical representation used in [46]) should be analysed.

Another area of further research, specially interesting for data mining applications, would be to study more deeply the effects of noise on the system performance, as well as the mechanisms to overcome it. The led problem has a 10% noise added in the training and test examples, and this makes XCS achieve a low performance, although no statistical degradation is observed in relation to the other methods. Some other informal experiments on the same dataset without noise (not reported here) allowed XCS to obtain better classification accuracy. Lanzi and Colombetti [30] designed a technique for avoiding performance degradation under conditions of action noise. The approach is based on a relative measure of the classifier's prediction error with respect to the minimum error in the action set. XCS performed nearly optimally in conditions of high noise, while keeping the ability of XCS to evolve generalizations. The same technique will probably be successful in noisy databases, as pointed out by Wilson [47], so its introduction and further testing remains as a certain area we want to explore.

Although XCS and GALE belong to different genetic-based machine learning approaches, they did not show significant differences in their prediction accuracy. In XCS, the individual members represent a partial solution (a single rule), whereas in GALE an individual is a complete solution (e.g., a set of rules). This seems to have no influence on the prediction accuracy, but may produce different rule sets, for example in terms of the number of produced rules. This could be another interesting area of research.

Acknowledgements

The authors would like to thank Alwyn Barry and Erick Cantú-Paz for valuable comments. The results of this work were obtained with the equipment co-funded by *Direcció de Recerca de la Generalitat de Catalunya (DOGC 30/12/1997)*. The authors acknowledge the support provided by *Comissionat per a Universitats i Recerca* under grant number 1999FI-00719, *Epson Ibérica*, under Rosina Ribalta Award, *Fondo de Investigación Sanitaria (Instituto Carlos III)* under grant number FIS-00/0033-2, as well as the support of *Enginyeria i Arquitectura La Salle*. We are also grateful to Ian H. Witten, Eibe Frank and Alwyn Barry for providing their code on-line, and to all the people who donated the datasets.

References

1. D. Aha and D. Kibler. Instance-based learning algorithms. *Machine Learning*, Vol. 6, pages 37–66, 1991.
2. Lee Altenberg. The Schema Theorem and Price's Theorem. In L. Darrell Whitley and Michael D. Vose, editors, *Foundations of Genetic Algorithms 3*, pages 23–49, Estes Park, Colorado, USA, 31 –2 1994 1995. Morgan Kaufmann.
3. Dieferson L.A. Araujo, Heitor S. Lopes, and Alex A. Freitas. Rule Discovery with a Parallel Genetic Algorithms. In D. Whitley, Goldberg D., E. Cantú-Paz, Spector L., Parmee I., and Beyer H., editors, *Workshop on Data Mining with Evolutionary Computation held in GECCO 2000*, pages 89–92. Morgan Kaufmann Publishers, 2000.
4. C.L. Blake and C.J. Merz. UCI Repository of machine learning databases, [http://www.ics.uci.edu/~mlearn/MLRepository.html]. University of California, Irvine, Dept. of Information and Computer Sciences, 1998.
5. Pierre Bonelli and Alexandre Parodi. An Efficient Classifier System and its Experimental Comparison with Two Representative Learning Methods on Three Medical Domains. In *4th. International Conference on Genetic Algorithms (ICGA'91)*, pages 288–295, 1991.
6. M.V. Butz and S.W. Wilson. An algorithmic description of XCS. IlliGAL Report (No. 2000017), University of Illinois at Urbana-Champaign, 2000.
7. Erick Cantú-Paz and Chandrika Kamath. Using Evolutionary Algorithms to Induce Oblique Decision Trees. In D. Whitley, Goldberg D., E. Cantú-Paz, Spector L., Parmee I., and Beyer H., editors, *Genetic and Evolutionary Computation Conference (GECCO 2000)*, pages 1053–1060. Morgan Kaufmann Publishers, 2000.
8. W.J. Conover. *Practical Nonparametric Statistics*. New York: John Wiley, pp.206–209, 383, 1971.
9. T. M. Covert and P. E. Hart. Nearest Neighbor Pattern Classification. *IEEE Transactions on Computers*, 13(1):21–27, 1967.
10. A De Jong, Kenneth, William M. Spears, and Diana F. Gordon. Using Genetic Algorithms for Concept Learning. *Genetic Algorithms for Machine Learning (John J.Grefenstette editor), A Special Issue of Machine Learning, 13, 2-3*, pages 161–188, 1993.
11. Thomas G. Dietterich. Approximate Statistical Tests for Comparing Supervised Classification Learning Algorithms. *Neural Computation*, 10(7):1895–1924, 1998.
12. Ian W. Flockhart. GA-MINER: Parallel Data Mining with Hierarchical Genetic Algorithms (Final Report). Technical Report EPCC-AIKMS-GA-MINER-REPORT 1.0, University of Edinburgh, 1995.
13. Eibe Frank and Ian H. Witten. Generating Accurate Rule Sets Without Global Optimization. In J. Shavlik, editor, *Machine Learning: Proceedings of the Fifteenth International Conference*, pages 144–151. Morgan Kaufmann, 1998.
14. P.W. Frey and D.J. Slate. Letter recognition using Holland-style adaptive classifiers. *Machine Learning*, 6:161–182, 1991.
15. Attilio Giordana and Filippo Neri. Search-Intensive Concept Induction. *Evolutionary Computation*, 3(4):375–416, 1995.
16. David E. Goldberg. *Genetic Algorithms in Search, Optimization and Machine Learning*. Addison-Wesley Publishing Company, Inc., 1989.
17. David Ferry Greene and Stephen F. Smith. Competition-Based Induction of Decision Models from Examples. *Machine Learning*, 13:229–257, 1993.
18. Jiawei Han and Micheline Kamber. *Data Mining. Concepts and Techniques.* Morgan Kaufmann Publishers, 2001.

19. Adrian R. Hartley. Accuracy-based fitness allows similar performance to humans in static and dynamic classification environments. In W. Banzhaf, Daida J., A.E. Eiben, M.H. Garzon, Honavar V., Jakiela M., and R.E. Smith, editors, *Proceedings of the Genetic and Evolutionary Computation Conference (GECCO'99)*, pages 266–273. Morgan Kauffmann, 1999.

20. John H. Holland. *Adaptation in Natural and Artificial Systems*. University of Michigan Press, Ann Arbor, 1975.

21. John H. Holland. Escaping Brittleness: The Possibilities of General Purpose Learning Algorithms Applied to Parallel Rule-Based Systems. *Machine Learning: An Artificial Intelligence Approach, Vol. II*, pages 593–623, 1986.

22. John H. Holland and J. S. Reitman. Cognitive systems based on adaptive algorithns. *Pattern directed inference systems*, pages 313–329, 1978.

23. John H. Holmes. Discovering Risk of Disease with a Learning Classifier System. In *Proceedings of the Seventh International Conference of Genetic Algorithms (ICGA97)*, pages 426–433. Morgan Kaufmann, 1997.

24. John H. Holmes. Applying a Learning Classifier System to Mining Explanatory and Predictive Models from a Large Clinical Database. In *Third International Workshop on Learning Classifier Systems*, 2000.

25. C.Z. Janikow. A Knowledge Intensive Genetic Algorithm for Supervised Learning. *Machine Learning*, 13:198–228, 1993.

26. George H. John and Pat Langley. Estimating Continuous Distributions in Bayesian Classifiers. In *11th. Conference on Uncertainty in Artificial Intelligence*, pages 338–345, 1995.

27. Tim Kovacs. XCS Classifier System Reliably Evolves Accurate, Complete and Minimal Representations for Boolean Functions. In Roy, Chawdhryand, and Pant, editors, *Soft Computing in Engineering Design and Manufacturing*, pages 59–68. Springer-Verlag, 1997.

28. Tim Kovacs. Deletion Schemes for Classifier Systems. In W. Banzhaf, Daida J., A.E. Eiben, M.H. Garzon, Honavar V., Jakiela M., and R.E. Smith, editors, *Proceedings of the Genetic and Evolutionary Computation Conference (GECCO'99)*, pages 329–336. Morgan Kauffmann, 1999.

29. John R. Koza. *Genetic Programing: On the Programing of Computers by Means of Natural Selection (Complex Adaptive Systems)*. MIT Press, 1992.

30. P. L. Lanzi and M. Colombetti. An extension to the XCS classifier system for stochastic environments. In W. Banzhaf, Daida J., A.E. Eiben, M.H. Garzon, Honavar V., Jakiela M., and R.E. Smith, editors, *Proceedings of the Genetic and Evolutionary Computation Conference, (GECCO'99)*, pages 353–360. Morgan Kaufmann, 1999.

31. Xavier Llorà and Josep M. Garrell. Automatic Classification and Artificial Life Models. *Proceedings of Learning00 Worshop*, 2000.

32. Xavier Llorà and Josep M. Garrell. Evolving Hierarchical Agents using Cellular Genetic Algorithms. In D. Whitley, Goldberg D., E. Cantú-Paz, Spector L., Parmee I., and Beyer H., editors, *Proceedings of the Genetic and Evolutionary Computation Conference, (GECCO 2000)*, page 868. Morgan Kaufmann, 2000.

33. Xavier Llorà and Josep M. Garrell. Inducing Partially-Defined Instances with Evolutionary Algorithms. In *Proceedings of the 18th International Conference on Machine Learning (ICML'2001)*. To appear, 2001.

34. Xavier Llorà and Josep M. Garrell. Knowledge-Independent Data Mining with Fine-Grained Parallel Evolutionary Algorithms. In *Proceedings of the Genetic and Evolutionary Computation Conference (GECCO'2001)*. To appear, 2001.

35. J. Martí, X. Cufí, and J. Regincós. Shape-based feature selection for microcalcification evaluation. In *Proceedings of the SPIE Medical Imaging Conference on Image Processing*, page 1215:1224, 1998.
36. J.Kent Martin and D.S. Hirschberg. Small Sample Statistics for Classification Error Rates I : Error Rate Measurements. Technical Report No. 96-21, Department of Information and Computer Science, University of California, Irvine, 1996.
37. E. Martínez and E. Santamaría. Morphological Analysis of Mammary Biopsy Images. In *8th Mediterranean Electrotechnical Conference on Industrial Applications in Power Systems, Computer Science and Telecommunications*, pages 1067–1070, 1996.
38. S. Murthy, S. Kasif, and S. Salzberg. A system for induction of oblique decision trees. *Jounal of Artificial Intelligence Research*, 2(1):1–32, 1994.
39. J. Platt. Fast training of support vector machines using sequential minimal optimization. In B. Schlkopf, Burges C., and Smola A., editors, *Advances in Kernel Methods-Support Vector Learning*. Cambridge, MA:MIT Press, 1998.
40. Ross Quinlan. Induction of decision trees. *Machine Learning*, 1(1):81–106, 1986.
41. Ross Quinlan. *C4.5: Programs for Machine Learning*. Morgan Kaufmann Publishers, 1993.
42. Shaun Saxon and Alwyn Barry. XCS and the Monk's Problems. In Stolzmann Lanzi and Wilson, editors, *Learning Classifier Systems: From Foundations to Applications*, pages 223–242, 2000.
43. S. F. Smith. Flexible Learning of Problem Solving Heuristics through Adaptive Search. In *Proceedings of the 8th International Joint Conference on Artificial Intelligence*, pages 422–425, 1983.
44. Stewart W. Wilson. Classifier Fitness Based on Accuracy. *Evolutionary Computation*, 3(2):149–175, 1995.
45. Stewart W. Wilson. Generalization in the XCS Classifier System. In J.Koza et al., editor, *Genetic Programming: Proceedings of the Third Annual Conference*. San Francisco, CA: Morgan Kaufmann, 1998.
46. Stewart W. Wilson. Get Real! XCS with Continuous-Valued Inputs. In L. Booker, S. Forrest, Mitchell M., and Riolo R, editors, *Festschrift in Honor of John H. Holland*. Center for the Study of Complex Systems, University of Michigan, 1999.
47. Stewart W. Wilson. State of XCS Classifier System Research. Technical Report No. 99.1.1, Prediction Dynamics, 1999.
48. Stewart W. Wilson. Mining Oblique Data with XCS. In *Third International Workshop on Learning Classifier Systems (IWLCS-2000)*, 2000.
49. Ian H. Witten and Frank Eibe. *Data Mining. Practical Machine Learning Tools and Techniques with Java Implementations*. Morgan Kaufmann, 2000.

A Preliminary Investigation of Modified XCS as a Generic Data Mining Tool

Phillip William Dixon, David W. Corne, and Martin John Oates

Department of Computer Science, University of Reading, Reading, RG6 6AY, UK
pwdixon@tesco.net, d.w.corne@reading.ac.uk,
moates@btinternet.com

Abstract. Wilson's XCS classifier system has recently been modified and extended in ways which enable it to be applied to real-world benchmark data mining problems. Excellent results have been reported already on one such problem by Wilson, while other work by Saxon and Barry on a tunable collection of machine learning problems has also pointed to the strong potential of XCS in this area. In this paper we test a modified XCS implementation on twelve benchmark machine learning problems, all real-world derived. XCS is compared on these benchmarks with C4.5 and with HIDER (a new and sophisticated GA for machine learning developed elsewhere). Results for both C4.5, HIDER and XCS on each problem were tenfold cross-validated, and in the case of HIDER and XCS a modest amount of preliminary parameter investigation was done to find good results in each case. We find that XCS outperforms the other techniques in eight of the twelve problems, and is second-best in two of the remaining three. Some investigation is then done of the variance in XCS performance, and we find this to be verging on significant, either when varying the data fold composition, or the algorithmic random seed. We also investigate variation of several XCS parameters around well-known default settings. We find the default settings to be generally robust, but find the mutation rates and GA selection scheme to be particularly worthy of exploration with a view to improved performance. We conclude that XCS has the potential to be a powerful general data mining tool, at least for databases without too many fields, but that considerable research is warranted to identify rules and guidelines for parameter and strategy setting.

1   Introduction

Learning Classifier Systems (LCSs) are machine learning systems based on seminal ideas due to Holland (1976, 1980). They maintain an adapting population of co-operating rules, also known as *classifiers*, which attempt to model a (possibly) adaptive environment, and learn appropriate actions to take in that environment based on some form of feedback which discriminates between rules based on the quality of the actions which they produce. Comprehensive tutorial and survey material are provided by Holland et al (2000) and Lanzi and Riolo (2000).

One application area for LCSs is that of data mining, where the environment to be modelled is a (typically) large and complex dataset, and the LCS is asked to map data

P.L. Lanzi, W. Stolzmann, and S.W. Wilson (Eds.): IWLCS 2001, LNAI 2321, pp. 133–150, 2002.
© Springer-Verlag Berlin Heidelberg 2002

instances to known categories. An early example of such work is Bonelli et al (1991), while a recent and successful spate of work in this area, involving medical and clinical databases, is due to Holmes (e.g. 2000). In particular, however, Wilson's XCS system (Wilson, 1995) has recently been applied to a hard, real-world benchmark machine learning dataset, the Wisconsin Breast Cancer (WBC) problem, and been found to achieve very strong performance in comparison to other methods which have been applied to the WCB (Wilson, 2000a). This success came through modifying the basic XCS system to allow it to deal with integer-valued rather than binary inputs. XCS has also been similarly modified and shown to perform well for real-valued data (Wilson, 2000b).

Spurred on by the impressive results from XCS on a real-world data mining benchmark problem, we sought to investigate a suitably modified version XCS with a view to identifying its general performance as a data mining tool. A closely related style of study has been done by Saxon and Barry (2000), who applied ternary-alphabet XCS (i.e. a vanilla representation, not modified to deal with numeric ranges) to the 'Monk's problems', a collection of test problems with known structure which present a series of specific and distinct types of challenge to a machine learning system. In this study, Saxon and Barry (2000) found XCS to perform at least as well as traditional techniques, and championed the notion of future research on applying XCS to real-world benchmark datasets. Wilson (2000a) echoed this appeal, having found modified XCS to perform so well on the WBC data.

Towards this end, in this paper XCS was first implemented and validated on the WBC problem, and then modified further to cope with a mixture of symbolic and numeric valued data. We chose twelve widely available real-world derived benchmark machine learning datasets, and explored the performance of our modified XCS on these problems. In this way, we considerably widen the depth of published experience with XCS on standard machine learning problems, enabling its performance in this arena to be more easily compared. In particular, we were interested in various questions relating to the potential of XCS as a generic data mining tool. The questions we begin to address in this paper are:

- How does XCS perform in comparison to rival machine learning techniques on a range of benchmark problems?
- How reliable and robust is XCS' performance in terms of the need to vary parameter and strategy settings?
- What types of data mining problem is XCS most suitable for?

Note that we will continue to use the term 'XCS' as shorthand for 'modified XCS', where the implicit modifications relate to data representation and operator issues, but not to the underlying algorithmic framework. Also, note that we currently eschew more complex versions of XCS (such as with adaptive parameters – e.g. Bull et al (2000)), in favour of exploring and understanding the basic mechanism first in a data mining setting.

The remainder of this paper is set out as follows. Section 2 describes our implementation of and modifications to the XCS system. In section 3 we note the datasets used for comparison, and describe the two comparative methods for which recent results on these datasets were available. Section 4 describes experiments and results in two phases. The first set of experiments performed 10-fold cross-validation tests on each of our twelve chosen benchmark datasets using 'default' parameter and strategy settings. This gave us a validation of our own implementation of XCS, while also providing material on the XCS comparison, reliability and robustness issues. In a second phase of experiments, a single one of these datasets was chosen (one which could be processed reasonably quickly) to support a parameter and strategy variation study. This gave us insight into the sensitivity of XCS with respect to parameter setting, and into how hard or easy it would generally be to tune XCS for best performance on a given data mining problem. Notably, we find that XCS achieved better than previous best results using sophisticated machine learning strategies on three of the twelve problems, while being broadly competitive on the remaining four. Following a discussion in Section 5, we conclude in Section 6, in which we broadly suggest, with certain caveats, that XCS is potentially a powerful and general data mining tool.

2   XCS and Modifications

2.1   Symbolic and Numeric Attributes

To ensure clarity, we will first note some terms and notation. In this paper we are dealing with machine learning datasets. A dataset consists of a number of *instances*, each of which has a known *category*. An instance is a vector of values, each drawn from a particular set or interval. A classifier is a vector of subsets, one per value, together with a prediction of the category value of any instance covered by all of the subsets. When we refer to a *symbolic* value, this means that it is drawn from a discrete and finite set, and that there is no sensible order-relation within that set. For example, a value for colour might be drawn from the set {red, green, brown, purple, black, white, orange, yellow}. Since there is no ordering relation, it does not make sense to restrict fields of classifiers to only represent 'interval' subsets of this set. For example, to allow '{brown, purple, black}' to be represented, but not '{red, black, yellow}', is inappropriate. Hence, if a symbolic value field is drawn from the set S, the corresponding field in a classifier must be capable of expressing any non-empty subset of S. In contrast, a *numeric* value is defined by a range of integers[1], The value associated with a numeric field can be any integer within the range. In this case, it makes sense for the corresponding field of a classifier to only represent subintervals within the range. For example, if the range was $[l, u]$, then we may restrict classifiers to represent subintervals of the form $[x, y]$, where $y \geq x$, $x \geq l$ and $u \geq y$. This worked well for Wilson (2000a), in which it supported impressive results on the Wisconsin Breast Cancer dataset. Notice, however, that there seems to be nothing particularly unwise about representing scattered subsets of integers such as {2, 6, 8}. For

---

[1] All datasets used here are either integer-valued, symbolic, or both; in some cases, real-valued fields have been pre-processed by us and approximated as integer ranges. We have not yet modified our XCS to deal directly with real-valued inputs.

example, consider addressing XCS to a data mining question in which categories depended on the whether certain fields were odd or even numbers. However, this omission in representational possibility did not deter Wilson's achievements in Wilson (2000a), and we similarly stick to interval subsets in our processing of numeric values. It can be posited that, where such a dispersed integer set is necessary to represent a category, it can be achieved via co-operation among a set of rules with relatively specific and distinct subintervals for the fields in question. Of course, enhancement of integer-handling implementations of XCS to allow the representation of such dispersed numeric subsets is an interesting future research issue.

2.2   Algorithmic Issues

Algorithmically, our implementation of XCS is based on the description in Butz and Wilson (2000), incorporating Wilson's modifications for integer-valued inputs garnered from Wilson (2000a). As hinted above, in our implementation, inputs may be from a symbolic alphabet, or an integer range. A given problem may contain a mixture of these two types of input field. A note is necessary here concerning our preprocessing of data. Although our XCS is not yet set up to address real-valued inputs, many fields of our test datasets are real-valued fields. We pre-process such a fields by discretising it across its range into a number of bins; by default, this number is 10. For example, if a real-valued input were in the range [0, 10), this corresponds to replacing each value with its 'floor' integer. In doing so we lose some information, of course, however this has not prevented us for achieving strong results.

We followed Wilson (2000a) in designing covering, mutation and crossover operators for coping with integer-interval fields. However, further modifications in these areas were required to deal with symbolic fields. We describe these modifications next; largely, we used simple and easily implemented strategy choices in each case, although we attempted to be sensible in terms of the type of variation introduced by the operators.

First, we decided to avoid having crossover points 'within' the classifier field of a symbolic variable. Hence, a crossover between the following two actions in a three variable (all symbolic) problem:

{a, b, c}	{Q, T}	{red, orange, white}
{d, e}	{P, S, Z}	{yellow, blue, green}

might yield one of the following children, among many other possibilities:

{a, b, c}	{Q, T}	{yellow, blue, green}
{d, e}	{P, S, Z}	{red, orange, white}

however not, for example, any of:

{a, b, c}	{P, Q, T}	{red, orange, white}
{c, d}	{P, S, Z}	{red, white, blue, green}

in which one or more of the individual classifier fields is some sort of recombination of that field from its two parents. As hinted here, it would not be difficult to dream up suitable ways to handle recombination 'within' a symbolic field, but we chose not to implement any such scheme yet.

Mutation of a symbolic variable amounted to increasing or decreasing the size of the subset by a number k of randomly chosen symbols, corresponding to slightly (depending, of course, on k) increasing or decreasing the generality of the mutated field. For example, if k is 2, then the subset: {yellow, blue, green} might be mutated to become: {yellow, blue, green, red, orange} – i.e. two randomly chosen values are added.

Covering of a symbolic variable is achieved by duplicating the input condition to the covering classifier and applying mutation as above but with the proviso that the variable is only made more general; the result is a variable in the classifier which is capable of matching both the covering input condition and variations around that input. For example, to cover a data example with "red" in a symbolic field, the covering classifier is simply initialized with {red} in the appropriate place and then immediately mutated as above with a positive value of k. Finally, missing values are handled by simply allowing the appropriate field of a classifier to always match the missing-value field(s) of a data example.

3   Benchmark Datasets and Comparative Algorithms

3.1   Benchmark Datasets

The datasets we use are named and described in Table 1. In all cases, the additional target category field was two-valued; i.e. the task in each case was to predict which of two categories an instance belonged to.

The choice of this particular collection arose by fortuity and elimination. We are fortunate to be acquainted with the work of Aguilar and colleagues, who are developing an evolutionary algorithm for machine learning, called HIDER, which evolves a collection of hierarchical decision rules (Aguilar et al, 2001). In common with Wilson's approach to the Wisconsin Breast Cancer dataset in Wilson (2000a), Aguilar et al (2001) also use ten-fold cross-validation on that and several other benchmark datasets, and they compare HIDER with C4.5 on all of the problems. Aguilar et al's results are the background for our own tenfold cross-validated XCS comparisons. Although the submitted paper we refer to (Aguilar et al, 2001) is not readily available, we have permission to report a subset of the results, while interested readers may find the ideas behind HIDER published in Aguilar et al (1998a, 1998b), and we also briefly describe it in this section. Finally, the particular subset of twelve datasets used here, chosen from the 20 investigated by Agular et al (2001), is due to the current limitations of our modified XCS implementation. The datasets chosen were those without any fields which were obviously 'troublesomely' real-valued (i.e. for which it seemed an integer discretisation was not a good idea), and for which there were only two target categories. The real-value input handling (a la Wilson, 2000b) modifications in our XCS are not yet fully implemented.

Table 1. Databases used in our experiments. Each has a two-class target field not included in the 'Input Field' information. All are available from the UCI Machine Learning Repository (Blake and Merz, 1998)

Database Title	Field information	Instances
BUPA Liver Disorders	7 fields, all numeric, no missing values, 2 classes	345
Wisconsin Breast Cancer (Mangasarian and Wolberg, 1990)	9 fields, all numeric, 16 missing values, 2 classes	699
Pima Indians Diabetes (Smith et al., 1988)	8 fields, all numeric, no missing values, 2 classes	768
Sonar Classification	60 fields, all numeric, no missing values, 2 classes	208
Hepatitis Domain (Diaconis and Efron, 1983)	20 fields, 6 numeric and 14 symbolic, 2 classes	155
Tic-Tac-Toe Endgame (Matheus and Rendell, 1989)	9 fields, all symbolic, no missing values, 2 classes	958
1984 US Congressional Voting (Schlimmer, 1987)	16 fields, all symbolic, 285 missing values, 2 classes	435
Wine Recognition (Aeberhard et al, 1992)	13 fields, all numeric, no missing values, 3 classes	178
Zoo Database	17 attributes, 15 Boolean and 2 numeric-valued, no missing values, 7 classes	101
Iris Database (Fisher, 1936)	4 numeric attributes, no missing values, 3 classes	150
Lenses Database (Cendrowska, 1987)	4 symbolic attributes (3 binary, 1 ternary), no missing values, 3 classes	24
Glass Identification (Evett and Spiehler, 1987)	9 numeric attributes, no missing values 6 classes	214

3.2   C4.5 and HIDER

C4.5 (Quinlan, 1993) is the well-known decision tree construction heuristic based on Quinlan's seminal ID3 algorithm (Quinlan, 1986). The results we present for C4.5 come from Aguilar et al (2001), who used the code distributed with Quinlan's C4.5 book (Quinlan, 1993). We additionally note here that there is negligible difference in terms of results quality between C4.5 and C5.0; C5.0 is the commercial version, which benefits from a variety of implementation efficiency improvements.

HIDER (Aguilar et al, 2001) uses a typical 'sequential covering GA' (Mitchell, 1997) to evolve a sequentially ordered list of rules. When using the evolved list to classify an instance, the condition part of each rule is tested in turn for matching the instance, and the first rule which matches is used to generate the predicted category. This is very similar to the use of *decision lists* (Rivest, 1987), but Aguilar et al (1998b, 2001) extend the concept to handle arbitrary types and mixtures of input values. The HIDER method generates rules in successive stages; in each stage, an evolutionary algorithm is run to completion to find a rule which best covers the remaining data. This is then added as the next rule in the list, reducing the data to be covered in the next step.

4   Experiments and Results

4.1   Default XCS Setup and Initial Tests

Table 2 gives the default parameter and strategy settings for our XCS setup in all experiments. In particular, these were the settings which formed the basis of the further tests on the Voting database described in section 4.2. However, for the tests described here, a small amount of preliminary tuning of XCS was done in each case, which led to a revised setting for (usually) the maximum classifier population size. Full details of these are available on request form the first author. We note that population size and other parameters in the main comparative technique (HIDER) were also preliminarily tuned for each database. These default settings are largely as in Butz and Wilson (2000) and Wilson (2000a), plus additional settings for parameters and strategies which were necessary to include due to our modifications. Our XCS implementation is essentially a 'vanilla' setup, without sophisticated operators or other devices which we leave for future exploration once we have completed studies of a basic XCS setup.

XCS was applied to the twelve datasets listed in Table 1, using ten-fold cross-validation in each case, and running XCS on each fold for 100 cycles (100 complete passes through the training set) The results, compared with comparable tenfold cross-validated results from C4.5 and HIDER reported by Aguilar et al (2001) are in Table 3. For each of the datasets, the tenfold cross-validation result from each of HIDER, C4.5, and our XCS is given, in terms of the *error rate*, which is just the percentage of instances mis-classified. For convenience, the best result from these tests for each dataset is underlined and in bold. Also included, to aid consideration of the results, are a value for 'Baseline Target Fraction Correct (BT). This simply indicates the performance of a method which just guesses that any example has the class with greatest incidence in that particular database. This can be thought of as the minimally achievable result for a minimally experienced system. For additional convenience, Table 3 also includes a reminder of the field types in each database.

XCS outperformed C4.5 in all cases except two, the Sonar database, which clearly causes problems for both of the rival methods too, and the Wine database. XCS outperformed HIDER on nine of the twelve databases, and was second best on two of the remainder, and worst on only one. To a first approximation (since XCS has eight 'best results' in Table 3, compared to three for HIDER and one for C4.5), XCS seems clearly the more robust of the three methods. These initial results are certainly encouraging from the point of view of XCS' potential as a general data mining tool, however it also points to problems and research issues: in the Tic-Tac-Toe case, it seems considerably worse than HIDER, and in the Sonar case it seems considerably worse than C4.5. It should also be noted that C4.5 is very fast when compared to HIDER or XCS. Both of the latter may typically take several hours on a modern desktop PC to provide a single ten-fold cross validation result on one of the larger of the databases tested here, however C4.5 takes a matter of minutes.

Table 2. Default parameter and strategy settings for our XCS implementation, as set up for all experiments unless explicitly indicated otherwise

Parameter	Role	Setting
Delete scheme	Classifier deletion selection method	roulette
Parent selection	Classifier parent selection method	roulette
Prob. of explore	Probability of exploration rather than exploitation	50%
θ_{del}	Deletion threshold	50
χ	Probability of crossover	90%
θ_{GA}	GA threshold	48
ε_0	Minimum effective error	10
β	Learning rate	0.2
α	Multiplier coefficient used in accuracy calculation	0.1
N	Power parameter used in accuracy calculation	25
θ_{sub}	Subsumption threshold	20
σ	Multiplier used in deletion vote calculation	0.1
μ_{action}	Probability of mutating the action	4%
μ (symbolic)	Probability of mutating a symbolic variable	1%
m_0 (symbolic)	Range of mutation	1
r_0 (symbolic)	Range of covering mutation (actual minimum =1)	0
Prob. of hash	Probability of mutating a cover	33%
Positive reward	Reward for a positive result	1000
Max number of classifiers	Limit of population	6400

It is of course tempting to try to understand these results in terms of the different features of the datasets involved. For example, the Sonar dataset has by far the greatest number of fields per instance among those tested here, and this was the only one for which C4.5 triumphed. Hence a tentative hypothesis is seeded which may suggest that C4.5's relative performance over XCS, say, improves with the number of fields, and when this number is particularly large the best choice of machine learning technique may be C4.5. Such a suggestion is not justified, of course, since the fundamental factor in a dataset's learnability is clearly the way in which the categories are clustered in feature space. However, there is alternative support for this hypothesis in the intuition that high numbers of fields may make it more difficult to appropriately set up parameters for systems such as XCS and HIDER. This is consistent with the view of Saxon and Barry (2000), who see a limit to the number of fields XCS can reasonably be expected to handle, and point to prior feature selection as the way through in such problems.

Table 3. Results of tenfold cross-validation tests. Error rates are given for C4.5 and HIDER as reported in Aguilar et al (2001), and the results of our XCS implementation using the settings in Table 2, with occasional variation in the classifier maximum population size. Bet results are underlined and in bold, while additional baseline targets are noted

Database	Fields/Classes	Baseline Target Fraction Correct error rate (%)	C4.5R8 (%)	HIDER (%)	XCS (%)
Bupa Liver	Numeric/2	42.03	34.73	35.71	**32.15**
Breast Cancer	Numeric/2	34.48	6.28	4.29	**3.73**
Pima Indians	Numeric/2	34.90	32.06	**25.9**	31.38
Sonar	Numeric/2	46.63	**30.31**	43.07	46.59
Hepatitis	Mixed/2	20.65	21.42	19.41	**18.71**
Tic-Tac-Toe	Symbolic/2	34.66	14.2	**3.85**	14.09
Voting	Symbolic/2	38.62	6.19	6.64	**5.77**
Wine	Numeric/3	60.11	6.71	**3.95**	7.26
Zoo	Mixed/7	59.41	7.0	8.0	**3.73**
Iris	Numeric/3	66.66	4.67	3.33	**2.00**
Lenses	Symbolic/3	37.50	29.99	25.0	**21.67**
Glasses	Numeric/6	64.49	32.73	29.41	**27.47**

In Table 4 we attempt a dissection of the databases tested in this paper into essential features, and map out XCS' performance against these features. Some clear hints at patterns start to emerge - further, in "periodic table" fashion, it suggested hypotheses for XCS performance on certain kinds of database untested here. It seems that XCS' niche for datamining may well be with databases of symbolic or mixed symbolic/numeric fields, and with few or medium numbers of fields.

Table 4. An attempt to relate relative performance of XCS to characteristics of the datasets. The table summarises performance in three dimensions (type of field, number of fields, and number of classes). XCS is given a grade (A = excellent to E = terrible) based on its performance on datasets of the given characteristics. To the left of "/" is a grade for 2-class database(s), and to the right of "/" is a grade for >2 class database(s). For example, we give XCS a B for numeric databases with few fields and 2 classes, but an A for numeric databases with few fields and more than 2 classes. "< >" indicates no databases were tested with this set of characteristics

	Field Types		
	Numeric	Symbolic	Mixed
Few fields	B / A	C / A	< >/< >
Medium	< >/ E	A /<>	A / A
Many fields	E / < >	< >/< >	< > / < >

Besides that observation, no apparent patterns arise. For example, XCS seems good on some numeric datasets, and bad on others; good on some symbolic datasets, and bad on others; and, pleasingly, good on the combined symbolic/numeric dataset. This lack of pattern is, on the other hand, evidence of a degree of robustness in the potential of XCS. On the majority (just about) of these datasets it has outperformed two good rival machine learning techniques, and does not seem *a priori* fazed by any particular feature, except perhaps when it comes comparatively large numbers of fields.

4.2   Further Study on the Voting Database

With an interest in the marketability of XCS as a general data mining tool, we were interested in how reliable results might be in the face of alternative stratifications of the data, and also in terms of algorithmic processing seed. The latter is the obvious question of reliability; i.e. how variable are the results across different trials on the same problem? It may seem reasonable to assume that tenfold cross-validation, by its very nature, gives a reliable account of the performance that can generally be expected on a dataset. However, we have observed that relatively significant variation can arise between complete tenfold trials, due to either fold-design seed or algorithm processing seed. A set of experiments in this section documents those observations.

The Voting database combined good comparative XCS performance with reasonable processing times (the number of instances was relatively low, and all categories were two-valued). We hence used this database as the substrate for a second series of experiments which tested variation in parameter settings. As previously noted, the 'default' XCS setup for the Voting database was precisely as in Table 2. In the following, we report on additional experiments to look at variation in performance due to random seed and fold-design using the Table 2 setup, and then we look at experiments on settings which minimally depart from the Table 2 setup.

Variability in Performance Due to Fold Seed.
It is important for industry-reading data-mining tools to be relatively robust and reliable. One possible source of variation concerns the way in which the data are stratified into folds. We perform tenfold stratified cross validation, where a random seed determines the particular way that the ten partitions are designed. We performed ten experiments on the Voting database using the setup in Table 2, but in each case using a different random fold-design seed. The results are in Table 5. This time we give accuracy instead of error rate, and also report on the mean generality of and number of unique classifiers evolved in an arbitrarily chosen fold in each case. We also provide a simple measure of the variation, which simply gives the difference between the best and worst results. The random number generator used in our experiments was the standard library routine provided with Borland Delphi 5.0.

Table 5. Results of tenfold cross-validation tests on the Voting database for each of ten different folding seeds. Also given are generality and number of unique classifiers for an arbitrarily chosen fold in each case

Fold Seed	Fraction Correct	Average Generality	No of (Unique) Classifiers
1	0.9054	0.5589	238
2	0.9426	0.5698	239
3	0.8987	0.4539	335
4	0.9131	0.2965	407
5	0.8848	0.5089	248
6	0.9194	0.6458	185
7	0.9150	0.5652	251
8	0.9218	0.6324	227
9	0.8806	0.4565	270
10	0.8965	0.5875	199
Mean	0.9078	0.5275	259.9
Variation	0.062	0.35	222

Clearly, the random partitioning of data into folds alone (these experiments all used the same algorithm processing seed) leads to marked variation in performance. It is hard to assess this without also determining the comparative measures for other techniques. Such data is not yet available at the time of writing for the comparative methods C4.5 and HIDER. However, we have done experiments using an alternative ruleset evolution system (for future submission/publication) on both the Wisconsin Breast Cancer and the Voting datasets, and examined the variation in performance of 10-fold cross-validation tests for different fold seeds. That is, we have obtained the data in column 2 of Table 5 for an alternative machine learning system on both the WBC and the Voting datasets. Respectively, these showed a mean of 92.9 with a variation of 6.2%, and a mean of 93.8% with a variation of 6.1%. It seems clear that variation due to fold seed is quite significant. Also, we can with some justification state that XCS is no more variable than other systems in its sensitivity to the fold seed. This certainly highlights the need for caution in inferring too much from a single tenfold cross-validation test.

Variability in Performance Due to Algorithm Seed.

In this test, we performed ten experiments on the Voting database using the setup in Table 2, and all using the same stratified ten-fold partition of the data, but with different random seeds for the algorithm The results are in Table 6, where we again give accuracy instead of error rate, and also report on the mean generality of and number of unique classifiers evolved in an arbitrarily chosen fold in each case.

Table 6. Results of tenfold cross-validation tests on the Voting database for each of ten different algorithm seeds. Also given are generality and number of unique classifiers for an arbitrarily chosen fold in each case

Processing Seed	Fraction Correct	Average Generality	No of (Unique) Classifiers
1	0.9105	0.5864	228
2	0.9128	0.4977	223
3	0.8987	0.4539	335
4	0.8574	1.0000	2
5	0.8941	0.5790	209
6	0.9013	0.5120	241
7	0.9149	0.5062	251
8	0.8851	0.5558	196
9	0.8900	0.5976	178
10	0.9127	0.5485	221
Average	0.8978	0.5837	208.4
Variation	0.054	0.55	333

Significant variation remains, of the same order as that due to fold-design seed.

Basic Parameter and Strategy Variation.

We then arbitrarily chose a single combination of seeds (which, with the Table 2 setup, produced 92.2% accuracy, mean generality of 0.5524, and number of unique classifiers of 225) and used these for a number of parameter variation experiments. The results of these are summarised in Table 7. Each row refers to a single ten-fold cross validation, the result of which is given as usual in the 'Fraction Correct' column.

It is worth noting in addition that the 'delete least fit' experiment showed a rapid reduction in the number of classifiers over time which led to erratic results. This finding agrees with those of Kovacs (1999), who points out that deletion of the least fit classifier amounts to baising deletion towards new classifiers (which tend to enter with relatively low fitness), hence stifling the system's exploratory ability.

Table 7: Results of tenfold cross-validation tests on the Voting database for each of 31 different variations in parameter settings, each minimally changed from the Table 2 setup

Variable Setting	Fraction Correct	Average Generality	No of (Unique) Classifiers	Effect compared to default
Delete least fit	0.7285	0.4754	4	much worse
Select most fit parents	0.9335	0.5562	290	better
Prob. of explore = 95%	0.8759	0.5201	291	worse
Prob. of explore = 5%	0.8827	0.4862	408	worse
θ_{del} = 95	0.8803	0.6136	290	worse
θ_{del} = 5	0.9194	0.4943	256	minimal
χ = 10%	0.8573	0.3419	312	much worse
N = 5	0.8874	0.5779	204	worse
μ_{action} = 96%	0.9130	0.5992	291	worse
θ_{GA} = 90	0.9151	0.5491	240	minimal
θ_{GA} = 10	0.9218	0.5174	288	minimal
ε_0 = 100	0.8777	0.5909	286	worse
ε_0 = 1	0.9172	0.4753	262	minimal
β = 0.1	0.8785	0.4436	394	worse
β = 0.3	0.8916	0.5225	247	worse
α = 0.05	0.9104	0.5471	274	worse
α = 0.15	0.9038	0.5104	331	worse
θ_{sub} = 10	0.8802	0.5142	268	worse
θ_{sub} = 30	0.8690	0.6035	237	worse
σ = 0.05	0.8784	0.4390	337	worse
σ = 0.15	0.9197	0.5602	236	worse
μ (symbolic) =10%	0.9058	0.4712	245	worse
m_0 (symbolic) =2	0.9383	04078	365	better
m_0 (symbolic) =3	0.9127	0.5156	360	minimal
r_0 (symbolic) =1	0.9220	0.5525	225	none
r_0 (symbolic) =2	0.9220	0.5525	225	none
r_0 (symbolic) =4	0.9173	0.6277	170	minimal
Prob, of Hash =66%	0.8475	0.7886	124	much worse
Prob, of Hash =5%	0.8829	0.2944	421	worse
Positive reward =5000	0.8898	0.4410	271	worse
Positive reward =100	0.8898	0.5856	293	worse

Examining the results for all of these setting changes relative to the initial reference it can be seen that almost all results fall within the 6% variation we noted in the tests which varied seed values over the default setup. The only result outwith this level of variation in accuracy was that for the classifier deletion scheme, which gave a very poor result.

Concerning strategy settings, not to use the 'delete least fit' scheme for classifier population update seems to be the clearest message which arises. Other than that, the simple (if intuitively unwise) expedient of selecting the fittest parents (rather than the standard classifier selection scheme) seems to be beneficial in this case.

The variation of probability of exploration, which tested heavy exploration/light exploitation and heavy exploitation/light exploration in turn, both produced worse performance. Presumably there is an optimal setting for this, and likely to be different for different problems, but the default setting of 50% balanced exploration/ exploitation is certainly far more in the right ballpark than not. Similar variations around the default deletion threshold also affected performance adversely, however a quite low deletion threshold does not seem to be convincingly damaging.

Shifting the crossover probability from 0.9 to 0.1 was indeed damaging, reflecting the important role of this operation in LCS's which has often been reported. Of the other variations, notable results seem to be that a considerable change in the probability of mutation an action (from 4% to 96%) did not affect performance too adversely. The GA threshold also seems to be a relatively insensitive parameter. However, correct setting of the range (step size) of mutation for covering seems important, while the range of mutation for the GA seems rather less sensitive.

5   Discussion

It can be seen that the results which were in general most improved over the Baseline Target error rate were those for Breast Cancer, Tic-Tac-Toe and Voting. In some cases, the results for all methods were not very different from the baseline target figure and for some worse results were produced. In the cases where XCS performance seemed particularly lacking, we note that the relatively large number of variables in the input data considerably slowed down exploration of system settings with our implementation, consequently hiding the true capabilities of XCS when used in these cases.

Databases which are wholly or partially symbolic in nature appear very difficult for identification of 'good' settings for the various system constants.

When the system is balanced on the point of providing the baseline target result it does appear to be very easy for the system to 'flip' over and produce the exact opposite response. In this situation a reliable error of, for example, 25% being produced with occasionally an error of 75% being generated. This effect is due to very similar highly generalised classifiers being present with opposing outcomes. Simply presenting the test dataset in a different order allows the system to learn a different strategy and thus produce a result based on the least frequent outcome of training.

Experimentation on the composition of the original datasets (folds) by varying the random seed for the data division routine was carried out. Results of these experiments show that the variation in the results can be quite large (of the order of 6%). Experiments to separate the component of error due to variations in the random seed used during processing were also carried out. Results of these experiments indicate that this contribution to system variability is also significant and attributes of the order of 6%. These errors may be dependent on the actual settings chosen, as yet, no attempt to broaden the parameters of these experiments either by the inclusion of different database data or by extensive variation in the settings of the system constants.

Variations due to fold composition should therefore be taken into account when comparisons are made between different settings being evaluated. It should be noted that changes in settings of system constants will be directly equivalent to random seed changes as the sequence of events and subsequent random function activations will be dependent on settings used.

It is almost certain (based on our experience) that with XCS the more training the better the final result though it has been shown that the incremental improvement in result diminishes quite rapidly. This being the case, then taking sample test runs of only 100 training cycles (as we have done – where a cycle is one complete pass through the training data) may not give the full picture to allow appropriate selection of system settings to achieve optimum performance. 100 cycles was chosen as a test sample since at this point covering tends to have finished and regular deletion has been established. Faster processing or longer test periods may produce better results with larger sample runs.

A preliminary investigation of parameter and strategy settings was done, which focussed on large variations in one parameter (or strategy) rather than fine-grained exploration around default settings. This was to help establish the general 'validity' of the default settings, and to gain a first appreciation of XCS' general sensitivity to the various parameters. The default settings seem very much in the ball-park of generally good settings. This probably reflects preliminary work done in Wilson's original implementation (1995), whose parameters have been used unchanged in much later work (e.g. Butz and Wilson (2000) and Wilson (2000a)). However, from our work it seems worth noting that the hash probability and crossover rate seem least wise to meddle with, while benefits seem achievable by exploring the GA's selection strategy and the mutation probabilities. We do not suggest by that that any significant benefit is achievable in exploring alterations to the well-known default XCS mutation rate for binary classifiers. Our point is that the introduction of new types of field (e.g. symbolic subset fields) requires dedicated mutation and covering operators with their own specialised rate parameters – it seems to be valuable use of preliminary tuning time to explore optimal settings for such new mutation parameters.

6   Summary and Conclusions

While it can be seen that the results which were in general most improved over the Baseline Target error rate were Breast Cancer, Tic-Tac-Toe and Vote it is felt that the other databases would benefit from more extensive examination and constant optimisation. Limited time has meant the focus of work was on the faster moving databases, as such the slower databases were not fully examined and it may be expected that improvements in results will be forthcoming in the future.

XCS outperformed C4.5 in all cases except two. XCS outperformed HIDER on eight of the twelve databases, and was second best on two. These results were achieved with little or no preliminary investigation of parameter settings in each case. When we later explored parameter settings in the context of a single test database, we found that the default settings (in Butz and Wilson (2000) and Wilson (2000a)) were generally well-chosen, and that the settings most worth examining for improved performance seemed to be the GA's parent selection method and the mutation probabilities. The results of these experiments generally demonstrate that, with certain caveats, and especially the need for much more research, that XCS is potentially a powerful and general data mining tool.

Based on our experience, some of which is documented here, we are able to draft the following preliminary guidelines for parameter and strategy setting in XCS applied to data mining problems.

- If covering is found to persist after the 'deletion phase' begins then increase the population size, since covering has a tendency to reoccur when the population has insufficient classifiers to hold a member relating to all inputs. This may require a much larger population than one may intuitively expect, as deletion and mutation will have eliminated potential input matches even though classifier experiences do not exceed set requirements.

- Simple superposition of constant settings which individually appear to produce advantageous results has been shown to be unreliable therefore this method of optimum constant search must be seen as a guide only.

Finally, much further work needs to be performed to include exploration of the various system constants in order to establish optimal conditions for maximal results. A future approach we favour is to attempt to use XCS itself to investigate system setting rules by compiling a database of results and using these results as an input to XCS in order to produce a set of classifiers which lead to a set of selection criteria for settings.

Acknowledgements
The authors wish to thank British Telecommunications Plc for ongoing support for this research, and we also thank Stewart Wilson for prompt and helpful replies to emails during our attempts to validate our XCS implementation on the WBC data. We are also grateful for the careful and very helpful comments of our anonymous reviewers. Finally, the 2nd and 3rd authors gratefully acknowledge sponsorship from Evosolve Ltd.

References

Aeberhard, S., Coomans, D., and de Vel, O. (1992) Comparison of Classifiers in High Dimensional Settings, Tech. Rep. no. 92-02, Dept. of Computer Science and Dept. of Mathematics and Statistics, James Cook University of North Queensland.

Aguilar, J.S., Riquelme, J.C., and Toro, M. (1998a) Decision Queue Classifier for Supervised Learning using Rotated Hyperboxes, in *Progress in Artificial Intelligence: IBERAMIA '98*, Springer LNAI volume 1484, pp. 326–335.

Aguilar, J.S., Riquelme, J.C., and Toro, M. (1998b) A Tool to Obtain a Hierarchical Qualitative Set of Rules from Quantitative Data, in *Progress in Artificial Intelligence: IBERAMIA '98*, Springer LNAI volume 1484, pp. 336–345.

Aguilar, J.S., Riquelme, J.C., and Toro, M. (2001) 'Evolutionary Learning of Hierarchical Decision Rules' paper submitted to the *IEEE Transactions on Evolutionary Computation*.

Blake, C.L. and Merz, C.J. (1998). UCI Repository of machine learning databases [http://www.ics.uci.edu/~mlearn/MLRepository.html]. Irvine, CA: University of California, Department of Information and Computer Science.

Bull, L. Hurst, J., and Tomlinson, A. (2000) Self-Adaptive Mutation in Classifier System Controllers. In J-A. Meyer, A. Berthoz, D. Floreano, H. Roitblatt, and S.W. Wilson (eds) *From Animals to Animats 6 - The Sixth International Conference on the Simulation of Adaptive Behaviour*, MIT Press.

Butz, M.V. and Wilson, S.W. (2000) YEAR, 'An Algorithmic Description of XCS', Technical Report 2000017, Illinois Genetic Algorithms Laboratory, IL, USA.

Cendrowska, J. (1987) PRISM: An algorithm for inducing modular rules, *International Journal of Man-Machine Studies*, **27**: 349–370

Diaconis, P. and Efron, B. (1983). Computer-Intensive Methods in Statistics. *Scientific American*, **248**.

Evett, I.W. and Spiehler, E.J. (1987) Technical Note, Central Research Establishment Home Office Forensic Science Service Aldermaston, Reading, Berkshire, UK RG7 4PN

Fisher, R.A. (1936) The use of multiple measurements in taxonomic problems, *Annual Eugenics*, 7, Part II, 179-188 (1936)

Holland, J.H. (1976) Adaptation, in Rosen, R., and Snell, F.M. (eds.), Progress in Theoretical Biology, New York: Plenum.

Holland, J.H. (1980) Adaptive algorithms for discovering and using general patterns in growing knowledge bases, International Journal of Policy Analysis and Information Systems, 4(3):245–268.

Holland, J.H., Booker, L.B., Colombetti, M., Dorigo, M., Goldberg, D.E., Forrest, S., Riolo, R.L., Smith, R.E., Lanzi, P.L., Stolzmann, W., and Wilson, S.W. (2000) What is a Learning Classifier System? In Lanzi, P.L., Stolzmann, W., and Wilson, S.W. (eds.), Learning Classifier Systems: From Foundations to Applications, Springer Lecture Notes in Computer Science 1813, pp. 3–32.

Holmes, J.H. (2000), Learning Classifier Systems Applied to Knowledge Discovery in Clinical Research Databases, in Lanzi, P.L., Stolzmann, W., and Wilson, S.W. (eds.), Learning

Classifier Systems: From Foundations to Applications, Springer Lecture Notes in Computer Science 1813, pp. 243–261.

Kovacs, T. (1999) Deletion schemes for classifier systems, in Wolfgang Banzhaf, Jason Daida, Agoston E. Eiben, Max H. Garzon, Vasant Honavar, Mark Jakiela, and Robert E. Smith, editors. *Proceedings of the Genetic and Evolutionary Computation Conference (GECCO-99)*. Morgan Kaufmann, pages 329–336.

Lanzi, P.L. and Riolo, R.L. (2000) A Roadmap to the Last Decase of Learning Classifier System Research (from 1989 to 1999), in Lanzi, P.L., Stolzmann, W., and Wilson, S.W. (eds.), Learning Classifier Systems: From Foundations to Applications, Springer Lecture Notes in Computer Science 1813, pp. 33–61.

Mangasarian, O.L. and Wolberg, W.H. (1990) 'Cancer diagnosis via linear programming', *SIAM News*, **23**(5):1 and 18.

Matheus, C.J. and Rendell, L.A. (1989). Constructive induction on decision trees, *in Proceedings of the Eleventh International Joint Conference on Artificial Intelligence*, Detroit, MI: Morgan Kaufmann, pp. 117–121.

Mitchell, T. (1997) *Machine Learning*, McGraw-Hill.

Quinlan, J.R. (1986) Induction of Decision Trees, *Machine Learning*, **1**(1): 81–106.

Quinlan, J.R. (1993) *C4.5: Programs for Machine Learning*, Morgan Kaufmann.

Rivest, R.L. (1997) Learning Decision Lists, *Machine Learning*, **1**(2): 229–246.

Saxon, S. and Barry, A. (2000) XCS and the Monk's Problems, in Lanzi, P.L., Stolzmann, W. and Wilson, S.W. (eds.), Learning Classifier Systems: From Foundations to Applications, Springer Lecture Notes in Computer Science 1813, pp. 223–242.

Schlimmer, J.C. (1987). Concept acquisition through representational adjustment. Doctoral dissertation, Department of Information and Computer Science, University of California, Irvine, CA.

Smith, J.W., Everhart, J.E., Dickson, W.C., Knowler, W.C., and Johannes, R.S. (1988). Using the ADAP learning algorithm to forecast the onset of diabetes mellitus, in *Proceedings of the Symposium on Computer Applications and Medical Care*, IEEE Computer Society Press, pp. 261–265.

Wilson, S.W. (1995) 'Classifier fitness based on accuracy', *Evolutionary Computation*, **3**(2):149–175.

Wilson, S.W. (2000a) 'Mining Oblique Data with XCS', Technical Report 2000028, University of Illinois at Urbana-Champaign, MI, USA.

Wilson, S.W. (2000b) 'Get Real! XCS with Continuous-Valued Inputs', in Lanzi, P.L., Stolzmann, W. and Wilson, S.W. (eds.), Learning Classifier Systems: From Foundations to Applications, Springer Lecture Notes in Computer Science 1813, pp. 209–219.

Explorations in LCS Models of Stock Trading

Sonia Schulenburg and Peter Ross

School of Computing, Napier University
10 Colinton Road, Edinburgh EH10 5DT
s.schulenburg@napier.ac.uk, peter@dcs.napier.ac.uk

Abstract. In previous papers we have described the basic elements for
building an economic model consisting of a group of artificial traders
functioning and adapting in an environment containing real stock market
information. We have analysed the feasibility of the proposed approach
by comparing the final wealth generated by such agents over a period of
time, against the wealth of a number of well known investment strategies,
including the bank, buy-and-hold and trend-following strategies. In this
paper we review classical economic theories and introduce a new strategy
inspired by the Efficient Market Hypothesis (named here *random walk*
to compare the performance of our traders. In order to build better
trader models we must increase our understanding about how artificial
agents learn and develop; in this paper we address a number of design
issues, including the analysis of information sets and evolved strategies.
Specifically, the results presented here correspond to the stock of IBM.

1 Forecasting Financial Markets

Modelling real financial markets is not an easy task, it was once said that:
"anybody doing applications of artificial intelligence (AI) in financial trading
and investment management must possess considerable determination and vast
reserves of optimism." [13] Why?

The generalised growth in complexity of financial markets has been one of
the most significant changes seen in the past decade. As a result, the difficulty of
the decision making process has increased dramatically, becoming more dependent upon the analysis of information gathered and available data coming from
many different sources and in various forms. The results of various quantitative
forecasting techniques, as well as human subjective skills and judgment, serve
as an important tool for strategic decisions to most financial institutions.

The high levels of activity seen in financial markets nowadays, along with the
vast amounts of information available, produce multidimensional financial time
series where the general mechanism that generates them is poorly understood.
Much research has been devoted to trying to find some kind of model that has
good explanatory power of the variables involved but is still of relatively low
complexity. With the hope of finding the key to increased wealth, a common approach to follow is to try to look for previously undetected nonlinear regularities
(such as daily or intra-daily fluctuations) from economic time series. This can
be done in several ways.

P.L. Lanzi, W. Stolzmann, and S.W. Wilson (Eds.): IWLCS 2001, LNAI 2321, pp. 151–180, 2002.

In some models, data derived from only one time series is used, such as a specific stock's price, a given index or the one-day rate of return to holding a stock. Readers interested in a neural net (NN) model of this type are referred to [42], where inputs are defined as the *one-day return of a stock* r_t[1], and for a genetic programming model where inputs are defined as the difference between the current price of a single stock and its moving averages, highest and lowest prices, refer to [40, 41, 26, 27].

In addition to using a single price series, other approaches use more variables and in different levels of sophistication (see [8, 18, 21]). These models can include over 120 inputs coming from other stock prices, volume of transactions, macro economic data, market indicators such as indexes, profit and earnings ratios, etc.

More recently, as a result of the fast growth of the Internet, other approaches started to emerge, such as the work on text in finance [43, 38, 39]. Much of this effort concentrates on finding profitable trading rules from the analysis of text information of financial interest publicly available on the Internet – chat boards or news stories. The problem of designing trader models with relevant indicators has been addressed in [32], where it is also proposed to use genetic algorithms to optimise simple trading models.

Also, a number of conferences report many papers on financial time series analysis and prediction. Specially, during the early nineties, when the use of neural networks appeared to be an area of great potential in securities forecasting, dozens of papers using neural networks were published. A good review of these results can be found in [1–4], and for a good summary of techniques used, see [30]. Although later on the revolution came to an end, what that era brought to the surface was perhaps the need to address the fallacies encountered with traditional approaches and the need to search for non-linear models capable of handling the complex task of forecasting. Too much was expected from NNs, and soon people were going to realise that, as pointed out by Halbert White when reporting his results, "in either case the implication is the same: the neural network is not a money machine" [42].

It then seems reasonable to suppose that in financial markets, investment decisions must involve taking into account a significant number of elements and their relationships, which due to the complex nature of economic systems, are usually difficult to understand and highly non-linear. Even though some investment managers and traders could factor in such dependencies in the analysis, they often cannot explain their decisions and point out the significant elements and relationships contributing to their current positions; other times, due to secrecy policies, they are just not willing to do so. This makes the problem of economic forecasting very hard, as there is no actual knowledge easily available and controversies and debates as to what is the right investment approach are still in question. In the following section we will review some of these.

---

[1] The one-day return of a stock is defined as $r_t = \frac{p_t - p_{t-1} + d_t}{p_{t-1}}$, where p_1 is the closing price of the stock in question on day t and d_t is the dividend it paid on day t. This value should be adjusted to stock splits and dividends if appropriate.

2   Classical Economic Theories

With tremendous impact in industry and academia, the Efficient Markets Hypothesis (EMH) has been perhaps one of the strongest weapons against the development of economic forecast approaches described in the previous section. The hypothesis first appeared in the famous and highly controversial PhD dissertation of Eugene F. Fama at the University of Chicago, under the title "The Behaviour of Stock Market Prices", and was originally published in the Journal of Business [15]. In addition to this work, Fama also published ideas of this kind in a number of journal papers, such as "Random Walks in Stock Market Prices" which appeared in, amongst others, the Institutional Investor [14], where the following excerpt is taken:

> "An 'efficient' market is defined as a market where there are large numbers of rational, profit-maximisers actively competing, with each trying to predict future market values of individual securities, and where important current information is almost freely available to all participants. In an efficient market, competition among the many intelligent participants leads to a situation where, at any point in time, actual prices of individual securities already reflect the effects of information based both on events that have already occurred and on events which, as of now, the market expects to take place in the future. In other words, in an efficient market at any point in time the actual price of a security will be a good estimate of its intrinsic value."

The great impact of EMH dispersed rapidly from academia to the investment community. Fama's 1970 paper on the topic "Efficient Capital Markets" [16] argues that on average, it is nearly impossible for an individual to consistently beat the stock market as a whole because of the broad availability of public information. Therefore markets are assumed to be efficient if all available information is reflected in current market prices [16, 17]. Some people think this is equivalent to saying that an investor who throws darts at a newspaper's stock listings has as much chance at beating the market as any professional investor. In summary, the statement that stock price behaviour is random and not predictable by any forecasting method had become a dominant paradigm used by economists to understand and investigate the behaviour of financial markets.

Looking for more evidence to sustain this theory, Fama later studied all the funds that survived during a 20-year period starting in 1976. But because these funds were naturally biased from being survivors during the period, he reduced the sample by choosing only the 20 biggest winners from the first ten years and analysed their performance over the second 10 years relative to a risk-corrected model. Not surprisingly for him, he found out that exactly half of them were above average and the other half below. This means that the best performers had a 50% chance to succeed over the next period. With this new evidence he continues to favour passive management[2] over active management[3]. But still, for those who do not follow the EMH, there were some winners over the whole period. (The biggest winner of all was Fidelity Magellan, credited to Peter Lynch.)

The EMH also comes in many strengths, the first one being the **"Weak form"** of efficiency, which asserts that in a market that assimilates information efficiently it is impossible to predict the future price of a security on the basis of its **past price** because all past market prices and data are fully reflected in security prices, so there cannot be investment strategies which yield extraordinary profits on the basis of past prices – technical analysis is of no use. An argument in favour of this form of efficiency says that a short-term market-timing rule cannot make money because the opportunity goes away if everyone follows the same strategy. So the belief is that markets do not follow major patterns in stock prices, and the minor patterns caused by momentum are costly to explore. Evidence suggests that prices do appear to be random.

The **"Semi-strong"** form refers to the degree of market reaction to events based on **public information**, which includes news announcements, annual reports, gossip columns, news clippings, etc. A market that impounds all of this information in its current price is known as semi-strong efficient. Most people believe that the U.S. equity markets by and large reflect publicly available information [19]. But the question of what is considered public information is still unanswered: is the information obtained through the Internet considered to be of public nature? Is *all* of this already impounded in the stock price? If so, at what rate was this information discounted in prices? A common guess is that the easier it was to get certain type of information, the more likely it is to have already been traded upon. Therefore in this view it is impossible to predict on the basis of publicly available fundamental information. Evidence supports that earnings and dividend announcements are incorporated into stock prices within 5 minutes.

It is easy to see that against these two types of efficiency are a great number of experienced financial professionals and financial groups who usually take positions from public information, even though there is no proof that they can actually beat the market. Such evidence would be impossible to obtain for obvi-

---

[2] Traditionally, investment managers have been categorised as active or passive types according to their trading profiles. Passive Management, also known as *index* management, focuses on the belief that people cannot get more than the market rate of return from the given category they are in because security prices are the best estimate of value, therefore no effort is needed to distinguish between one security over another to try to 'beat the market'. Portfolios are created to resemble the performance of well-known indexes and price adjustments are made in response to changes in the underlying universe or index.

[3] Active management states that there are people who can make valuation judgements that are superior to the market; portfolios are constructed by using a variety of strategies which are believed to offer excess returns. There are more costs associated with this investment strategy than with passive investment because portfolios are usually more dynamic.

ous reasons, but the fact is that it is hard to believe that they do not outperform the market somehow.

Finally, the **"Strong form"** of efficiency analyses whether investors have **private information** to take advantage of. Private information includes insider information such as a personal note passed from a CEO to the CFO regarding a major financial decision, which according to this form of efficiency, would suddenly have an impact in the stock price! Not many people believe that the market is strong-form efficient. In this view it is, therefore, impossible to predict from any information at all.

As previously stated, EMH became the dominant paradigm used by economists to understand financial markets. From the EMH derives the Random Walk Hypothesis (RWH), which states that future price movements cannot be predicted from past price movements alone; changes in prices are uncorrelated. The expected average change in price is zero and the best guess of price at time $t + 1$ is the price at time t given the information set available at time t. A commonly used analogy for the random walk is the flipping of a coin.

In addition to the EMH and the RWH, a considerable body of economic theory and research centers on the notion of "rational expectations," a classical economic theory formalised in the 1970s by Nobel laureate (1995) Robert E. Lucas, Jr. from the University of Chicago, who is believed to have the greatest influence in macroeconomics research since 1970. The basic assumptions of the Rational Expectations Theory (RET) are:

1. Economic actors (such as consumers or investors) behave rationally by collecting and studying carefully current and historical conditions
2. Markets are highly competitive
3. People act in response to their expectations

The idea that in an efficient market a trading model cannot generate any excess returns is based on the assumption that all investors act according to the rational expectations model. Broadly speaking, the Rational Expectations Theory (RET) suggests that, in a stationary world, if all investors have the same data, they will all entertain the same expectations and those expectations will be true (or rational). The theory suggests that most participants in the stock market are "smart investors," whose individual expectations, on average, anticipate the future correctly.

3   Against the Classical Hypotheses

In favour of the EMH, Burton G. Malkiel in his book entitled "A Random Walk Down Wall Street" [29] agrees with a relaxed market efficiency in which transaction costs end up reducing any of the advantages a given strategy could offer, so that a buy-and-hold strategy of index funds produces higher returns. He shows that a broad portfolio of stocks selected by chance performs as well as one that has been carefully chosen by the experts. In this book he also compares the *holes* of the EMH to proverbial $10 bills lying in the gutter. The idea is that a given person cannot find \$10 bills in gutters because someone else has already picked them up. However, as a response to these claims, Andrew W. Lo and A. Craig MacKinlay have provided important evidence showing that financial markets are not completely random. They have edited a number of their papers in the book entitled "A Non-Random Walk Down Wall Street" [28]. In this volume they put RWH to the test, finding that predictable components do exist in recent stock and bond returns. They also explain various techniques for detecting predictabilities and evaluating their statistical and economic significance and offer some of their views of the financial technologies of the future.

By looking at a given historical sequence it is clear that price tends to trend in one direction for too long at each time. Another idea against RWH is that some people reinforce trends by not buying until they see a price trending upwards to assure their decision to buy that asset, confirming the idea that "the more people share a belief, the more that belief is likely to be true." Therefore the behaviour of people second-guessing the expectations of others produces a self-fulfilling prophecy [33] where it follows that the price behaviour of each day depends, up to a certain point, on the price of past days. People then generate price movements, changing the dynamics of the market in ways that do not appear to be random. Such prophecies can deliver some elements of predictability that could be captured by some systems in practice.

While there is no doubt as to the merit of RET in explaining many economic relationships, one must admit that it also departs from observed behaviours. The theory has two immediate limitations: first, we do not live in a stationary world but in one that is subject to change; and second, all investors will not necessarily reach the same conclusions, even when acting under the same observables. In addition to these, there are other factors such as emotions which often seem to play a significant role in economic decisions by bringing a certain degree of irrationality to our true perceptions. If the assumption of rational expectations is wrong to begin with, then the validity of its conclusion in the form of the EMH becomes also questionable.

One could argue that markets are becoming more efficient in their handling of information, which is becoming easily and rapidly available, but the rate in which it is compounded into the prices is still subject of debate. The way people react to events can not be factored out immediately, their expectations are based on what they expect that others expect and therefore many differing actions affect the price dynamics in different ways. Some of these price changes can be predicted with some success by a number of important players in financial markets such as Olsen Group, D. E. Shaw & Co., Prediction Company, Parallax, and many other research boutiques.

Finally, inconsistent with the EMT, one could also argue that not everybody would pick up the \$10 bill even if they are the lucky ones to find it. There are a number of reasons why EMH may not be correct, because investors have a wide variety of reasons for trading, e.g. for a short-term profit or a steady profit with long-term stability, or some even to lose money. Transactions are also performed by reasons other than to make a profit; for example, the Government of France, buying francs to support their price rather than to make a profit.

In this paper we have shown that there exists mixed evidence regarding market efficiency and trading profitability. Under classical economics security prices adjust rapidly to the arrival of new information, which comes to the market randomly and prices adjust rapidly to reflect the new information. Price adjustments are imperfect, yet unbiased, so that buying and selling securities as an attempt to outperform the market is just a game of chance rather than skill. As a result, the average investor can not beat the market and a prudent strategy to follow would be to buy some index funds or good stocks and hold them for a long period of time. But does this work in real markets? Are they efficient? Is the movement of the price really unpredictable? Is the reaction to news immediately adjusted and the stock market fully reflects the new information? As pointed out earlier, many investors disagree with this view, arguing that "new information is absorbed differently by different investors at different rates; thus, past price movements are a reflection of information that has not yet been universally recognised but *will* affect future prices" [34].

Still there are some open-end questions surrounding these concepts because EMH does not explicitly say that an individual cannot make money in the stock market (just the average of individuals cannot) or that it does not matter what such individual invests in – he/she will earn the same return in any case (again it is *the* average investor). It doesn't say either that flipping a coin or throwing darts is an equally good method as any other for selecting stocks. It is implied that some methods will be good and others bad.

By looking at history one can see that it has been possible to make money by *anticipating*. Whether it is economic shifts around the world or the possible outcome of a stock's price in a short period of time, trying to *anticipate events right* is a crucial factor in financial markets. But this is not an easy task, Peter Lynch said in a recent interview "In this business if you're good, you're right six times out of ten. You're never going to be right nine times out of ten"[5].

4 Previous Work and New Objectives

In the previous sections we presented different approaches, beliefs and theories concerning financial markets. It is not the purpose of this work to strongly agree with either one of them. However, we believe that it is likely that proper use of information can indeed help in the discovery of a set of trading rules which could perform better than the average (outperform the buy-and-hold strategy). We believe that if such rules could be found, they would *not* be profitable for a long period of time because market behaviour continuously changes, it never settles down. In this context the motivation of this work is based in the development of a number of artificial traders capable of generating and updating useful strategies in a continuous manner in order to check the consistency of the forecasting model over a long period of time.

This paper follows on a number of topics addressed in our previous papers [36, 37], where we provided full description of both, the Learning Classifier System (LCS), and the variables used in the rule conditions for each of the three types of evolving traders of our stock market model. Such traders learn, forecast and trade their holdings in a real stock market scenario that is given exogenously, in the form of easily-obtained stock statistics such as various price moving averages, first difference in prices, volume ratios, etc. These artificial agent-types trade during a 10-15 year period with a fixed initial wealth to trade over two assets: a bond (represented by the bank with a fixed interest rate i) and a stock. To make the experiments as real as possible, agents also pay a fixed commission on every trade. The agent's learning process is modelled by LCS; that is, as sets of bit-encoded rules. Each condition bit expresses the truth or falsehood of a certain real market condition. The actual conditions used differ between agents.

In our previous papers, forecasting performance of our artificial agents has been compared against the performance of the buy-and-hold strategy, a trend-following strategy and the bank investment. In addition, in this paper we also compare performance against a new type of agent we have recently implemented, called the *random walk agent*. In [37] we addressed the question of whether it would be worth using a fixed random strategy for comparison purposes. Our response was negative, made on the grounds that because in this model all the agent-types start with random strategies, we have observed that those random strategies have not survived long; they have been replaced quickly by better ones because of the constant changes in the market environment and the learning process involved. We decided investigate this issue further by contributing to the already controversial topics surrounding traditional economic theories on Market Efficiency, Rational Expectations and Random Walk. We perform additional tests with the goal of addressing whether, on average, the performance of the agent-types is consistently better than the *random walk agent*.

We have also addressed that this model allows us to experiment and learn more about important issues regarding the financial data involved in the decision-making process. Determining which items of information are more relevant than others or whether they are important at all can be achieved by looking at what the overall effect of subtracting these bits of information could have on performance. For example, there is considerable scope for experimenting with the mixture of rule conditions as a way of assessing whether we could manage to improve performance even further. In this paper we attempt to gain a better understanding of these issues in order to guide us in the design of better trader models. While choosing the right information set, it is important to explore whether a trader could benefit from more, or maybe less, information. Using more factors provides more clues but also multiplies the size of the search space so that the evolutionary process may come to be governed more by neutral genetic drift than by genuine selective pressure. Other sorts of information, such as external political or economic conditions, might be introduced in a simplistic way by, say, adding the behaviour of an index or similar gross indicators as an extra factor. We will address these issues in more detail in the following sections.

5   Reviewing the Model

This section briefly describes the structure of the model, consisting of the following elements and the roles they play in the trading process:

1. **Time**, which is discrete and indexed by t, represents one cycle equivalent to one *real* trading day in the market. There are only about 253 trading days in a calendar year due to weekends and holidays, so when we refer to a ten year period of historical data in the following sections, it roughly corresponds to a total of 2,530 days.

2. Two assets traded, both with infinite supply: a **risk free bond** paying a fixed interest rate. In this case it is equivalent to a real bank's investment, and a **risky stock** whose return will be ruled by the specific stock in question, with the restriction that the agent must be able to afford the amount of shares it wishes to buy.

3. One **buy-and-hold agent** which represents the so called *buy-and-hold* strategy – in this case, this agent simply puts all available cash into the stock at the start and then keeps it there, buying the stock at the initial price P_t, and of course paying a commission percentage when doing this single transaction.

4. The **bank agent**, which keeps all money in the bank at a good rate of interest, never buying the stock. Therefore this agent does not own any shares, all its possessions are cash, compounded in the bank at an interest rate of 8% p.a. (but the user can alter this). When given shares, it immediately sells them, paying the appropriate commission for the transaction.

5. One **trend-following agent**, representing a strategy that varies according to price moves. This is a type of *momentum trader* that buys all its money available in stocks at the end of the day if the price increased with respect to the previous day. Otherwise, it sells all the shares owned. This agent also pays commission for every transaction performed.

6. One **random walk agent**, who makes a daily random decision of whether to buy, sell or hold the stock, paying the corresponding commission. If the decision is to buy, 100% of its cash available is used for the purchase; in the same way, when the decision is to sell, it sells all the stocks in possession and the money obtained from the sale is all invested in the bank at the given interest rate.

7. Three **heterogeneous agents** (also referred as *trader-types*), whose decision making process is represented by a Michigan-style, strength-based LCS as described in [35–37]. These agents are designed to learn and adapt to a market environment that is partially understood and where the domain characteristics can change rapidly over time.

   In order to keep the model as simple as possible, only three types of traders have been introduced at this stage in the market and to make them truly heterogeneous, they all receive different sets of market information and make their own decisions by using different models. In what follows, these three types (agents) are called **Tt1**, **Tt2**, and **Tt3**. One type can not evolve into another type, but it can go broke and thus halt while another one can get rich. It is also possible for an agent to learn to ignore any particular field in the daily market information it receives, but it cannot ask for extra fields beyond those given to it.

Note that the stock price does not change according to the supply and demand governed by the artificial trader-types, but rather by changes of real phenomena outside their scope.

8. The **information set**. This is comprised by the available raw data about the market, as well as data which has been processed in various ways. The raw data includes basic daily information about the stock such as its current price, volume of transactions, splits and dividends.

   The following represents a typical format in which most financial data is freely obtained through the Internet. This portion of data was taken from http://quote.yahoo.com and it corresponds to the Coca Cola stock during the month of April, year 2001:

```
Date,Open,High,Low,Close,Volume
30-Apr-01,46.75,46.75,45.85,46.19,3837000
27-Apr-01,47.50,47.50,46,47,3480900
26-Apr-01,47.60,47.98,46.90,46.90,4296400
25-Apr-01,47.50,48.40,47.40,48.20,3247700
.
.
.
2-Apr-01,45.40,46.92,44.86,45.85,5212400
```

   As it can be seen, it starts with the date. Date formats vary between sources. The following four columns describe the various prices that are recorded daily, starting from the opening-price of the day, then the highest and lowest of the day, followed by the closing-price. Finally, the last column displays the volume of transactions relative to that stock. Note that dates are given in descending order, so they need be re-ordered in ascending order before being processed, this is a simple step which can be done by using almost any spreadsheet package.

   In our model this raw data and some other information is processed by the agents in different ways. For instance, an agent might take into consideration factors such as (i) the first difference in price, (ii) certain moving averages of the stock's price or volume, (iii) the current wealth of the buy-and-hold and bank investments, etc.

9. An **accounting procedure**. This procedure calculates and updates the possessions of every trader according to the new price. Possessions at any given time include the shares owned by each *trader-type*, their current holdings, interest payments, cash available, and their current wealth. The procedure works as follows: at the beginning of each trading cycle, the agent's holdings and cash accounts are updated, including stock splits, cash dividends and commissions for all transactions executed. For instance, if the trader decides to buy, it must own all the cash incurred in the transactions, including the

commission fee. When selling, the trader must own all the shares it wants to sell. Agents cannot borrow money or sell short. At the end of the day, the wealth of each trader is updated by adding the interest paid during one cycle to the cash account. The wealth $W_{i(t)}$ at time t of agent i is thus given by the equation:

$$W_{i(t)} = (1 + r)M_{i(t)} + H_{i(t)}p(t), \tag{1}$$

where $(1 + r)M_i(t)$ is the cash invested at an interest rate r and $H_{i(t)}p(t)$ are the holdings calculated at the current price of the stock $p(t)$.

6 Analysing Agent Dynamics

Now that we have briefly described the basic elements of the model, we begin this section by addressing some important issues about artificial stock markets, explaining the main differences between these and our model. Then, in order to analyse the agents, we describe in separate subsections the market environment and the structure of the classifier rules.

Building an Artificial Stock Market (ASM) is not a trivial task. Blake LeBaron has done extensive research in this new and emerging area of building artificial markets. For a good review, refer to [22–24, 9, 10]. These papers point out that there are a large number of questions about market and agent design that still remain unanswered. Perhaps one of the most difficult issues to tackle when building an ASM is how to represent and implement ideas of evolution and learning in populations of agents while trying to keep the model as simple as possible.

Usually, in an ASM, active traders, through their consumption and portfolio decisions, endogenously determine the price sequence of the stock they are dealing with, allowing us to learn properties about the market being modelled; for instance, whether it exhibits certain phenomena seen in real markets such as bubbles and crashes, high volatility, etc. Important properties of real markets have been reported in successful ASM, such as [7, 25] and [11, 12]. However, partly due to the complexity of agents' decision processes and sets of strategies and partly due to the global structure of an ASM, we have learned very little about the agents when not viewed via the market they generate, i.e. inferences are usually made about the agent from the endogenously created market.

This is achieved by analysing the consequences of the agents' behaviours and then deduce, by the use of economic theories, an approximation of what is going on inside the artificial trader, rather than studying the dynamics of the actual strategies. In this sense ASMs try to reproduce qualitative features of the real market, but in this quest of knowledge about market dynamics, not much is revealed about the agent per se. The dynamics of the agents is still unknown and there is no consensus or standards established as to how exactly these agents adapt, what type of models they develop, test and improve upon. A number of simple questions have not been answered yet: are the market hypothesis these agents generate meaningful and consistent throughout different markets? Can they keep improving or they reach a plateau and become less and less susceptible to market changes? In this model, by exploring information sets and the evolved pool of strategies even further, we can search for better ways of improving these agents. Although not all possibilities can be analysed in this paper and perhaps many questions will still be left unanswered, our intention is to contribute to increase the interest and to open more ways of exploring and expanding our current knowledge of how these agents operate and interact under different market conditions and how such learning process can be improved.

Trader strategies are difficult – or even impossible – to analyse directly by some ASMs. Chen and Chia-Hsuan Yeh in their paper describing an ASM model where the learning mechanism is represented by Genetic Programming (GP), [12], point out that it would be "interesting to know what kind of useful lessons traders learn .... However, this is a very large database, and is difficult to deal with directly. But, since all forecasting trees are in the format of LISP trees, we can at least ask *how complex these forecasting models are.*" The authors define this complexity measure according to the number of nodes and the depth of the trees evolved. As it can be appreciated here, it can be a difficult task to try to understand trader's strategies and the tendency will be to try to avoid it by defining other types of measures that could give an approximation of what is going on inside the trader. In the same way, the Santa Fe Artificial Stock Market [6, 31] analyses strategy complexity (a measure of the rule's specificity); [20] analyses the effects of changing the learning rate in market behaviour. In these experiments it would be difficult to analyse each agent because their ASM runs for hundreds of thousands of cycles. In our model, traders' strategies are easier to handle and, in terms of computational cost, can be evolved very cheaply.

We believe that increasing our understanding about how agents learn and develop is essential for the development of better trader models. It is the purpose of this paper to address these issues. One way to achieve this is in our model is by analysing the relevance that certain bits of information have in the agent's overall performance. In our previous papers we have described results where the agents were analysed from a broad perspective; for instance, by looking at how successful the agents can be at learning useful strategies, how they react to certain changes in the real market environment they live in, etc. These properties are important to describe, many relevant issues were addressed when viewing the agent from this perspective. This type of analysis of agent behaviour will be referred as the *macroscopic* approach to agent dynamics.

However, one would also like to know more about another aspect of the learning process: the agent's internal composition. For instance, it would be important to address how the agent's structure of beliefs is formed, how it changes over time and whether it would be possible to control some aspects of the learning process. This model provides ways to learn more about the agent internally, in addition to the external behaviour already described. This refers to the second way in which one can learn about the agent dynamics: the *microscopic* approach, which we will illustrate in the following sections by providing a number of feasible ways in which the agent's evolved rule sets and the effect of changing various market environments can be analysed; but first, let's describe the market environment.

6.1   Market Environment

The US stock that will be considered for the purpose of analysing the agent from a *microscopic* perspective is shown in Table 1, where the profile and dates of the series analysed are described. From now on, the stock will be addressed by its symbol, as shown in the table, and its properties and trends by day numbers rather than the actual dates when they occurred.

Table 1. Profile of stock analysed – IBM Corporation

Sector	Symbol	Index Membership	From	To	No. of Days
Tech./Comp.Hardware	IBM	Dow Ind., S&P 500	03/01/85	14/01/00	3,800

Figure 1 displays the price of IBM stock from Jan 03, 1985 to Jan 13, 2000. Note that the price tends to decrease during the first half of the period (bear market) and increases dramatically during the second half (bull market). This is indeed a very difficult stock to analyse because initial indications would seem to suggest that this stock shows a very erratic behaviour. The aim is to find out if the artificial traders are able to learn some regularities when none seem to exist and furthermore, how do they react to a price behaviour such as this one when they are exposed to different information sets?

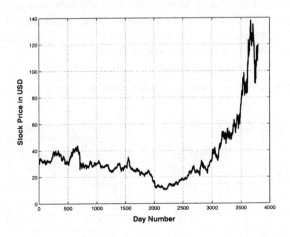

Fig. 1. IBM Stock, closing price Jan 03 1985 - Jan 14 2000

6.2 Classifier Rules

For a full description of the rules refer to [36]. Classifier rules contain two parts: $<$ *condition* $>:<$ *action* $>$. The condition part is a bit string matching the current market state vector. Tt1's state vector is seven bits long, Tt2's is five, Tt3's is 6. Table 2 shows the meaning of each bit position for Tt1 and Tt2 during the current trading period t. The actual value of each cell is 1 if the condition is satisfied. For example, bit number 1 is 1 if the price today is higher than yesterday's: P_t is the price on day t, P_{MA5} is the five-day price moving average, $P_{highest}$ and $V_{highest}$ are the highest price and volume for any day so far, etc.

Table 2. Condition part of traders Tt1 and Tt2

Trader Type 1

Bit Number	Representation
1	$P_t > P_{t-1}$
2	$P_t > 1.2 * P_{MA5}$
3	$P_t > 1.1 * P_{MA10}$
4	$P_t > 1.05 * P_{MA20}$
5	$P_t > 1.025 * P_{MA30}$
6	$P_t \geq P_{highest}$
7	$P_t \leq P_{lowest}$

Trader Type 2

Bit Number	Representation
1	$P_t > P_{t-1}$
2	$V_t > V_{t-1}$
3	$V_t > V_{MA20}$
4	$V_t \geq V_{highest}$
5	$V_t \leq V_{lowest}$

The action is a bit string of length 4 indicating the decision of whether to buy, sell or hold possessions on the current day. The first bit represents a buy (1) or sell (0) signal, followed by three more bits which represent the percentage of available cash to use if buying, or the percentage of shares to sell if selling. Table 3 shows the mapping between bits 1 to 4 and the percentage to trade. Buying or selling 0% corresponds to simply holding.

Table 3. Action Part: Transaction and percentage to trade

Bit 1	Bit 2	Bit 3	Bit 4	Action	Trade
0	0	0	0	H	0%
0	0	0	1	S	15%
0	0	1	0	S	30%
0	0	1	1	S	45%
0	1	0	0	S	60%
0	1	0	1	S	75%
0	1	1	0	S	90%
0	1	1	1	S	100%

Bit 1	Bit 2	Bit 3	Bit 4	Action	Trade
1	0	0	0	H	0%
1	0	0	1	B	15%
1	0	1	0	B	30%
1	0	1	1	B	45%
1	1	0	0	B	60%
1	1	0	1	B	75%
1	1	1	0	B	90%
1	1	1	1	B	100%

7   Results of IBM Stock

Table 4 displays some numeric results. The top block in this table shows the final wealth of bank, buy-and-hold, trend-following and the new *random walk* strategy; the performance of the agents can be compared with these. Of these three, buy-and-hold is the best, worth $39,833 by the end. For other stocks, this one may not be the winner, of course.

We have named the new strategy we introduce in this paper the *random walk* after the classical economics views we detailed in Section 2. This strategy is explained in Section 5 and seems relevant because we want to compare if the agents manage to outperform a daily random decision that involves no learning. Note that because we run this strategy for a number of times (1001), we provide two different values, the maximum and the average.

The next three blocks describe the performance of the three agent types over 1001 runs; remember that every run starts with new random strategies, i.e no previous knowledge is transferred from one run to the next. In the block labelled *GA 050*, the GA runs every 50 days; in *GA 100* it is every 100 days; in the third it is every 150 days. The reader interested in parameter settings should refer to [36]. As pointed out in previous papers, results with *GA 100* and *GA 150* seem to be the most appropriate for the stocks and periods analysed.

Table 4. IBM Stock returns

Bank	$33,294
Buy-and-Hold	$39,833
Trend-Following	$12,557
Random Walk Ave	$15,640
Random Walk Max	$43,718

GA 050	Average	Best	Beat B&H
Tt1	$37,941	$182,475	31.8%
Tt2	$47,525	$216,144	50.6%
Tt3	$33,590	$163,885	17.9%

GA 100	Average	Best	Beat B&H
Tt1	$43,314	$195,859	43.4%
Tt2	$49,347	$209,519	47.0%
Tt3	$35,444	$208,200	21.0%

GA 150	Average	Best	Beat B&H
Tt1	$49,357	$174,481	52.0%
Tt2	$47,811	$211,729	42.7%
Tt3	$36,669	$173,713	22.1%

The 'Average' column shows the trader's final wealth averaged over 1001 separate runs. The 'Best' column shows the best performer. The 'Beat B&H' column shows the percentage of runs in which that trader type beat the buy-and-hold strategy. In all three blocks, Tt2 shows the highest average and best performers, although in the *GA 150* block Tt1 was slightly ahead on the average. As it can be seen, the performance of our best performers is far better than the random walk. All of our averages are also superior to the average random walk performance, and most are superior to the max random walk. These results are encouraging.

Figure 2 shows the wealth of the best of every trader type. These graphs display interesting behaviours. For the first 2,200 days the price was heading downwards (see Figure 1) and not much could be done to achieve profits other than leaving the money in the bank, as the agents quickly learned. Look at Figure 3, which shows the distribution of shares of all three traders. Even though it looks like Tt2 was behaving fairly erratically during the first 500 days, a closer look at the graph reveals that by day 330, Tt2 had already managed to outperform the buy-and-hold strategy.

Closer examination of the evolved rule-sets of this trader shows that sets of highly accurate strategies had been developed as early as day 330. However, due to space limitations, such strategies can not be explained in detail in this paper. As an illustration, a rule developed by this type of trader might look like this: 0111#:0101, meaning that the agent will: sell 75% of its possessions of IBM stock when *today's price* is not higher than *yesterday's price*, and *todays' volume* is higher than *yesterday's volume*; and *todays' volume* is higher than the *20-day volume moving average*; and *todays' volume* is higher or equal than *the highest volume* seen so far; regardless of whether *todays' volume* is lower or equal than the *lowest volume* seen so far.

Overall, one can see that these traders trade at the beginning of the period (days 1-500 approx.) more or less randomly, and without accumulating excess profits (no large deviations are observed from the *buy-and-hold*). After these transactions, in all traders a large period of tranquility is observed from day 500 to day 2,200 approximately.

As seen in the graphs, just before the market starts crimping up, the agents decide to buy IBM stock and spend all their available cash. They do that in different ways. Although trader behaviours are never exactly the same, they exhibit certain similarities, such as the ones just described. After day 2,200 they seem to be quite comfortable holding large possessions of the stock, and because they bought it cheaper than *buy-and-hold*, they end up owning about 2,000 shares, as opposed to just over 300 from *buy-and-hold*.

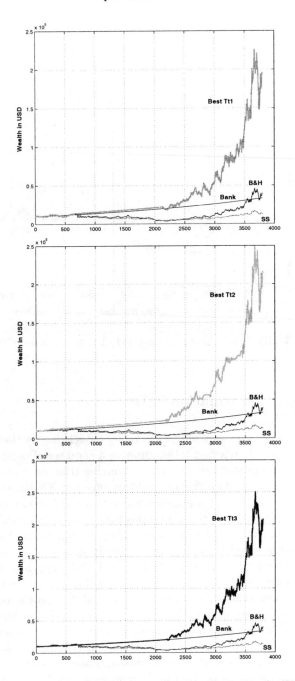

Fig. 2. IBM Stock. Wealth in USD of Tt1, Tt2, Tt3, Bank, BuyAndHold (B&H) and TrendFollowing (SS) strategies, Corresponding to Table 4. Final wealth Tt1 = $195,859; Tt2 = $216,144 and Tt3 = $208,200

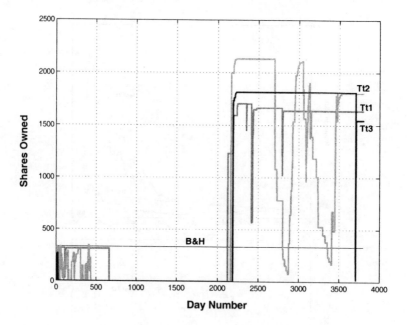

Fig. 3. IBM Stock. Shares of Best Tt1, Tt2 and Tt3 from Table 4

8   Analysing Information Sets

One of the most relevant problems forecasting models face is that many indicators can be potentially relevant. "Determining a good set of indicators is crucial in generating good predictions as well as reducing training times to reasonable levels" [8]. This represents a crucial problem affecting NN-based systems reliability, and it is undoubtedly, a problem which is present in any system.

The aim of this section is to analyse this potential problem and how a system of this type would handle such constraints. There are a number of ways in which a sensitivity analysis might be performed. Typically, in NNs, the values of a certain variable are altered by a small percent (usually 5-10%) while keeping all the others fixed as they were, and the outputs after this change are then compared with the output using the original values. This is called a *weak sensitivity measure* because the whole idea is that there are non-linear relationships between the variables and therefore the change in one should affect the others as well. For instance, if one tests the relevance of variable 4, obtaining a negative change in performance of 25% and variable 8 showing a decrease of 10%, then if both variables are changed, the drop in performance cannot be added i.e, expecting a decrease of 35% in performance; it is not a linear relationship.

The true result of altering variables is not easy to infer because of the non-linear interactions of such variables. In addition to this difficulty, sensitivity analysis also vary over time, i.e., changing one variable over one period of time might not have the same effect of changing it over another period of time. However, a *sensitivity analysis* of this type can give us at least an idea of which are the most influential indicators in a model, providing an alternate way of understanding the evolved sets of strategies (in a NN it would be a way of understanding a trained net and which inputs are emphasised, as reported in [8]). This type of analysis seems to be useful in our LCS model.

To illustrate this point, table 5 shows an arbitrary segment of Tt1's rule set, evolved from a run with Forest Oil, a stock whose *buy-and-hold* performs worse than the *bank* investment; its price steadily falls, so that in very few occasions the current price will be the highest ever. This small segment of rules is divided in two blocks, on the left are the *buy rules* and on the right *sell rules*. At any given point of the period analysed, the rules evolved can be observed to assess their relevance and they can provide us with useful information about the environment being analysed. For instance, this set of rules reflects important information about the stock. It is clear that most values of bits 1-7 are set to 0, revealing that the current price of the stock is, most times, *not* higher than the variables it is compared with, such as previous price, moving averages of various days, etc. Specifically, bit number 6 in most cases indicates a 0, which means that P_t is not higher than $P_{highest}$. Bit No. 7, indicating that P_t is lower than P_{lowest} is set to 1 or # more often in the second block, where the sell rules are.

Table 5. An arbitrary segment of Forest Oil Set of evolved rules. Buy Rules are in the top half, Sell Rules in the bottom half

Condition			Action		Condition			Action
Bits 1-5	Bit 6	Bit 7			Bits 1-5	Bit 6	Bit 7	
00#00	0	0	1001		00101	0	0	0100
0#0#0	0	0	1010		#0##0	0	#	0101
#111#	0	0	1101		00##0	0	0	0111
#111#	0	1	1101		00001	0	0	0111
#0001	0	0	1101		10000	0	1	0010
#1110	0	0	1101		#000#	1	#	0011
#1100	0	0	1101		10#0#	0	1	0101
10001	0	0	1101		1000#	0	0	0101
10#00	#	0	1111		10001	#	0	0101
10#00	0	1	1111		10011	1	1	0101

Because they are stock-dependent, the evolved sets of strategies provide useful information about the stock being analysed. In this model, one could also easily asses whether one bit of information is relevant or not by discarding that bit completely. For example, after analysing the rule set evolved by a trader, one might just create an alternative trader that does not have that particular bit of information in the condition part of its rules and evolve it in the absence of that piece of information. Then, both performances can be measured in order assess the how important it was. This analysis is similar to the *sensitivity analysis* explained earlier, except that instead of changing the value by a small percent, this approach deletes the entire variable. This will be exemplified in the following section, where we will also change some of the percentages associated with the variables.

9   Developing New Traders

In order to develop better trader models, this section addresses ways in which trader's internal composition can be analysed and further improved. The environmental message of Tt1 was defined in table 2. No additional explanations were given regarding the percentages that compare the variables because these thresholds were defined arbitrarily. For instance, bit No. 2 of Tt1 considers whether the price today is 20% higher than the moving average of the previous week. Why 20%? The idea was to make the agents less susceptible to small price changes and to account for transaction costs. Suppose the average of the past week is $10. If that bit is ON, it means that the price today is higher than $12. This is a large price increase and the agent must be aware of it. But some stocks do not show too many increases as high as this; certainly IBM does not look like a very volatile stock, so perhaps this high threshold is not a good idea for this stock. On the other hand, many stock prices tend to increase in prices more than 50% of the times, which was the main motive to add a threshold. In this model we can easily test whether adding the thresholds was a good design decision or not.

One simple way to do this is to create another Tt1, one that does not exhibit those arbitrary thresholds. Table 6 shows the environmental message of both Tt1s, the old (called v1) and the new (v2). However, a second test will be performed in this section. Still regarding Tt1, one might wonder if the information it receives is useful or not; perhaps it could benefit with one bit less. To test this hypothesis, a new type of Tt1 will be created. A new version is implemented (v2), which is very similar to Tt1v1, (our previous one) except that it has no thresholds. Then, a third version is implemented (v3), which does not have the 7th bit of information (whether the price today is the lowest ever).

Our first insight is that thresholds will help the trader get more wealth; that is, that performance of Tt1v1 will be higher than the performance of Tt1v2, this is our first hypothesis. The second one is that Tt1v3 (the one without P_{lowest}) will not perform as well as Tt1v2 (the one with P_{lowest}) because by looking at the stock price series, one can see that it presents many lows during the first half of the period. However, it is difficult to say because not many lows appear during the second half.

Table 7 reports the results obtained with the three versions of Tt1 described above. Note that Tt1v1 is the same Tt1 that has been reported in our previous papers. The new traders are Tt1v2 and Tt1v3. With *Ga_period=50* (this corresponds to very fast learning, every 50 days 20% of the population is modified by the GA), Tt1v1 (the old one) is a better performer than Tt1v2, which means that the thresholds introduced originally were indeed favourable for the trader

Trader Type 1V1	
Bit Number	Representation
1	$P_t > P_{t-1}$
2	$P_t > 1.2 * P_{MA5}$
3	$P_t > 1.1 * P_{MA10}$
4	$P_t > 1.05 * P_{MA20}$
5	$P_t > 1.025 * P_{MA30}$
6	$P_t \geq P_{highest}$
7	$P_t \leq P_{lowest}$

Trader Type 1V2	
Bit Number	Representation
1	$P_t > P_{t-1}$
2	$P_t > P_{MA5}$
3	$P_t > P_{MA10}$
4	$P_t > P_{MA20}$
5	$P_t > P_{MA30}$
6	$P_t \geq P_{highest}$
7	$P_t \leq P_{lowest}$

Trader Type 1V3	
Bit Number	Representation
1	$P_t > P_{t-1}$
2	$P_t > P_{MA5}$
3	$P_t > P_{MA10}$
4	$P_t > P_{MA20}$
5	$P_t > P_{MA30}$
6	$P_t \geq P_{highest}$

Table 6. IBM Stock. Environmental message for Tt1 versions 1.0, 1.1 and 1.2

because the average performance of Tt1v1 dropped from \$37,941 to \$36,016 and the best performer dropped from \$182,475 to \$121,274, which is a considerable amount. Then, with Tt1v3, which has one less bit than Tt1v2, the average performance dropped even more, from \$36,016 to \$33,949; however, the best performer increased from \$121,274 to \$138,867.

Results for best performers with *Ga_period=100* and *Ga_period=150* suggest that removing the thresholds helps, increasing the average wealth from \$43,314 to \$45,766 and from \$49,357 to \$49,790 respectively, but Ttv3 is still lower than Tt1v2 in both cases. Best performer is Tt1v1 under *Ga_period=100*, but it is Tt1v3 under *Ga_period=150*.

The main point addressed in this section is to show that it is indeed possible to analyse the traders even deeper; and secondly, it is important to point out that many times we are concerned with finding best performers rather than better averages. For the purpose of this paper, the latter one has been emphasised more. A lesson to learn from these experiments is that results should no be generalised; stocks are very different from each other. What works well in one might not work well in another. Also, an interesting piece of information revealed from table 7 is that all the highest percentages that beat *buy-and-hold* come from Tt1v2, which means they have no thresholds. This shows that after analysing trader's behaviours, one can easily change their make up and improve them. For example, if one is interested in getting the best performers, then the thresholds showed to be a better alternative. But, in the other hand, if one is interested in more

Table 7. IBM Stock. Returns of Old(v1) vs two new Tt1(v2 and v3)

Bank $33,294	Buy-and-Hold $39,833	Trend-Following $12,557	Random Walk $15,640

GA 050	Average	Best	Beat B&H
Tt1v1	$37,941	$182,475	31.8%
Tt1v2	$36,016	$121,274	31.9%
Tt1v3	$33,949	$138,687	27.8%

GA 100	Average	Best	Beat B&H
Tt1v1	$43,314	$195,859	43.4%
Tt1v2	$45,766	$174,830	52.2%
Tt1v3	$44,280	$153,154	48.9%

GA 150	Average	Best	Beat B&H
Tt1v1	$49,357	$174,481	52.0%
Tt1v2	$49,790	$160,386	60.5%
Tt1v3	$48,360	$177,565	58.7%

traders that beat the *buy-and-hold* strategy, then it would be best not to have thresholds. As of the P_{lowest} bit, it seems more reasonable to leave it because the averages were consistently lower during its absence.

A similar experiment was performed with Tt2. A new version of Tt2 was created, which has the same information in bits 1-3 as before, except that bit 4 and 5 (the ones about volume highs and lows) were replaced by bits 3 and 4 of Tt1. This new trader is denoted as Tt2v2 and is described in table 8 and analysed in table 9. These results show a better Tt2v1 than Tt2v2 in both, averages and best performers for *Ga_period = 50* and *Ga_period = 100*, but the opposite for *Ga_period = 150*. A plausible explanation for the difference between the *Ga_periods* is that under fast learning the agents are able to adjust more quickly to the changes in the market environment, thus making better use of the information about highs and lows of volume. A large *Ga_period* may not inject new strategies as fast as they are needed and the agent could end up using other not so accurate rules, therefore not being able to pick up the trends. The information about the high and lows is with respect to the current day only, so it may provide information that needs to be learned and used more rapidly than the information about the price moving average of the past five and ten days.

Table 8. IBM Stock. Old (v1) vs new (v2) environmental message for Tt2

Old Trader Type 2

Bit Number	Representation
1	$P_t > P_{t-1}$
2	$V_t > V_{t-1}$
3	$V_t > V_{MA20}$
4	$V_t \geq V_{highest}$
5	$V_t \leq V_{lowest}$

New Trader Type 2

Bit Number	Representation
1	$P_t > P_{t-1}$
2	$V_t > V_{t-1}$
3	$V_t > V_{MA20}$
4	$P_t > P_{MA5}$
5	$P_t > P_{MA10}$

Table 9. IBM Stock. Old (v1) vs new (v2) Tt2

Bank $33,294	Buy-and-Hold $39,833	Trend-Following $12,557	Random Walk $15,640

GA 050	Average	Best	Beat B&H
Tt2v1	$47,525	$216,144	50.2%
Tt2v2	$42,474	$174,021	44.6%

GA 100	Average	Best	Beat B&H
Tt2v1	$49,347	$209,519	47.0%
Tt2v1	$48,095	$190,946	50.3%

GA 150	Average	Best	Beat B&H
Tt2v1	$47,811	$211,729	42.7%
Tt2v2	$48,610	$213,876	52.0%

10   Examining the Rules

The agents' evolved strategies are perhaps the most interesting outcome of any complex adaptive system model, yet they have traditionally been the least important focus of attention of researchers, probably because of their intrinsic complexity. Such ecologies represent various interactions and non-linear dependencies of rules which are involved in competitive and cooperative relations with each other.

The analysis of such evolved sets of rules is not an easy task. But let's not be disappointed by such difficulties: these rules seem easier to study and explain than those derived from other paradigms such as NN, Fuzzy Systems or even GP (rules here can be extremely large and therefore difficult to understand). This section is devoted to provide the reader with several ways of gaining understanding of the relevance of the behaviours learned. As these come in many flavours, an example to illustrate where they apply will also be given in the following sections.

The relevance of each rule of the evolved set can easily be studied by the following procedure, see figure 4: in chronological order, divide the total period analysed in two parts, a *training* set, composed of about 90% of the cases (year 1 to 9) and a *testing* set, with the remaining 10% (the 10th year). Initialise the training set with random strategies and run the simulation as normal, with both components, Reinforcement Learning (RL) and the GA enabled in order to allow the agent to evolve its own new set of rules. After passing through the training period once, i.e. going from year 1 to year 9 of the market environment, stop and take **one** rule out along with its exact duplicates and run the test scenario where there should be no macro-adaptation involved (GA off), but only the micro-adaptation level is on (improvement of present rules, i.e. RL on). Measure and compare the performance of the trader during this testing period in two distinct cases, one with and one without the rule present in the set. Run the simulation without one of the rules each time, for a total of N times, the number of rules in the original set.

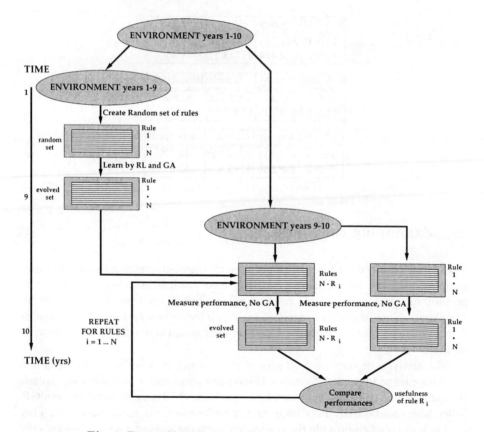

Fig. 4. Testing the relevance of each rule of the evolved set

What can we learn by doing this? On one hand, in the case of decreasing performance by removing the rule, one can easily infer that the rule in question was indeed a relevant one (note that this assertion is only valid for the testing period analysed). But on the other hand, if performance improves without the use of that rule, the rule had no importance during that period. Let's emphasise what *during that period* means. Situations in the stock market are never guaranteed to reappear, and the successful use of a learned strategy in the near future only means that conditions have not changed dramatically. This would not be the case if the testing set was chosen to be in the year 2000 when many technical stocks dropped dramatically. However, even in this case, if would be a good idea to find out if the rule appeared in the continuous learning case, because perhaps it is a rule that was going to be out of the set anyway.

In previous sections, the effect of different information sets was examined. This section looks at some of the rules evolved during those experiments. Table 10, column 1 shows some examples of *buy-rules* evolved from Tt1v1 over different runs. Because the LCS used in these experiments is based on specificity, the second column displays the *strength* or every rule, where it can be seen, for instance, how the more general rules have lower strengths. The next columns show the *specificity* of each rule and the number of times the rule matched and was *correct* (i.e. when suggested a buy/sell before the price increased/decreased by at least 2%, etc.). The total number of *matches* appears in the next column, followed by its *age*, which indicates how many days old is the rule since it was created and inserted in the population. Considering that the runs were performed with a total of 3,800 days, observe that rules appear to be fairly young. Old rules that were bad (like all the initial random rules) have been replaced by better ones, and those which were good have been replaced by similar or identical descendants. The age of identical or new versions of old rules inserted in the population is set to 0. This explains why, in the case in which there was a very good random rule created at the beginning of the period, it does not appear to be 3,800 days old. Notice also that the system is indeed finding and developing highly accurate rules.

Due to space limitations, hold and sell-rules have not been added in this table, but they exist. Hold-rules represent the majority of rules in the evolved sets. As they are also rewarded, they achieve perfect accuracy, just like these buy-rules, but their use does not make the agent richer directly, like the buy/sell rules do when their action is taken. It seems that the main duty of hold-rules is to avoid great losses, as shown in the results of the previous sections.

Because the rule specifies in its first part the actual conditions encountered in the market, a closer examination of the sets of such rules can give a broad description of certain properties the stock analysed. For instance, the system could count the number of 0s, 1s and #s in the entire rule set and determine, according to the bits of information considered per agent, whether the market was more bullish or bearish, whether information such as $P_{highest}$ was relevant or not, etc. For instance, one can observe that bit No. 2, describing whether today's price is higher than 20% of the moving average of the past week, is 0 in most rules.

This might explain why, in the previous section, the average of the experiments where such threshold was removed proved to be higher than with it. Another bit which is almost always set to 0 is the last one, indicating whether the current price is the lowest ever. This again, explains why the hypothesis that it was an important bit did not hold for the best performers. The table also shows that these rules are reasonably young. The old ones that were describing states when the market was dropping have started to disappear. This system adjusts quickly to new market information.

And finally, observe that bit No. 5 is set to 1 in most buy rules. This provides important information too. The rule suggests to buy the stock when (among others), the current price is higher than 2.5% of the moving average of the past six weeks. These rules proved to be 100% accurate, as shown in column *No. correct*. Overall, it can be concluded that analysing the rules has shown to provide with useful information about the market.

Table 10. IBM Stock. Examples of evolved buy-rules

Condition[Action]	Strength	Specificity	No. Correct	Matches	Age
1011110 [1010]	47.79	7	3	3	185
000#100 [1101]	49.69	6	122	122	650
10001#0 [1111]	45.13	6	57	57	550
1001#00 [1111]	43.35	6	184	184	1600
1000100 [1111]	49.73	7	75	75	750
1###1#0 [1001]	23.30	3	155	155	500
100#11# [1001]	29.02	5	14	14	200
000#1#0 [1001]	33.55	5	72	72	350
1001##0 [1001]	33.90	5	114	114	650
000#1#0 [1001]	38.01	5	122	122	650
10#11#0 [1001]	35.21	5	236	236	1400
1001##0 [1001]	34.87	5	253	253	1700
1001#00 [1001]	35.07	6	290	290	3800
#0001#0 [1010]	32.26	5	17	17	50
00#1### [1101]	26.47	3	6	6	50
1#0#1#0 [1101]	26.51	4	58	58	200
00##1#0 [1101]	28.86	4	254	254	1400
0#00100 [1101]	25.75	6	31	31	350
##0#1#0 [1001]	24.55	3	35	35	50
##0010# [1101]	28.52	4	407	407	1900
00#01#0 [1101]	34.76	5	178	178	1700
00#01## [1111]	31.55	4	70	70	800
1#0#110 [1111]	32.79	5	69	69	1100

11   Conclusions

Using a limited number of factors from the real stock market, we have shown how the best performers of all three types of traders were able to survive and furthermore, outperform the bank, buy-and-hold, trend-following and the new *random walk* strategy in the stock analysed. The agents were successful in finding some profitable rules exploiting the market inertia. The model seems to be able to at least represent competent traders.

The experiments presented in this paper show that the model is capable of producing sensible results:

- The agent's **average wealth** is in most cases, higher than the buy-and-hold, and in all cases higher than the bank, trend following and *random walk* strategies.
- The **best performers** are outstanding, all three types of traders outperformed the bank, buy-and-hold, trend-following and the *random walk* strategies by far.
- The agents found **successful strategies** which are easy to understand and analyse. With these, market behaviour and important properties of the specific stock can be learned.

We have illustrated how to analyse the relevance of financial indicators. It is important to realise that in each run, each agent sees each day's price just once – unlike, say, a neural net model. Because performing thousands of runs only takes a few seconds on a PC, the first simple alternative we propose after observing the rules set evolved is to discard completely a particular bit of the information set and compare performances with and without it. The second alternative is to modify only a small particular value or variable from the information set. Both of these approaches were illustrated by developing new traders with different information sets and comparing the results. If one is interested in obtaining high performers, it is also perfectly reasonable to do a large number of runs and take the best performer. In this paper we also described ways of analysing the ecology of rules evolved.

This economic model is limited in the sense that it captures only a small fraction of the whole repertoire of a real trader's behaviour, where the total number of strategies analysed is, indeed, far greater and more complex than the simple market models (i.e. trader-types) used here. However, this system offers perhaps one of the fastest ways of intelligently exploring vast amounts of information, an imperative property which adds great computational complexity when attempting to model modern financial markets. We recall that the idea supported here is that there should be no need to learn market behaviour by passing the data more than once. In real life this hardly happens, the world is a very dynamic system where one learns to generalise with very limited examples and by trial and error. The argument is that circumstances never repeat exactly and therefore there is no need to repeatedly be faced with previous examples to be tested on future unknown states. We propose that the generalisation that one must try to achieve is one of a higher level, in a context that is made throughout the whole life-span of the agent rather than through separate training and testing phases.

So far, the model works entirely autonomously, i.e. learns and adapts without any human intervention nor any initial clues given to it, and results shown with no prior knowledge about the market are encouraging, strongly suggesting that it is feasible to model a trader's behaviour in such a simplistic way and that LCS can be a good tool to do so. However, further research still needs to be done in this fairly new and emerging area.

References

1. In Robert R. Trippi and Efraim Turban, editors, *Neural Networks in Finance and Investing. Using Artificial Intelligence to Improve Real-World Performance.* Probus Publishing Company, Chicago, Illinois, 1993.
2. In Apostolos-Paul N. Refenes, editor, *Neural Networks in the Capital Markets.* John Wiley & Sons, March 1995.
3. In Apostolos-Paul N. Refenes, Yaser Abu-Mostafa, John Moody, and Andreas Weigend, editors, *Neural Networks in Financial Engineering: Proceedings of the Third International Conference on Neural Networks in the Capital Markets.* World Scientific Publishing Company, June 1996.
4. In Yaser S. Abu-Mostafa, Blake Lebaron, Andrew W. Lo, and Andreas S. Weigend, editors, *Computational Finance 1999.* MIT Press, 1999.
5. Betting on the Market. An Interview with Peter Lynch. http://www.pbs.org, Consulted May, 2001.
6. W. B. Arthur, J. H. Holland, B. LeBaron, R. Palmer, and P. Tayler. Asset pricing under endogenous expectations in an artificial stock market. Working Paper 96-12-093, Santa Fe Instituite, December 1996.
7. W. B. Arthur, J. H. Holland, B. LeBaron, R. Palmer, and P. Tayler. Asset Pricing Under Endogenous Expectations in an Artificial Stock Market. In W. B. Arthur, S. Durlauf, and D. Lane, editors, *The Economy as an Evolving Complex System II*, pages 15–44. Addison-Wesley, Reading, MA, 1997.
8. Dean S. Barr and Ganesh Mani. Using Neural Nets to Manage Investments. *AI EXPERT*, pages 16–22, February 9th 1994.
9. Nicholas Chan, Blake LeBaron, Andrew W. Lo, and Tomaso Poggio. Information Dissemination and Aggregation in Asset Markets with Simple Intelligent Traders. Technical Report C.B.C.L No. 164, Massachusetts Institute Of Technology, Artificial Intelligence Laboratory and Center for Biological and Computational Learning, 1998.
10. Nicholas Chan, Blake LeBaron, Andrew W. Lo, and Tomaso Poggio. Agent-Based Models of Financial Markets: A Comparison with Experimental Markets, September 1999.
11. Shu-Heng Chen and Chia-Hsuan Yeh. Modeling Speculators with Genetic Programming. In Peter J. Angeline, Robert G. Reynolds, John R. McDonnell, and Russ Eberhart, editors, *Proceedings of the Sixth Conference on Evolutionary Programming*, volume 1213 of *Lecture Notes in Computer Science*, pages 137–147, Indianapolis, Indiana, USA, 1997. Springer-Verlag.

12. Shu-Heng Chen and Chia-Hsuan Yeh. Genetic Programming in the Agent-Based Modeling of Stock Markets. In David A. Belsley and Christopher F. Baum, editors, *Proceedings of the Fifth International Conference on Computing in Economics and Finance*, Boston College, MA, USA, 1999.

13. James Essinger. *Artificial Intelligence. Applications in Financial Trading and Investment Management.* Euromoney Publications Plc., 1st edition, 1990.

14. Eugene F. Fama. Random Walks in Stock Market Prices. Paper No. 16 in the series of Selected Papers of the Graduate School of Business, University of Chicago, 1965. Reprinted in the Financial Analysts Journal (September-October 1965), The Analyst Journal, London (1966), The Institutional Investor, 1968.

15. Eugene F. Fama. The Behavior of Stock Market Prices. *Journal of Business*, 38:34–105, January 1965.

16. Eugene F. Fama. Efficient Capital Markets: A Review of Theory and Empirical Work. *Journal of Finance*, 25:383–417, May 1970.

17. Eugene F. Fama. Efficient Capital Markets: II. *Journal of Finance*, 46(5):1575–1617, December 1991.

18. Mani Ganesh and Dean Barr. Stock-specific, non-linear neural net models: The AXON System. In *Proceedings of the Neural Networks in the Capital Markets Conference*, November 1994.

19. William N. Goetzmann. An Introduction to Investment Theory. http://viking.som.yale.edu/will/finman540/classnotes/notes.html, Consulted May, 2001.

20. Shareen Joshi and Mark A. Bedau. An Explanation of Generic Behavior in an Evolving Financial Market. Working Paper 98-12-114, Santa Fe Institute, 1998.

21. Takashi Kimoto and Morio Yoda. Buying ans Selling Timing Prediction System for Stock Based on Modular Neural Networks. *Fujitsu Scientific & Technical Journal*, 29(3):257–264, Autumn 1993.

22. Blake LeBaron. Experiments in Evolutionary Finance. SSRI Working Paper No. 9528, Department of Economics, University of Wisconsin-Madison, August 1995.

23. Blake LeBaron. Building Financial Markets With Artificial Agents: Desired Goals, and Present Techniques. Technical report, Graduate School of International Economics and Finance, Brandeis University, February 1999.

24. Blake LeBaron. Agent Based Computational Finance: Suggested Readings and Early Research. *Journal of Economic Dynamics and Control*, 2000.

25. Blake LeBaron, W. Brian Arthur, and Richard Palmer. The Time Series Properties of an Artificial Stock Market. *Journal of Economic Dynamics and Control*, 23:1487–1516, 1999.

26. Jin Li and Edward P. K. Tsang. Improving Technical Analysis Predictions: An Application of Genetic Programming. 1999.

27. Jin Li and Edward P. K. Tsang. Reducing Failures in Investment Recommendations using Genetic Programming. Barcelona, Spain, July 2000.

28. Andrew W. Lo and A. Craig MacKinlay. *A Non-Random Walk Down Wall Street.* Princeton University Press, 1999.

29. Burton G. Malkiel. *A Random Walk Down Wall Street.* W.W. Norton & Company, 6th edition, 1999.

30. Timothy Masters. *Neural, Novel & Hybrid Algorithms for Time Series Prediction.* John Wiley & Sons, October 1995.

31. R. G. Palmer, W. Brian Arthur, John H. Holland, Blake LeBaron, and P. Tayler. Artificial economic life: a simple model of a stockmarket. *Physica D*, D 75:264–274, 1994.

32. Olivier V. Pictet, Michel M. Dacorogna, Rakhal D. Davé, Bastien Chopard, Roberto Schirru, and Marco Tomassini. Genetic Algorithms with collective sharing for Robust Optimization in Financial Applications. Working Paper OVP.1995-02-06, Olsen & Associates Research Group, January 1996.
33. Matt Ridley. Frontiers of Finance. *The Economist*, pages 3–22, October 9th 1993.
34. Sheldon M. Ross. *An Introduction to Mathematical Finance. Options and Other Topics*. Cambridge University Press, Cambridge, UK, 1999.
35. Sonia Schulenburg and Peter Ross. An Evolutionary Approach to Modelling the Behaviours of Financial Traders. In *Genetic and Evolutionary Computation Conference Late Braking Papers*, pages 245–253, Orlando, Florida, 1999.
36. Sonia Schulenburg and Peter Ross. An Adaptive Agent Based Economic Model. In Pier Luca Lanzi, Wolfgang Stolzmann, and Stewart W. Wilson, editors, *Learning Classifier Systems: From Foundations to Applications*, volume 1813 of *Lecture Notes in Artificial Intelligence*, pages 265–284. Springer-Verlag, Berlin, 2000.
37. Sonia Schulenburg and Peter Ross. Strength and Money: An LCS Approach to Increasing Returns. In Pier Luca Lanzi, Wolfgang Stolzmann, and Stewart W. Wilson, editors, *Advances in Learning Classifier Systems*, volume 1996 of *Lecture Notes in Artificial Intelligence*. Springer-Verlag, Berlin, 2001.
38. James D. Thomas. Thesis Proposal, Carnegie Mellon University, Department of Computer Science, 2000.
39. James D. Thomas and Katia Sycara. Integrating Genetic Algorithms and Text Learning for Financial Prediction. In Alex A. Freitas, William Hart, Natalio Krasnogor, and Jim Smith, editors, *Proceedings of the GECCO-2000 Workshop on Data Mining with Evolutionary Algorithms*, pages 72–75, Las Vegas, Nevada, USA, 2000.
40. Edward P. K. Tsang, Jin Li, and James M. Butler. EDDIE Beats the Bookies. *International Journal of Software, Practice and Experience*, 28(10):1033–1043, August 1998.
41. Edward P. K. Tsang, Jin Li, Sheri Makrose, Hakan Er, Abdel Salhi, and Giulia Iori. EDDIE in Financial Decision Making. *Journal of Management and Economics*, November 2000.
42. Halbert White. Economic Prediction Using Neural Networks: The Case of IBM Daily Stock Returns. In *Proceedings of the IEEE International Conference on Neural Networks*, July 1988.
43. Beat Wuthrich, D. Permunetilleke, S. Leung, Vincent Cho, J. Zhang, and W. Lam. Daily Prediction of Major Stock Indices from Textual WWW Data. In *Knowledge Discovery and Data Mining – KDD-98*, pages 364–368, 1998.

On-Line Approach for Loss Reduction in Electric Power Distribution Networks Using Learning Classifier Systems

Patrícia Amâncio Vargas[1], Christiano Lyra Filho[2], and Fernando J. Von Zuben[1]

[1] School of Electrical and Computer Engineering (FEEC)
State University of Campinas (UNICAMP)
Department of Computer Engineering and
Industrial Automation (DCA),
Campinas, S.P., Brazil C. P. 6101, 13081-970
{pvargas,vonzuben}@dca.fee.unicamp.br
[2] School of Electrical and Computer Engineering (FEEC)
State University of Campinas (UNICAMP)
Department of Systems Engineering (DENSIS)
Campinas, S.P., Brazil C. P. 6101, 13081-970
chrlyra@densis.fee.unicamp.br

Abstract. - The problem of minimization of energy losses in power distribution systems can be formulated as obtaining the "best" network configuration, through the manipulation of sectionalizing switches. Using graph terminology, we have a combinatorial optimization problem, whose solution corresponds to finding a minimum spanning tree for the network. As an on-line approach to loss reduction in electric power distribution networks, this paper relies on Learning Classifier Systems to continually proposed network configurations close to the one associated with minimum energy losses, in the case of time-varying profiles of energy requirement. In order to evolve the set of rules that composes the Classifier System, operators for selection, reproduction and mutation are applied. Case studies illustrate the possibilities of this approach.

1 Introduction

This work explores the flexibility of Classifier Systems [5] to obtain a solution to the problem of loss reduction in electric power distribution systems with time-varying demands.

Based on the purpose of the system and the present state of the environment, the Classifier System defines, through a computational process of evolutionary adaptation, a set of classifiers (rules) that defines which sectionalizing switches should be opened and closed in the distribution network. In order to determine the set of optimal classi-

P.L. Lanzi, W. Stolzmann, and S.W. Wilson (Eds.): IWLCS 2001, LNAI 2321, pp. 181-196, 2002.

fiers, considered here as a population, we apply all the evolutionary computation inner procedures, such as selection, reproduction and mutation.

Using graph terminology, the solution to the problem of loss minimization in electric power distribution corresponds to finding the minimum spanning tree for the network [1]. However, when the arc costs (directly linked to energy losses) vary according to the level of demand on each graph node, the problem can not be solved by applying classic algorithms, very efficient, but developed for situations where all the arcs have fixed costs. The presence of varying demands also implies a higher computational complexity.

Merlin and Back [12] proposed the first algorithms for loss reduction in distribution systems with fixed demand. They also identified that the computational cost to obtain an optimal solution was prohibitive. In fact, the most utilized approaches, like "successive opening of switches" [12,15,17], and "branch-exchange" [2,7,15], lead to approximated solutions.

Nara et al. [14] were the first authors to investigate the use of evolutionary computation (EC) to reduce losses in electric power distribution systems. The strategy developed by Nara et al. [14] may produce solutions that violate the radial constraint, and the process of identification and elimination of infeasible solutions degrades the performance of the approach. Costa [8] addressed this issue proposing two levels of codification : indirect and direct code. He also added methodological innovations to the evolutionary algorithm and explored the possibility of using these concepts together with tabu-search [9].

The approaches described above normally suppose that energy demands are fixed. Recently, Zhou et al. [18] have addressed the problem of reconfiguration of the distribution network under time-varying demand. They proposed an operation decision support tool responsible for reducing the cost over a specific time period.

In the present paper, on-line reconfiguration will be considered, based on a Learning Classifier System that will make use of the two levels of codification proposed by Costa [8].

2   Problem Formulation

The graph representation in Fig.1 shows the main entities for assessing loss minimization in electric power distribution systems [6]: load blocks (L1, L2, ..., L10), comprising a set of energy customers nodes, switches for network reconfiguration (S1, S2, ..., S16), and substations (SS1, SS2). Line resistance and reactance are aggregated in the arcs that represent switches. Electric loads demand active and reactive power at each node L_k (P_{Lk} and Q_{Lk}, respectively).

As distribution networks operate radially, a unique energized path must link any node in the graph to the corresponding substation. The total power is drawn from the transmission network at the root node (R). Using a graph terminology, the energized network must be a spanning tree for the graph [1].

The position (opened or closed) of the sectionalizing switches defines which paths in the graph will supply energy to the nodes L_k ($k = 1, ..., 10$). The essence of the problem is to uncover the set of paths that leads to minimum energy losses.

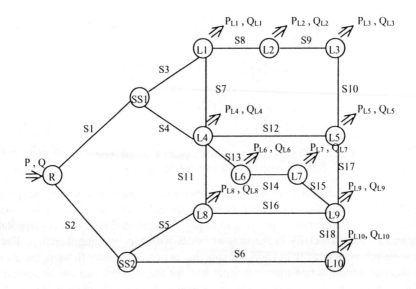

Fig. 1. Simplified graph model for a Distribution System

We understand as network parameters all the specifications treated as invariable: the number of demand nodes, the number of arcs, the connections between nodes, resistance, reactance, maximum demands and voltage at substations' nodes.

Formally, the problem of finding a network configuration that minimizes energy losses can be formulated as follows [3]:

$$Min \sum_{c \in \Omega} \sum_{k \in N} \sum_{i \in A_k} r_{ki} \frac{\left(P_{ki}^2 + Q_{ki}^2\right)}{V_k^2} . \tag{1}$$

s.t. $P_k = \sum_{i \in A_k} P_{ki} + P_{Lk}$

$Q_k = \sum_{i \in A_k} Q_{ki} + Q_{Lk}$

$\left(V_{ki}\right)^2 = \left(V_k\right)^2 - 2\left(r_{ki} P_{ki} + x_{ki} Q_{ki}\right)$

$\Omega = \{j : c_j = 1\}$

where Ω is the set of all spanning trees for the network, c is a vector of boolean variables which define the state of the sectionalizing switches, N is the set of nodes in the distribution network, A_k is the set of arcs with origin at node k, P_k is the active power flow at switch k (refer to Fig. 2), Q_k is the reactive power flow at switch k, V_k is the voltage at node k, r_{ki} e x_{ki} are, respectively, resistance and reactance of lines aggregated in switch ki.

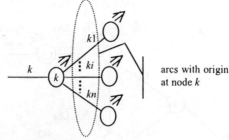

Fig. 2. A Branch of an operation tree for a Distribution
Network, emphasizing switch k and node k

This is a combinatorial optimization problem with constraints, where the computational effort to find the optimal solution through exhaustive evaluations involves the consideration of all feasible spanning trees [3]. This exhaustive search is computationally intractable, especially in the case of nodes with time-varying demands. Because arc costs are associated with energy losses that depend on power flows in the arcs, the problem of finding a minimum spanning tree for the network can not be solved with classic algorithms, developed for situations where arcs have fixed costs. Time-varying demands adds to the complexity of the problem.

In the case of on-line reconfiguration, computation tractability is conquered as we apply methods capable of providing a good solution, though with no guarantee of being the optimal one. Taking into account this fact, and the requirement of finding a new configuration for each significant demand variation, we investigate in this paper the possibility of obtaining good on-line solutions to the problem by means of Classifier Systems [5].

3   A Brief Review of Learning Classifier Systems

Holland [11] introduced the structure and mechanisms associated with Learning Classifier Systems. Basically, they refer to a methodology for creating and updating rules (the classifiers), which code alternative specific actions according to the purpose of the system and the present state of the environment. In the context of this application, each classifier will directly provide the next action, without chaining. So, there is no need for bucket brigade or alternative reinforcement learning algorithms.

The Classifier System communicates with the environment through his message detectors (Fig. 3). These detectors are responsible for the reception and codification of messages received by the system, turning them into an intelligible language for the Classifier System. The system acts on the environment through his effectors, which decodes the system's proposed actions. The appropriate reward applied to the active classifier is determined by the nature of the consequences of each action (environment's feedback).

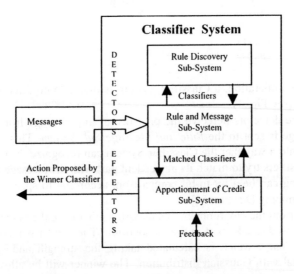

Fig. 3. Simplified flow (Classifier System ↔ Environment)

Each classifier or rule represents a candidate to act on the environment and the Classifier System is composed of a population of classifiers (Table 1). The classifiers themselves are composed of an antecedent and a consequent part. The antecedent part of the classifier is a string of fixed size composed of elements of the ternary alphabet set {0,1,#}. The symbol "#" is known as the "don't care" symbol and can assume value "1" or "0" during the matching phase. The consequent part of the classifier is generally given by a string of fixed size composed of elements of the binary alphabet set {0,1}, but in the case of floating point codification, we have a string of fixed size composed of real numbers. The use of floating point representation at the consequent part of the classifier will be discussed in Section 4.

Associated with each classifier, there is a "strength" that is used to express the energy or power of the classifier during the evolutionary process. It is the matching of the classifier's antecedent part with the messages of the environment that will define which classifiers will compete to act on the environment. This competition is based on the strength of the selected classifiers.

Another important concept is the "specificity" of each classifier, which is a measure inversely proportional to the quantity of symbols "#" on the classifier's antecedent part.

Table 1. An Example of a Set of Classifiers

Classifiers or Rules	Strength
1#1## : 11	8,5
1110# : 01	15,2
11111 : 11	5,9
##0## : 10	19,0

In terms of internal operation, a Classifier System is divided into three interactive distinct sub-systems (see Fig. 3).

When the message detectors perceive the presence of any message from the environment, this message is sent to the *Rule and Message Sub-System*. This sub-system codes the message into a way that the Classifier System can recognize. From this moment on, all the classifiers try to match its antecedent part with the message (matching phase). This matching can be a bit-to-bit comparison, according to specific rules, or just based on the Hamming Distance [4].

Given a message from the environment, the classifiers that have the highest level of matching will be allowed to take part in the competition. The winner is recognized by a parameter called *"bid"*, which is calculated taking the strength and specificity, modulated by a signal with Gaussian distribution. The winner will be allowed to act on the environment.

The environment will reply in response to the action proposed by the winner classifier, providing a feedback to the Classifier System. It is the responsibility of the *Apportionment of Credit Sub-System* to incorporate a reward or punishment value, based on the feedback of the environment to the strength of the active classifier at that moment.

Once the feedback is received from the environment and the credit is attributed to the winner classifier, a new message will be provided by the environment, describing its actual state. Then, once again the message is treated by the *Rule and Message Sub-System*. The process continues for one epoch of iteration, defined as a sequence of actions adopted by the Classifier System between evolutionary phases.

As already mentioned, we do not implement the bucket brigade algorithm mainly because no classifier is directly responsible for the activation of other classifiers: the consequent part always represents an action to be decoded by the effectors.

At the end of each epoch, the Classifier System will take part in another process of evolution: the discovery of new rules at the *Rule Discovery Sub-System*.

At this time, the genetic operators are applied to produce the next generation of rules. The evolutionary process tends to produce a Classifier System with an improved performance.

Basically, the genetic algorithm chooses the classifiers with greater strength and promotes the reproduction between them, applying the genetic operators of crossover and mutation. The generated children will be introduced into the population at the next generation, replacing the weakest individuals (the ones with the lowest strength) according to the replacing mechanism adopted by Richards [16].

In a simplified way, the whole algorithm is depicted in Fig. 4.

4   Classifier Systems Applied to the Problem

As mentioned in Section 2, losses are reduced by network reconfiguration, through opening and closing switches. The function of the Classifier System is to propose the most suitable switch configuration for loss reduction, given a specific demand profile in the network.

Classifier Systems communicate with the environment through "detectors", "effectors" and "feedback". The electric power distribution network sends as a message to the Classifier System the energy flow associated with each arc of the graph. Once the message is detected, it is coded in order to be internally processed. In this paper, each arc flow is a real number that will be quantified into a two-bit string representation, indicating 4 discrete levels (see Table 2).

Once the appropriate sector is identified for each arc flow, the message is transformed into a binary sequence. As an example, let $f_1 = 1680$ kW be the flow on arc 1 and $fmax = 3140$ kW. In this case f_1 belongs to the third discrete level (medium-high) and it is represented by the sequence "10". Therefore, the number of bits in the antecedent part of each classifier will correspond to only two times the number of arcs in the graph. This parsimonious representation is necessary to allow the application of the same codification to high dimension networks.

The consequent part of each classifier is represented with an extended version of the two levels of codification proposed by Costa [8]: indirect and direct code. The indirect code is initially composed of a vector of virtual costs (real values - indirect code), randomly generated in the interval [0,1], and associated with each arc of the graph that represents the distribution network. Applying Sollin's minimum spanning tree algorithm [1] to this data, we always generate a unique radial configuration for the network with the opened and closed switches (binary values – direct code) satisfying feasibility constraints. So, each set of virtual real-valued costs will produce a feasible switch configuration to the power distribution system. .

The reason why we have two levels of codification is the necessity to produce a feasible network configuration all the time. In this case, all the genetic operators are applied at the level of virtual costs, with no constraints, and the associated network configuration is obtained using the Sollin's minimum spanning tree algorithm.

The unusual way adopted here to codify the consequent part of each classifier deserves a step-by-step explanation:

- The antecedent part of each classifier will be associated with a specific range of demand profiles.
- Each range of demand profile will require a proper network configuration that minimizes the losses, and this network configuration should be indicated by the consequent part of the corresponding classifier.
- An straightforward approach to codify the consequent part would be the adoption of a binary representation, with each bit indicating the state of one switch (opened or closed).

```
  ┌─── START OF THE EVOLUTION PROCESS
  │ ┌─── START OF ONE EPOCH
  │ │ Step 1    : Detect environment messages.
  │ │ Step 2    : Code messages.
  │ │ Step 3    : Select matched classifiers.
  │ │ Step 4    : Begin Competition:
  │ │                  - Calculate each competitor's bid.
  │ │                  - Point out the winner.
  │ │                  - Collect taxes from competitors and the winner.
  │ │ Step 5    : Act on the environment.
  │ │ Step 6    : Receive environment's feedback.
  │ │ Step 7    : Reward or not the winner classifier.
  │ │ Step 8    : Charge life tax from all classifiers.
  │ │ Step 9    : If it is not the end of an epoch, go to Step 1.
  │ └─── END OF ONE EPOCH
  │
  │   Step 10 : Select classifiers to apply genetic operators (gener-
  │               ally, the more adapted ones).
  │
  │   Step 11 : Apply crossover and mutation operators to generate the
  │               children.
  │
  │   Step 12 : Select classifiers to be replaced (generally the less
  │               adapted ones).
  │
  │   Step 13 : Insert  the generated children of Step 11 into the
  │               population, to replace the classifiers selected on
  │               Step 12.
  │
  │   Step 14 : If it is not the end of the evolution process, go to
  │               Step 1.
  └───
```

Fig. 4. Classifier System: Basic algorithm

- However, the state of the switches can not be arbitrary. Only a subset of the possible states guides to a feasible network configuration, i.e., a radial configuration (with no cycles).
- If we adopt the binary representation at the consequent, the infeasible configurations (much more frequent than the feasible ones) must be discarded, dramatically reducing the efficiency of the evolutionary process.
- Instead of operating in a search space composed of feasible an infeasible solutions, we adopted two levels of codification.

Table 2. Power flow codification

SECTORS			
Flow : 0 to *fmax* (kW)			
Each Sector : *fmax* / 4 (kW)			
1 (low)	2 (medium-low)	3 (medium-high)	4 (high)
[0, *fmax*/4]	(*fmax*/4, *fmax*/2]	(*fmax*/2, 3*fmax/4]	(3*fmax/4, *fmax*]

- At the first level, the consequent part of the classifier will assign virtual real-valued costs to each arc of the network.
- Then, in the second level, the Sollin's minimum spanning tree algorithm is used to map every set of real-valued costs to a feasible solution.
- In this sense, the space of real-valued costs is always feasible, and the application of genetic operators at the first level of codification may be considered with no restriction (e.g. crossover disruption).
- As a consequence, the purpose of the genetic algorithm is to search for classifiers with a coherent antecedent part, capable of matching the messages form the environment (which reflects the current demand profile) and a corresponding consequent part, that will guide to a network configuration with minimum energy losses.

The initial population of individuals (classifiers or rules) is randomly created. At the antecedent part, the initial probability of finding the symbol "#" is of 70 % – remember that the symbol "#", known as the "don't care" symbol, will assume value "1" or "0" during the matching phase.

Each "epoch" (sequence of actions adopted by the Classifier System between evolutionary phases) comprehends 150 steps – a number considered to be adequate to allow the competition among classifiers. The reward mechanism, based on Richards [16] and specified in Equation (2), is calculated for each feedback of the environment, in response to the proposed configuration indicated by the winner classifier.

$$R_t = \left(\frac{2*P_{t-1} - P_t}{P_{t-1}} \right) * Tax\_r . \qquad (2)$$

where R_t is the reward value at step t, P_{t-1} and P_t are system's energy losses at step t-1 and t, and Tax_r is the reward factor with the value of 7.5 [16].

Genetic operators are applied to 10% of the selected classifier in the population, based on the strength of each one (fitness) – a Roulette Wheel selection is adopted [10]. One-point crossover is applied to all selected pair of individuals and mutation rate is 1% per individual, i.e., each offspring will undergo mutation with a 1% of probability. At the antecedent part, each allele selected for mutation will be replaced by another with equal probability, among the remaining options. At the consequent part, a specific mutation operator for floating point representation is adopted [13].

5   Case Studies

In all the cases considered, we used the electric power distribution network first proposed by Baran & Wu [3] and illustrated in Fig. 5. It is composed of 37 arcs, 33 nodes and sectionalizing switches associated with each arc. At the configuration presented in Fig. 5, the opened sectionalizing switches are those associated with arcs 33, 34, 35, 36 and 37.

Several other papers in the literature, including Augugliaro *et al.* [2] and Cavellucci and Lyra [6], consider this network as a benchmark. However, these papers deals with fixed demand profiles, and no comparison is possible with the results presented here.

Before investigating the case of variable demand profile, we performed an experiment to attest the efficacy of evolving the consequent part of the classifiers. We know that a proper rule is the one that becomes active at a given demand profile, indicating a set of virtual costs (indirect code) that guides to a feasible network configuration with minimum cost (direct code).

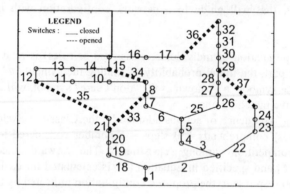

Fig. 5. Electric power Distribution Network [3]

Two questions are then raised:

- Given a population of consequents (each one associated with an active rule), is it possible to improve their performance through evolution?
- If yes, does each demand profile require a specific network configuration to minimize the cost?

Both questions have positive answers based on the application of genetic algorithms to six (randomly generated) fixed demand profiles for the network presented in Fig. 5.

Table 3. Optimal network configuration for 6 (six) distinct and fixed demand profiles proposed by the Genetic Algorithm

Demand Profile (DP)	Network configuration in terms of opened switches					Minimum energy losses (in $p.u.$[1])
1	7	10	14	16	28	0.0135
2	7	10	14	17	28	0.0207
3	7	9	14	17	28	0.0202
4	10	14	15	28	33	0.0222
5	7	9	14	28	36	0.0178
6	7	9	14	32	37	0.0204

The opened switches that allow the best results for each randomly generated demand profile are presented in Table 3.

As a result of this study, we verified that the set of sectionalizing switches that provides optimal loss reduction varies significantly for different demand profiles. Genetic algorithm was able to produce the optimal configuration (the one with minimum energy losses) in all cases.

Notice that here, as the demand profile is fixed, very efficient optimization tools are available to produce the optimal configuration for each profile [2,6]. Genetic algorithms were considered here because they will be used to optimize the classifier systems, in the case of time-varying demand profiles.

Table 4 illustrates the raise of losses, in percentage, when a specific optimal configuration found for the demand profile P_i (i=1,...,6), is applied to another profile P_j (j=1,...,6, $j \neq i$). For example, the application of the best configuration found for the profile P_1 (opened switches: 7, 10, 14, 16 e 28) to P_6, resulted in a raising of 6,4485 % in losses when compared to the best configuration found for profile P_6 (opened switches: 7, 9, 14, 32 e 37).

The second experiment that we have conducted corresponds to situations in which the demand profile goes through four abrupt variations (stepwise). The presence of variations justifies the use of Classifier System from now on. In this case, the best classifiers found for a given demand profile probably will not present good performance in response to a subsequent demand profile, guiding to a reevaluation of the classifier set.

Results obtained with four normalized demand profiles, illustrated in Fig. 6, indicate that the Classifier System is capable of evolving from a set of inadequate solutions (initial configuration just after a stepwise variation) to improved solutions.

The horizontal lines presented at each 20 epochs represent the optimal performance level, in terms of loss reduction, for each demand profile. The results obtained by the Classifier System are slightly above the optimum. This is due to the Classifier System's requirement of keeping its flexibility to adapt to new situations.

---

[1] The values of all energy losses are presented in $p.u.$(per unit basis), a representation normally adopted by the IEEE Power Engineering Society to express energy power in kW.

Table 4. Application of optimal network configurations, developed for a specific demand profile, to other demand profiles

	P_1	P_2	P_3	P_4	P_5	P_6
P_1	0	0,2911	2,2553	0,3059	1,7839	6,4485
P_2	1,7181	0	1,0184	12,602	0,4144	4,2648
P_3	1,5189	2,5179	0	13,277	0,1080	4,1104
P_4	2,7524	2,8187	12,481	0	9,4363	12,819
P_5	3,8348	2,4171	3,9084	16,925	0	1,5433
P_6	17,918	32,532	21,187	26,369	17,757	0

According to the sequence of the demand profiles presented, the opened switches indicated by the Classifier System are illustrated in Table 5.

Based on the four demand profiles presented above, the Classifier System was sufficiently flexible to always indicate new solutions as soon as the variation in demand begins to interfere significantly with the level of energy losses for a specific network configuration.

Table 5. Best network configuration proposed by the Classifier System for the stepwise variation case study

Demand Profile (DP)	Network configuration in terms of opened switches	Minimum energy losses (in $p.u.$)
1	10 15 25 33 34	0.0143
2	7 10 15 27 34	0.0156
3	7 10 12 16 28	0.0181
4	7 9 12 16 28	0.0220

Observe in Fig. 6 that the Classifier System showed a relative stability in the last two profiles presented. This behavior reflects the adaptation process of the Classifier System to the environment, promoting only the activation of effective rules.

In the last case study illustrated in Fig. 7, we presented to the Classifier System a periodic variation in demand profile. We migrated smoothly from one profile to another, among the ones already considered in the previous case study. This is accomplished at each 15 epochs in the following order: 1-2-3-4-3-2-1-2-3-4.

Once again, the horizontal lines presented in the last four transitions (at epochs 90, 105, 120 and 135), represent the optimal network energy losses for each demand profile

We can notice in Fig. 7 the proper performance achieved by the Classifier System, in terms of loss reduction, attesting its potential as an adaptive complex system.

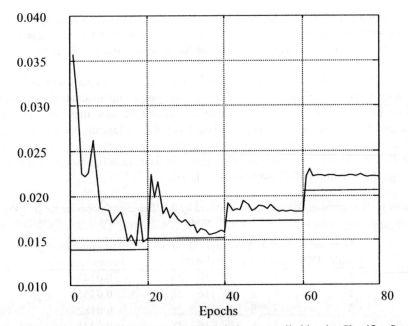

Fig. 6. Average loss for the Distribution Network being controlled by the Classifier System, and subject to 4 stepwise variations in the demand profile: at 0, 20, 40 and 60 epochs

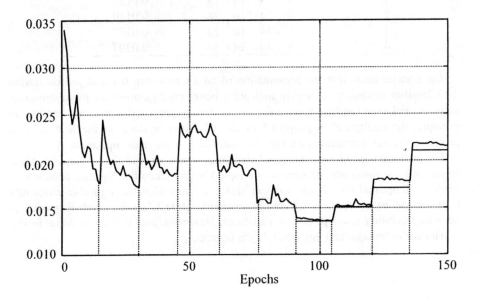

Fig. 7. Classifier System's Performance and Average Loss for the Distribution Network (smooth transitions among 4 distinct demand profiles)

We point out in Table 6 the best network configuration in terms of opened section-alizing switches proposed by the Classifier System for the periodic case study (Fig. 7), stressing the level of energy loss achieved for each demand profile at each transition point.

For these variable and cyclic demands, the Classifier System was able to react promptly to changes in the environment, not only proposing adequate distinct configu-rations for each new demand profile, when necessary, but also improving its perform-ance in terms of secondary responses. This has led the Classifier System to an almost stable condition during the last periods, characterized by already presented stimulus (see Fig. 7). This happens because of an immediate reconfiguration of the network through the activation of already evolved classifiers.

Table 6. Best network configuration proposed by the Classifier System for the periodic case study

Demand Profile (DP)	Network configuration in terms of opened switches					Minimum energy losses (in $p.u.$)
1	7	8	9	16	25	0.0148
2	7	8	9	16	28	0.0155
3	7	8	9	16	28	0.0182
4	7	8	9	16	28	0.0221
3	7	8	9	17	28	0.0181
2	7	9	14	16	28	0.0150
1	7	9	14	16	28	0.0135
2	7	9	14	16	28	0.0150
3	7	9	14	16	28	0.0177
4	7	9	14	28	36	0.0207

The conclusion is that the presentation of an already seen demand profile leaded the Classifier System to promptly indicate a better configuration for the distribution network, and even improve the configuration already proposed at the last time. As an example, the configuration proposed by the Classifier System for the first demand profile in the last simulation (see Fig. 7) is only 0.25% above the optimum.

For stationary environments (fixed demands), we observed that a Genetic Algo-rithm, with the same genetic operators adopted by the Classifier System, obtains net-works with optimal loss characteristics. This is because Genetic Algorithm efficiently explored stationary features of the environment, while Classifier System needed to keep its flexibility to adapt to new situations. New situations will never come in sta-tionary environments, and this flexibility is useless.

6 Conclusions

The paper presented the mathematical formulation and computational aspects to allow the application of Classifier Systems as an on-line approach to loss reduction in electric power distribution networks.

The Classifier Systems have shown to be able to learn by continued exposition to an environment. Also they have shown effectiveness on the production of secondary responses to previously presented stimulus.

Although they depend on the definition of several parameters for the success of their operation, they are sufficiently flexible to be considered as a promising tool when applied to combinatorial optimization problems subject to time-varying conditions. This is the case of the electric power distribution networks with variable and previously unpredictable demand on each node. A fundamental aspect is the requirement of distinct configurations for each demand profile in order to minimize losses.

Based on case studies, which gave us some guidelines on the possibilities of the approach, we can state that Classifier Systems are promising approach for self-adaptation to time-varying demands in electric power distribution networks.

Acknowledgements

This research was sponsored by grants from CNPq (Brazilian National Council for Scientific and Technological Development) and FAPESP (Research Supporting Foundation of the State of São Paulo, Brazil).

The authors thank the reviewers for the numerous suggestions.

The authors also thank Celso Cavellucci (CPFL) for the collaboration and fruitful discussions.

References

1. Ahuja, R.K., Magnanti, T.L., and Orlin, J.B. (1993). *Network Flows: Theory, Algorithms, and Applications.* Prentice Hall, Englewood Cliffs, NJ.

2. Augugliaro, A., Dusonchet, L., and Mangione, S. (1995). *An Efficient Greedy Approach for Minimum Loss Reconfiguration of Distribution Networks.* Electric Power Systems Research, vol. 35, pp. 167-176.

3. Baran, M.E. and Wu, F.F. (1989). *Network Reconfiguration in Distribution Systems for Loss Reduction and Load Balancing.* IEEE Transactions on Power Delivery, vol. 4, no. 2, pp. 1401-1407.

4. Booker, L.B. (1985). *Improving the Performance of Genetic Algorithms in Classifier Systems.* Proceedings of an International Conference on Genetic Algorithms and their Applications, pp. 80-92.

5. Booker, L.B., Goldberg, D.E., and Holland, J.H. (1989). *Classifier Systems and Genetic Algorithms.* Artificial Intelligence, vol. 40, pp. 235-282.

6. Cavellucci, C. and Lyra, C. (1997). *Minimization of Energy Losses in Electric Power Distribution Systems by Intelligent Search Strategies.* International Transactions in Operational Research, vol. 4, no. 1, pp. 23-33.

7. Civanlar, S., Grainger, J.J., Yin, H., and Lee, S.S.H. (1988). *Distribution Feeder Reconfiguration for Loss Reduction.* IEEE Transactions on Power Delivery, vol. 3, pp. 1217-1223.

8. Costa, M.F.N. (1999). *Evolutionary Computation for Resistive Loss Minimization on Electric Power Distribution Systems.* Master Thesis, FEEC, Unicamp, July (in Portuguese).

9. Glover, F. and Laguna, M. (1997). *Tabu Search.* Kluwer Academic Publishers.

10. Goldberg, D.E. (1989). *Genetic Algorithms in Search Optimization, and Machine Learning.* Addison-Wesley, Inc.

11. Holland, J.H. (1975). *Adaptation in Natural and Artificial Systems: An Introductory Analysis with Applications to Biology, Control, and Artificial Intelligence.* The MIT Press, Ann Arbor, MI.91.

12. Merlin, A. and Back, H. (1975). *Search for a Minimal-Loss Operating Spanning Tree Configuration in Urban Power Distribution Systems.* Proc. of 5 th Power Systems Comp. Com., Cambridge, U.K., Sept. 1-5.

13. Michalewicz, Z. (1996). *Genetic Algorithms + Data Structures = Evolution Programs..* Springer-Verlag Berlin Heidelberg, New York.

14. Nara, K.A., Shiose, M., Kitagawa, and Ishihara, T. (1992). *Implementation of Genetic Algorithm for Distribution Systems Loss Minimum Reconfiguration.* IEEE Transactions on Power Systems, vol.7,no.3, pp.1044-1051.

15. Peponis, G.J., Papadopoulos, M.P., and Hatziargyriou, N.D. (1995). *Distribution Network Reconfiguration to Minimize Resistive Line Losses.* IEEE Transactions on Power Delivery, vol. 10, no. 3, pp. 1338-1342.

16. Richards, R.A. (1995). *Zeroth-Order Shape Optimization Utilizing Learning Classifier Systems.* http://www.stanford.edu/~buc/SPHINcsX/book.html

17. Shirmohammadi, D. and Hong, H.W. (1989). *Reconfiguration of Electric Distribution Networks for Resistive Line Losses Reduction.* IEEE Transactions on Power Delivery, vol. 4, pp. 1492-1498.

18. Zhou, Q, Shirmohammadi, D., and Liu, W. –H.E. (1997). *Distribution Feeder Reconfiguration for Operation Cost Reduction.* IEEE Transactions on Power Systems, vol. 12, n. 2, pp. 730-735.

Compact Rulesets from XCSI

Stewart W. Wilson

Department of General Engineering
The University of Illinois, Urbana-Champaign IL 61801, USA
Prediction Dynamics, Concord MA 01742, USA
wilson@prediction-dynamics.com

Abstract. An algorithm is presented for reducing the size of evolved classifier populations. On the Wisconsin Breast Cancer dataset, the algorithm produced compact rulesets substantially smaller than the populations, yet performance in cross-validation tests was nearly unchanged. Classifiers of the rulesets expressed readily interpretable knowledge about the dataset that should be useful to practitioners.

1 Introduction

Desirably, machine learning systems for data inference not only perform well on new data but permit the user to see and understand the "knowledge" that the system has acquired. In principle, learning classifier systems (LCS) have both properties. XCS [6], a recently developed LCS, shows good performance and knowledge visibility in many problem domains. Good performance results from evolution of rules (classifiers) that accurately predict reinforcement (payoffs, rewards) to the system, resulting in correct decisions (yes/no, turn left/turn right/go straight, etc.) that maximize the reinforcement the system receives. At the same time, the rules evolve to be as general as possible while still maintaining accuracy; they compactly express input domain regions over which the same decision is appropriate. Accurate, general rules are a natural and understandable way of representing knowledge to users. Thus XCS has both performance and knowledge visibility properties suitable for data inference.

XCS takes binary inputs, but many data inference problems involve integer attributes. XCSI is an adaptation of XCS for the integer domain, but the essential aspects of XCS are carried over. XCSI was recently applied [8][3] to the Wisconsin Breast Cancer (WBC) dataset [1] with performance results comparable to or exceeding those of other machine-learning methods. In addition, the evolved rules suggested interesting patterns in the dataset, especially when the evolutionary process was continued for very large numbers of random dataset instances. The rules were plausible medically, but knowledge visibility was impeded because there were more than 1000 distinct rules in all. It is natural to ask whether there exists a minimal subset of the classifiers that is sufficient to solve the problem, i.e. to correctly process all instances in the dataset. If so, how small—"compact"— would such a subset be and would its rules be relatively simple?

P.L. Lanzi, W. Stolzmann, and S.W. Wilson (Eds.): IWLCS 2001, LNAI 2321, pp. 197–208, 2002.

We present a technique that on the WBC problem reduces the evolved classifier set to approximately two dozen classifiers while maintaining performance on both training and test sets. The rules of this compact set appear to "make sense medically"[1] and may be amenable to use by practitioners in several ways, one of which is illustrated. The technique for deriving the compact rulesets may be extensible to other data domains.

The next section briefly discusses XCSI, the WBC dataset, and previous experiments. Section 3 introduces a *macrostate* concept, important for visualizing classifier populations and in forming compact rulesets. The Compact Ruleset Algorithm is presented in Section 4, followed in the next section by its application to the WBC dataset. A cross-validation experiment is reported in Section 6. Section 7 has conclusions.

2   XCSI and the Wisconsin Breast Cancer Problem

We used the "original" Wisconsin Breast Cancer Database which contains 699 instances (individual cases). Each instance has nine attributes such as Clump Thickness, Marginal Adhesion, etc. Each attribute has an integer value between 1 and 10 inclusive. Sixteen instances contain an attribute whose value is unknown. The outcome distribution is 458 Benign (65.5%), 241 Malignant (34.5%). The upper line of Figure 1 uses a graphic notation to illustrate a particular instance. Each interval between vertical bars represents an attribute. The attribute's value is indicated by the position of the star within the interval. For example, the value of the first attribute (which happens to be Clump Thickness) is 5, the second is 1, etc. The outcome of the instance is indicated by the digit at the end of the line, 0 for Benign and 1 for Malignant; this case was benign.

```
I    *   I*        I*        I*       I *      I*       I *     I*        I*        I 0
I0000000...I0000000000I0000000000I00........I00........I0000000000I0000000000I0000000000I0000000000I  o 1000
```

Fig. 1. Example of an input data instance (upper line) matched by a classifier (lower line). See text for notation explanation.

The second line of Figure 1 shows a classifier that matches the data instance on the first line. The vertical bars separate attribute fields of the classifier's *condition*. Note that each field has exactly ten positions, corresponding to the ten possible attribute values. The string of "0" symbols in the first field indicates that that field matches the first attribute of an instance if the attribute's value is between 1 and 7, inclusive. Similarly, the second field matches *any* value for its attribute, the fourth matches values 1 or 2, and so on. A classifier matches an instance if and only if each of its fields matches the corresponding attribute value.

---

[1] Personal communication, 25 April 2001, William H. Wolberg, MD. Dr. Wolberg compiled the WBC dataset.

The last two numbers in the classifier are its *action* (its decision) and its payoff *prediction*, respectively. In the illustrated classifier, the action is 0 (benign); the prediction is 1000, which is the highest possible payoff, indicating that this classifier is probably always correct (its action is the same as the outcome of every instance it matches).

Note that the illustrated classifier is quite *general*: it potentially matches a large number of possible instances. At the same time, observe that the fourth and fifth fields are restricted to just two possible values, and the first field is somewhat restricted. The assertion made by this classifier can be read, "If Clump Thickness is less than 8 and Marginal Adhesion is less than 3 and Single Epithelial Cell Size is less than 3, then the case is benign".

Internally, XCSI represents the classifier's condition by a concatenation of *interval predicates* $int_k = (l_k, u_k)$ where l_k and u_k are integers and denote the lower and upper limits, inclusive, of the range represented in Figure 1 by the "0" strings. The action is an integer. The prediction is one of several estimates associated with the classifier; the others are *prediction error*, *fitness*, and *action set size*. Two further associated quantities are the classifier's *numerosity* and *experience*.

A full description of XCSI may be found in [8]. Information on basic XCS is in [6], [7], and in the updated formal description of [2] that XCSI follows most closely. The present work concerns a method for *post-processing* classifier populations already evolved by XCSI. We therefore omit a review of XCSI's mechanisms except for some observations relevant to the post-processing.

XCSI trains on a dataset like WBC roughly as follows. An instance is randomly selected from the dataset and presented to XCSI which forms a *match set* [M] consisting of classifiers that match the instance. The system then randomly picks an action from among those advocated by the matching classifiers and presents that action to a separate *reinforcement program* which knows the correct answer (outcome of the case) and gives the system a reward of 1000 if the system was right and 0 if it was wrong. The system then updates the prediction and other quantities mentioned above of all match set classifiers that advocated the selected action—the so-called *action set* [A]. Broadly, the update process is designed to associate high fitness with classifiers that, when they are in the action set, *accurately* predict the reward that will be received.

Each presentation of an instance is called a *time-step*; the training continues for a predetermined number of time-steps or until some other termination criterion is met.

On some time-steps, a genetic algorithm takes place in [A]. Since fitness depends on accuracy, over time the population comes to consist of increasingly accurate classifiers. In addition, however, the classifiers become more general while still remaining accurate. This is because classifiers that are more general tend to occur in more action sets, giving them more reproductive opportunities. Genetic operations are constantly varying classifiers' interval predicates; variations toward greater generality win out over variations toward greater specificity as long as the more general versions retain accuracy–i.e., don't start making mistakes.

Increasing population generality can be observed in Figure 2, taken from [8]. In this experiment, XCSI was trained on the full WBC dataset for 2 million training time-steps. To monitor the system's performance, the training time-steps (called *explore problems* on the graph) alternated with testing time-steps or *test problems*. On a test problem, XCSI made its action choice deterministically (i.e., it picked the action with the highest likely payoff), and a moving average of the fraction correct was plotted.

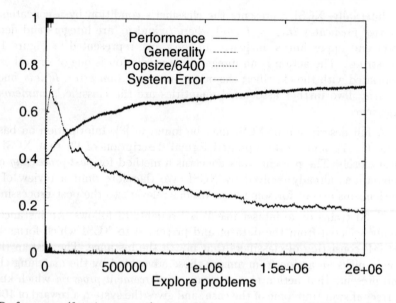

Fig. 2. Performance (fraction correct), generality, population size (/6400), and system error vs. number of explore problems in a training experiment on the Wisconsin Breast Cancer dataset.

Note that the performance curve reaches 100% early, at approximately 50,000 explore problems. The system error curve also falls quickly to a low level (system error measures the error in the system's expectation of payoff). The other two curves, however, develop over the whole experiment and are still changing at its end. The generality curve averages individual classifier generality over the whole population. Classifier generality is defined as the sum of the widths $u_k - l_k - 1$ of the interval predicates, all divided by the maximum possible value of this sum, in this case 90. Generality increases via genetic operations on the interval predicates as explained above. The result is to increase the widths of the interval predicates, some of which go to the full width of 10 and in effect remove the corresponding attributes from consideration in matching (they match unconditionally) and the classifier becomes simpler. Note that while generality steadily increases, the performance stays at 100%: the classifiers though more general are still accurate.

Corresponding to the generality increase, the population size decreases. Specialized classifiers are replaced by more-general ones, so fewer classifiers are needed. At the end, however, the population still has over 1000 classifiers in it, with extension of the experiment unlikely to produce much further improvement. The question arises: are all these classifiers really necessary (for high performance), or can a subset—ideally a *small* subset—be found that performs just as well? The remainder of the paper is devoted to providing an answer. In the next section we describe a simple technique for examining populations.

3 Macrostates

Classifier populations are basically unordered and no aspect of the operation of a classifier system depends on the order in which the classifiers occur. It may be that the classifiers actually form a list structure and those at the beginning were more recently generated than those further on. This makes no difference in principle, however, since the matching and GA processes are conceptually parallel. Nevertheless, as a tool for analysis, it can be useful to order the population according to certain classifier properties. This places classifiers of interest at the head of the list and brings out properties of the population as a whole. Such an ordering of the population is termed a *macrostate*[2].

As an example, consider a *numerosity macrostate* in which the classifiers are ordered in descending order of numerosity. A classifier that is often selected for the GA tends to attain high numerosity. When, as often happens under the GA, an offspring is unchanged from one of its parents (it was not mutated or crossed, or crossing had no effect), it does not enter the population as a separate classifier but the parent's numerosity is instead incremented by one. Thus if a classifier is frequently selected, its numerosity will grow more rapidly than that of less frequently selected classifiers. In general, the frequency of selection depends on fitness as well as the frequency with which a classifier occurs in an action set, which depends on its generality. Consequently, classifiers that are both accurate and maximally general will tend to have high numerosity and so will tend to appear at the top of the numerosity macrostate.

For both performance and knowledge visibility, we would regard accurate and maximally general classifiers as among the "best" in the population, so that calculating the numerosity macrostate is a way of finding these classifiers and bringing them to the fore. Other macrostates, for example based directly on fitness or on experience (the number of times a classifier has occurred in an action set) also tend to place "good" classifiers at the top. Not all orderings do this, however. For example, a generality macrostate will emphasize some highly general but *in*accurate classifiers that have not yet been eliminated from the population.

---

[2] There is a parallel with the macrostate concept of statistical mechanics; see [5].

Certain macrostates, then, tend to place the "best" classifiers at the top. In the next section, an algorithm is introduced that makes use of this fact to derive high-performance compact rulesets from the macrostates.

4   Compact Ruleset Algorithm

To state the algorithm it is useful first to define a macrostate $\mathbf{M}$ as an ordered set of classifiers c_i, $0 < i < M$, where i is an ordering index, the c are the members of a population [P], M is the total number of classifiers in [P], and the c_i are ordered according to a classifier property $prop$ such that $i < j$ if $prop_{c_i} > prop_{c_j}$. For example, $prop$ could be numerosity. $\mathbf{M}$ would then be in descending order of classifier numerosity, except that classifiers with equal numerosity would be adjacent in the ordering.

Define also a *sequential subset* $\mathbf{M}_n$ of $\mathbf{M}$ to be the subset consisting of all classifiers c_i such that $i \leq n$, $0 \leq n \leq M$. The nth sequential subset of $\mathbf{M}$ then consists of all classifiers starting with the 0th (at the "top" of $\mathbf{M}$) down through the nth.

The basic idea of the algorithm is heuristic: it is assumed that classifiers closer to the top of a macrostate are "better" (in terms of performance and generality) than those further down. The algorithm has three steps.

1. Find the smallest $\mathbf{M}_n$ that achieves 100% performance when tested on the dataset D. Letting n^* equal the corresponding value of n, call this set $\mathbf{M}_{n^*}$.
2. Then, because there might have been some c_i such that the performance of $\mathbf{M}_i$ was not greater than the performance of $\mathbf{M}_{i-1}$, $0 < i < n^*$, eliminate such c_i from $\mathbf{M}_{n^*}$. Call the resulting set $\mathbf{B}$.
3. Now process $\mathbf{B}$ as follows. First find the classifier in $\mathbf{B}$ that matches the largest number of instances of D. Place that classifier in an initially empty set $\mathbf{C}$ and remove the matched instances from D. Again find the classifier of $\mathbf{B}$ that matches the most instances of D, add it to $\mathbf{C}$, and remove the matched instances from D. Iterate this cycle until D is empty. Call the final $\mathbf{C}$ a *compact ruleset* for $\mathbf{M}$, and denote it by $\mathbf{M}_{comp}$.

Steps 1 and 2 do most of the work; step 3 places the classifiers of $\mathbf{B}$ in descending order of marginal contribution with respect to D, which is one way of measuring their relative importance. In principle, step 3 can also result in $\mathbf{M}_{comp}$ being slightly smaller than $\mathbf{B}$.

On the basis of experience and analysis of the algorithm, it is believed that if $\mathbf{M}$ has 100% performance on D, so will $\mathbf{M}_{comp}$.

Note that there is no guarantee that $\mathbf{M}_{comp}$ is *minimal*, i.e. that there is not some smaller subset of $\mathbf{M}$ that would also produce 100% performance. And it is not clear *a priori* that $\mathbf{M}_{comp}$ will be appreciably smaller than $\mathbf{M}$. Still, the heuristic of "seeing how many of the best you actually need" seemed reasonable, and worth testing experimentally.

5   Compact Rulesets for the WBC Data

The compact ruleset algorithm (CRA) was applied to the numerosity macrostate of the final population of the experiment of Figure 2, which consisted of 1155 classifiers. The resulting compact ruleset (CR), shown in Figure 3, contained 25 classifiers, a reduction of 97.8%. As expected, the ruleset scored 100% on the dataset, but it is interesting to examine how much of the ruleset is needed for a given level of performance.

```
 0. |0000000000|0000000000|0000......|0000000000|0000000000|00........|0000000000|00........|0000000000|  0 1000
 1. |......0000|....000000|0000000000|0000000000|0000000000|0000000000|0000000000|0000000000|0000000000|  1 1000
 2. |0000000000|0000000000|0000000000|0000000000|0000000000|.....00000|....000000|0000000...|0000000000|  1 1000
 3. |0000000000|0000000000|0000000000|0000000000|0000000000|0000000000|0000000000|.........0|0000000000|  1 1000
 4. |0000000...|0000000000|0000000000|00........|00........|0000000000|0000000000|0000000000|0000000000|  0 1000
 5. |00000.....|0000000000|.....00000|.000000000|0000000000|0000000000|0000000000|0000000000|0000000000|  1 1000
 6. |......0000|0000000000|0000000000|0000000000|0000000000|.......000|0000000000|0000000000|0000000000|  1 1000
 7. |000000....|0000000000|000000000.|000000000.|..00000000|000000....|000000000.|.0000000..|00........|  0 1000
 8. |0000000000|0000000000|..00000001|...0000000|0000000000|0000000...|000000....|0000000000|0000000000|  1 1000
 9. |00000000..|0000000000|0000000000|0000000000|0000000000|0000......|00........|0000000000|0000000000|  0 1000
10. |0000000001|.00000....|0000000000|0000......|1..000000001|.....00000|0000000000|0000000000|0000000000|  1 1000
11. |........001|0000000000|0000000000|0000000000|0000000000|0000000000|0000000000|0000000000|0000000000|  1 1000
12. |0000000000|000.......|0000000000|00000.....|0000000001|..0000000.|0000000001|.00000....|0000000000|  1 1000
13. |.....00000|000.......|1.0000000000|0000000001|....000000|000.......|0000000000|0000000000|0000000000|  1 1000
14. |00000000..|0000000000|000000000.|....0.....|1..00000001|...00000000|000000....|0000000...|000000000.|  0 1000
15. |0000000001|....000000|0000000000|0000000000|0000000000|0000000000|0000000000|0000000000|.000000000|  1 1000
16. |0000000000|0000000000|..00000001|.....00000|0000000000|0000000000|0000000...|0000000...|.000000000|  1 1000
17. |000000....|1...00000..|1..000000...|000000....|1..00000...|1..00000..|0000......|1...00000000|000000....|  0 1000
18. |0000000000|0000000000|0000000000|.000000000|0.........|1..0000....|0000000000|0000000000|0000000000|  1 1000
19. |0000000000|0000000000|0000000000|0000000000|0000000000|0000000000|.......000|0000000000|0000000000|  1 1000
20. |.....000..|1..0000000000|0000000000|.000000...|0000......|0000......|0000000000|0000000....|0000......|  0 1000
21. |....000001|000.......|0000000000|0000000000|00000.....|1.000000...|1....0......|0000......|000.......|  1 1000
22. |0000000000|0000000000|0000......|0000000000|0000000000|0000......|1000......|1.0000000000|0000000000|  0 1000
23. |....000001|.000......|1..0000...|1....0.....|00000000.|.1..0000000|....00000|0000000000|0000000...|  0 1000
24. !.00000000.|0000......|0000000....|1......0000|0000000000.|1..0000....|0000000....|00000000..|0000000....|  0 1000
```

Fig. 3. Compact ruleset derived from the numerosity macrostate of the final population of Figure 2 using the algorithm of Section 4.

Step 3 of the compact ruleset algorithm orders the classifiers according to their marginal contribution; that is, the classifiers are ordered such that a given one matches the maximum number of data instances not matched by previous classifiers in the set. Figure 4 shows how performance increases as classifiers are added (in effect, with a numbering adjustment, the graph shows performance vs. sequential subsets of the CR).

The first classifier in the set, number 0 in Figure 3, is alone sufficient to achieve 57.7% performance on the dataset; the first five classifiers raise performance to 90.0%; the first ten to 95.6%, and so on. Here, performance means number correct divided by the size of the dataset; since all classifiers of the CR are accurate, the number not correct consists entirely of instances that are not matched, i.e., not recognized. So the figures mean that classifier 0 has enough knowledge of the dataset to correctly classify 57.7% of it, etc. The CRA clearly shows that the knowledge about the WBC dataset that was contained in the original final population can be completely represented by a small number of selected classifiers.

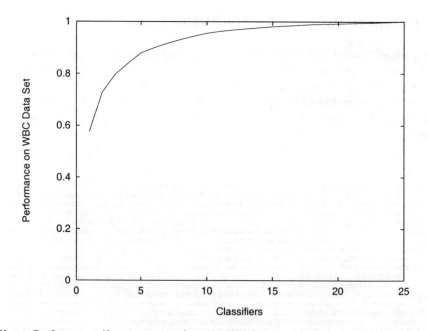

Fig. 4. Performance (fraction correct) on the WBC dataset using progressively increasing numbers of classifiers from the compact ruleset of Figure 3, starting with the first classifier.

It is interesting to ask why the original final population was so large—even though action of the GA and subsumption deletion [8] had reduced it considerably. In a nine-attribute, integer-valued problem like the WBC, the search processes (crossover and mutation) result in a huge number of candidate "better" classifiers, which are only very slowly either eliminated or emphasized. Furthermore, since the dataset occupies only a minuscule fraction of the input space, many different accurate generalizations are possible. They overlap only partially, so the GA and subsumption mechanisms have difficulty eliminating the less general of them. Fortunately, however, a small number of classifiers sufficient to accurately process the dataset are evolved, among all the others, and these can apparently be identified and selected by the CRA.

The classifiers of the CR in Figure 3 are straightforward to translate into English language descriptions, as was done in Section 2 for the classifier of Figure 1 (which is number 4 of the CR). In English (or other language), the rules could be directly useful to physicians, especially the first 10 rules (covering 95.6% of cases), most of which depend on just one, two or three attributes. These rules could be applied to cases or studied in themselves, as representing broad classes of cases.

A somewhat different way the rules could be employed is illustrated in Figure 5. As in Figure 1, the star rows represent particular cases (the block of stars is an example of a missing attribute value, matched unconditionally). With each case

```
        1        2        3        4        5        6        7        8        9
     |  *     |*       |*       |*       | *      | *      | *      |*       |*       |  0
  0. |0000000000|0000000000|0000......|0000000000|0000000000|00........|0000000000|00........|0000000000|  0 1000
  1. |0000000...|0000000000|0000000000|00........|00........|0000000000|0000000000|0000000000|0000000000|  0 1000
  2. |0000000000|0000000000|0000......|0000000000|0000000000|0000......|000.......|0.........|0000000000|  0 1000


     |      *|*   *   |    *  |*       | *      | *      | *      |  *     |   *|  *   |  1
  0. |0000000000|0000000000|0000000000|0000000000|0000000000|0000000000|0000000000|.........0|0000000000|  1 1000
  1. |........00|0000000000|0000000000|0000000000|0000000000|0000000000|0000000000|0000000000|0000000000|  1 1000


     |     *  |   *    |   *   |*       | *      |**********|    *   | *      |*       |  1
  0. |0000000000|0000000000|0000000000|0000000000|0000000000|.....00000|....000000|0000000...|0000000000|  1 1000
  1. |......0000|0000000000|0000000000|0000000000|0000000000|.......000|0000000000|0000000000|0000000000|  1 1000


     |*       |*       |*       |*       |  *     | *      |*       |*       |*       |  0
  0. |00000000..|0000000000|0000000000|0000000000|0000000000|0000......|00........|0000000000|0000000000|  0 1000
  1. |0000000000|0000000000|0000......|0000000000|0000000000|0000......|000.......|0.........|0000000000|  0 1000
```

Fig. 5. WBC cases and matching classifiers from the compact ruleset of Figure 3. Notation is the same as for Figure 1.

are the two or three classifiers from the CR that matched it. It can be imagined that a physician, with a case in hand, has the system display the classifiers that match the case in order to see what knowledge the ruleset, and through it the underlying dataset, might contribute.

For example, the first two classifiers matching the first case suggest that if either attributes 6 and 8 or attributes 4 and 5 have values less than 3, the case is benign. Each classifier has another non-general attribute, but it is not so sharply defined and may not matter so much. The third classifier is more complicated, but it also appears in the fourth case. Together, the two cases suggest that low values of attributes 6 and 7 also imply benign, and that if they are indeed low, the value of attribute 8 doesn't matter.

The second case suggests strongly that either a 10 on attribute 8 or 9-10 on attribute 1 implies malignant. Recall that a classifier tends to be generalized up to the point where it begins making mistakes. The narrow dependence of these two classifiers on high values of attributes 8 and 1, respectively, suggests that cases with values even slightly less will need to have additional attributes looked at (by other classifiers), but that values within these ranges are decisive by themselves. The third case in Figure 5 contains an unknown attribute value, but since the decision is correct, it probably depends on other attributes. The key variables are probably the relatively high value of either attribute 1 or attribute 7, since the other attributes are generalized out (except for the counter-intuitive predicate in field 8 of the first classifier, which might have generalized out had the evolution gone farther),

An interesting observation about Figure 5 is that attributes 2 and 9 are irrelevant to all four decisions. In fact, from looking at further cases, it turns out that attribute 2 is sometimes important, but attribute 9 hardly ever.

These examples are meant to indicate how the compact ruleset can assist a practitioner in gaining understanding of a database, and thus the real-world problem behind it. They bring out which attributes are important and which not, and they show how a given case can often be decided from more than one perspective. It seems likely that access to software that matched compact ruleset classifiers to cases would aid practioners in the important process of developing intuition.

6 Cross Validation Experiment

The CRA produced a quite compact and apparently insightful ruleset for the breast cancer data that retained 100% performance. However, it is important to know whether such rulesets have good performance on *new* cases. Since truly new cases were not available, stratified ten-fold cross-validation (STFCV) experiments were performed using the original dataset.

An STFCV is typically done as follows. The dataset is divided into 10 parts called "folds". The system is then tested on each fold (which functions as a set of "new" cases), after being trained on the balance of the dataset (the *fold complement*). Then the results on the 10 test folds are averaged giving the final score. The folds are made as equal in size as possible, given the size of the actual dataset. "Stratification" means that in each fold the possible outcomes have approximately the same prevalences as in the whole dataset. For more details, see [8] and [9].

Table 1. Results of stratified tenfold cross-validation tests on WBC dataset. Each line has results for one fold. Last line is mean of fold scores. See text for explanation of tests.

Fold	Pop. @ 50,000	Pop. @ 2 mill.	nCR of Pop. @ 2 mill.	eCR of Pop. @ 2 mill.
1	0.9714	.9714	.9429	.9714
2	0.9857	.9857	.9714	.9857
3	0.9286	.9143	.9000	.9143
4	0.9429	.9429	.9000	.9286
5	0.9286	.9429	.9286	.9286
6	0.9143	.9429	.9571	.9429
7	1.0000	.9429	.9143	.9286
8	0.9857	.9857	.9286	.9571
9	0.9420	.9565	.9420	.9275
10	0.9571	.9429	.9429	.9286
Mean	0.9556	.9528	.9328	.9413

Table 1 gives the results of four experiments. The second column reproduces performance results from the STFCV experiment in [8]. For each fold, XCSI was trained for 50,000 problems (on the fold complement), and the final population was tested with the performance (fraction correct) given in the table. For the third column, these populations were further trained (on the same fold comple-ments) out to 2,000,000 problems and then tested on the same folds as before. For the fourth column, the numerosity macrostate was computed for each of these populations, and the CRA applied to yield a numerosity compact ruleset, "nCR". Then the ten nCR's were tested on the folds with the results shown. The fifth column is like the third, except that *experience* compact rulesets, "eCR's", were computed and tested.

The table suggests several inferences. First, the means of the second and third columns are close, indicating that for full populations, the generalization achieved by training out to 2,000,000 problems does not come at the expense of performance. (The generalization and population size reductions were simi-lar to those in the experiment of Figure 2). Second, the results on the CR's, though worse, are only slightly so, suggesting that the large ruleset size reduc-tion achieved by the CRA comes without significant performance cost and thus that "the knowledge" made visible by the CRA is essentially as correct as the knowledge in the full populations. Finally, it is interesting that the eCR per-forms slightly better on this problem than the nCR, suggesting that classifier experience is at least as good a basis as numerosity for forming compact rulesets.

7 Conclusion

This paper presented a technique, the Compact Ruleset Algorithm, for reducing the size of evolved classifier populations. On the Wisconsin Breast Cancer dataset problem, the CRA produced compact rulesets substantially smaller than the evolved populations, yet performance on new data was nearly unchanged. Clas-sifiers of the CR's expressed readily interpretable knowledge about the dataset, and may be usable by practitioners in a variety of ways.

The CRA technique should be tested on other datasets, and variations in the technique itself need to be explored. The value of compact rulesets that make knowledge visible and can be easily worked with is clear, even if their performance is slightly less than that of full evolved populations. In a devel-oped software system, it would be desirable to make available *both* the evolved population—for maximum performance on new data instances—and the corre-sponding compact ruleset—as a summary of "the knowledge", a tool for quick evaluations, and an aid to intuition.

References

1. C.L. Blake and C.J. Merz. UCI repository of machine learning databases, 1998. http://www.ics.uci.edu/~mlearn/MLRepository.html.
2. Martin V. Butz and Stewart W. Wilson. An Algorithmic Description of XCS. In Lanzi et al. [4].
3. Chunsheng Fu, Stewart W. Wilson, and Lawrence Davis. Studies of the XCSI classifier system on a data mining problem. In Lee Spector, Erik Goodman, Annie Wu, William B. Langdon, Hans-Michael Voigt, Mitsuo Gen, Sandip Sen, Marco Dorigo, Shahram Pezeshk, Max Garzon, and Edmund Burke, editors, *Proceedings of the Genetic and Evolutionary Computation Conference (GECCO-2001)*, page 985. Morgan Kaufmann: San Francisco, CA, 2001.
4. Pier Luca Lanzi, Wolfgang Stolzmann, and Stewart W. Wilson, editors. *Advances in Learning Classifier Systems: Proceedings of the Third International Workshop (IWLCS-2000)*, LNAI-1996. Springer-Verlag, Berlin, 2001.
5. Stewart W. Wilson. Classifier Systems and the Animat Problem. *Machine Learning*, 2:199–228, 1987.
6. Stewart W. Wilson. Classifier Fitness Based on Accuracy. *Evolutionary Computation*, 3(2):149–175, 1995.
7. Stewart W. Wilson. Generalization in the XCS classifier system. In John R. Koza, Wolfgang Banzhaf, Kumar Chellapilla, Kalyanmoy Deb, Marco Dorigo, David B. Fogel, Max H. Garzon, David E. Goldberg, Hitoshi Iba, and Rick Riolo, editors, *Genetic Programming 1998: Proceedings of the Third Annual Conference*, pages 665–674. Morgan Kaufmann: San Francisco, CA, 1998.
8. Stewart W. Wilson. Mining oblique data with XCS. In Lanzi et al. [4].
9. Ian H. Witten and Eibe Frank. *Data Mining: Practical Machine Learning Tools and Techniques with Java Implementations*. Morgan Kaufmann, San Francisco, CA, 2000.

Part III

Appendix

An Algorithmic Description of ACS2

Martin V. Butz[1] and Wolfgang Stolzmann[2]

[1] Department of Cognitive Psychology
University of Würzburg, Germany
butz@psychologie.uni-wuerzburg.de
[2] DaimlerChrysler AG
Research and Technology
Berlin, Germany
wolfgang.stolzmann@daimlerchrysler.com

Abstract. The various modifications and extensions of the anticipatory classifier system (ACS) recently led to the introduction of ACS2, an enhanced and modified version of ACS. This chapter provides an overview over the system including all parameters as well as framework, structure, and environmental interaction. Moreover, a precise description of all algorithms in ACS2 is provided.

1 Introduction

Anticipatory learning classifier systems (ALCSs) are a new type of classifier system. The major addition in ALCSs is that they comprise the notation of anticipations in their framework. Doing that, the systems predominantly are able to anticipate perceptual consequences of actions independent of a reinforcement prediction. Thus, ALCSs are systems that are able to form a complete anticipatory representation, that is, they build an environmental model. The model specifies which changes take place in an environment after the execution of a specific action with respect to the current situation. The essential intention behind the framework is that the representation of an environmental model allows faster and more intelligent adaptation of behavior or problem classification. By anticipating the consequences of actions with the evolving model, the system is able to adapt its behavior faster and beyond the capabilities of reinforcement learning methods (Stolzmann, Butz, Hoffmann, and Goldberg, 2000, Butz, 2001a).

The system ACS2 is derived from the original ACS framework as introduced in Stolzmann (1997) and Stolzmann (1998). Moreover, ACS2 embodies the more recently introduced genetic generalization mechanism (Butz, Goldberg, and Stolzmann, 2000). This paper provides a precise algorithmic description of ACS2. The description starts in a top down manner detailing first the overall learning cycle. The following subsections specify the single parts of the cycle in more detail. This article should be read in conjunction with Butz (2001a) in which a more comprehensive introduction of ACS2 is provided as well as a previous version of this algorithmic description. The interested reader is also referred to the other cited literature above for further background.

P.L. Lanzi, W. Stolzmann, and S.W. Wilson (Eds.): IWLCS 2001, LNAI 2321, pp. 211–229, 2002.

The next section gives an overview of ACS2's framework, rule structure, and environmental interaction. Section 3 provides the actual algorithmic description. We hope that the description in combination with the explanations about framework, structure, parameters, and environmental interaction facilitates research with ACS2. We would like to encourage feedback regarding potential problems or ambiguities. Moreover, the usage of the available ACS2 code is encouraged (Butz, 2001b).

2   Environment, Knowledge Representation, and Parameters

Before rushing into the algorithmic description, we provide an overview of the basic environmental interaction of ACS2, as well as its internal structure. Moreover, a list of all parameters in ACS2 is provided with additional suggested parameter settings and possible hints of how to set the parameters with respect to a specific problem.

2.1   Environmental Interaction

Similar to reinforcement learning agents, ACS2 interacts autonomously with an environment. It perceives situations $\sigma \in \mathcal{I} = \{\iota_1, \iota_2, ..., \iota_m\}^L$ where m is the number of possible values of each environmental attribute (or feature), $\iota_1, ..., \iota_m$ are the different possible values of each attribute, and L is the string length. Note, each attribute is not necessarily coded binary but can only take on discrete values. Moreover, the system acts upon the environment with actions $\alpha \in \mathcal{A} = \{\alpha_1, \alpha_2, ..., \alpha_n\}$ where n specifies the number of different possible actions in the environment and $\alpha_1, ..., \alpha_n$ are the different possible actions. After the execution of an action, the reinforcement program evaluates the action in the environment and provides scalar reward $\rho(t) \in \Re$ as feedback.

Figure 1 illustrates the interaction. Hereby, the *reinforcement program* is denoted by a separate module. In accordance to Dorigo and Colombetti (1997) we separate the reinforcement from the environment, since the reinforcement could not only be provided by the environment itself, but also by an independent teacher, or even ACS2 itself, viewing the system in this case as an adaptive agent with certain needs that produce an internal reinforcement once being satisfied. ACS2 could represent certain motivations and intentions that would influence the reinforcement provision. For example, certain environmental properties might be highly desired by ACS2 so that the achievement of one of the properties would trigger high reinforcement. Thus, to what extend the actual reinforcement is influenced by the ACS2 agent is highly problem dependent.

The figure also represents the basic knowledge representation and main intuition behind ACS2. Reinforcement and perceptual feedback trigger learning in ACS2. Reinforcement as well as anticipations are represented in a common model. The knowledge represented in the model controls the action selection, i.e. the behavioral policy. Moreover, the model is intended to be exploited for improving the behavioral policy. How the model is represented in ACS2 is addressed in the following section.

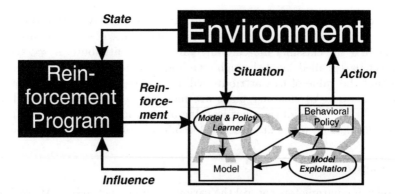

Fig. 1. ACS2 interacts with an environment perceiving environmental situations and executing actions in the environment. Reinforcement is provided by a separate reinforcement program that evaluates the current environmental state and might be more or less influenced by ACS2.

2.2 Knowledge Representation

As in other LCSs the knowledge in ACS2 is represented by a population $[P]$ of classifiers. Each classifier represents a condition-action-effect rule that anticipates the model state resulting from the execution of the specified action given the specified condition. A classifier in ACS2 always specifies a complete resulting state. It consists of the following components.

C The *condition part* ($C \in \{\iota_1, \iota_2, ..., \iota_m, \#\}^L$) specifies the set of situations (perceptions) in which the classifier can be applied.

A The *action part* ($A \in \mathcal{A}$) proposes an available action.

E The *effect part* ($E \in \{\iota_1, \iota_2, ..., \iota_m, \#\}^L$) anticipates the effects that the classifier 'believes' to be caused by the specified action.

M The *mark* ($M = (m_1, m_2, ..., m_L)$ with $m_i \subseteq \{\iota_1, \iota_2, ..., \iota_m\}$) records the properties in which the classifier did not work correctly before.

q The *quality* (q) measures the accuracy of the anticipations.

r The *reward prediction* (r) predicts the reward expected after the execution of action A given condition C.

ir The *immediate reward prediction* (ir) predicts the reinforcement directly encountered after the execution of action A.

t_{ga} The *GA time stamp* ($t_{ga} \in \mathbb{N}$) records the last time the classifier was part of an action set in which a GA was applied.

t_{alp} The *ALP time stamp* ($t_{alp} \in \mathbb{N}$) records the time the classifier underwent the last anticipatory learning process (ALP) update.

aav The *application average* ($aav \in \Re$) estimates the ALP update frequency.

exp The *experience counter* ($exp \in \mathbb{N}$) counts the number of times the classifier underwent the ALP.

num The *numerosity* ($num \in \mathbb{N}$) specifies the number of actual (micro-)classifiers this macroclassifier represents.

The condition and effect part consist of the values perceived from the environment and '#'-symbols. A #-symbol in the condition called 'don't-care'-symbol denotes that the classifier matches any value in this attribute. A '#'-symbol in the effect part, called 'pass-through'-symbol, specifies that the classifier anticipates that the value of this attribute will not change after the execution of the specified action. All classifier parts are modified by the anticipatory learning process (ALP), the reinforcement learning application, and the genetic generalization mechanism, which are described in 3.6, sections 3.7, and 3.8, respectively.

2.3   Parameters

The following parameters control the various learning methods in ACS2. We first provide a list of all parameters and then reveal their usage and default values in further detail.

θ_i The *inadequacy threshold* ($\theta_i \in [0,1]$) specifies when a classifier is regarded as *inadequate* determined by its quality q.

θ_r The *reliability threshold* ($\theta_r \in [0,1]$) specifies when a classifier is regarded as *reliable* determined by q.

β The *learning rate* ($\beta \in [0,1]$) is used in ALP and RL updates affecting q, r, ir, and aav.

γ The *discount factor* ($\gamma \in [0,1)$) discounts the maximal reward expected in the subsequent situation.

u_{max} The *specificity threshold* ($u_{max} \in \mathbb{N}$) specifies the maximum number of specified attributes in C that are anticipated to stay the same in E.

ϵ The *exploration probability* ($\epsilon \in [0,1]$) specifies the probability of choosing a random action similar to the ϵ-greedy policy in reinforcement learning.

θ_{ga} The *GA application threshold* ($\theta_{ga} \in \mathbb{N}$) controls the GA frequency. A GA is applied in an action set if the average delay of the last GA application of the classifiers in the set is greater than θ_{ga}.

μ The *mutation rate* ($\mu \in [0,1]$) specifies the probability of changing a specified attribute in the conditions of an offspring to a #-symbol in a GA application.

χ The *crossover probability* ($\chi \in [0,1]$) specifies the probability of applying crossover in the conditions of the offspring when a GA is applied.

θ_{as} The *action set size threshold* ($\theta_{as} \in \mathbb{N}$) specifies the maximal number of classifiers in an action set which is controlled by the GA.

θ_{exp} The *experience threshold* ($\theta_{exp} \in \mathbb{N}$) specifies when a classifier is regarded as *experienced* determined by exp.

Although seemingly influenced by a lot of parameters, studies showed that ACS2 is relatively robust to any chosen parameter setting. Usually, all parameters can be set to standard values. In the following, we specify default values and give the basic intuition behind the parameters.

The inadequacy threshold θ_i is usually set to the standard 0.1. Even values of 0.0 showed to not negatively influence the performance of ACS2 since in that case genetic generalization takes care of inadequate classifiers. A classifier is regarded as inadequate once its quality q falls below θ_i. In general, since inadequate classifiers are deleted by the ALP (see section 3.6), θ_i should be set to a low value. The reliability threshold θ_r on the other hand determines when a classifier is regarded as reliable and consequently becomes part of the internal environmental model. The standard value is 0.9. Generally, the higher the value is set, the longer it takes to form a complete model but the more reliable the model actually is. A more crucial parameter is the learning rate β which influences the update procedure of several parameters. The usual value is 0.05 which can be regarded as a rather passive value. The higher β, the faster parameters approach an approximation of their actual value but the more noisy the approximation is. The discount factor γ determines the reward distribution over the environmental model. A usual value is 0.95. It essentially specifies to what extend future reinforcement influences current behavior. The closer to one, the more influence delayed reward has on current behavior. The specificity threshold u_{max} constraints the specialization mechanism, namely the ALP, to what extend it is allowed to specialize the conditions. A save value is always L, the length of the perceptual string. However, if knowledge is available about the problem, then the learning process can be strongly supported by a restricted u_{max} parameter. The exploration probability ϵ determines action selection and consequently behavior. The fastest model learning is usually achieved by pure random exploration. Further biases in action selection are not considered in this description. The interested reader should refer to (Butz, 2002) in this volume.

The following parameters manipulate the genetic generalization mechanism. The GA threshold θ_{ga} controls the frequency with which genetic generalization is applied. A higher threshold assures that that the ALP has enough time to work on a generalized set if necessary. A default threshold is 100. Lower thresholds usually keep the population size down but can cause information loss in the beginning of a run. The mutation rate μ is set unusual high since it is a directly generalizing mutation. The default is set to 0.3. Lower values decrease the generalization pressure and consequently decrease the speed of conversion in the population. Higher values on the other hand can also decrease conversion because of the higher amount of over-general classifiers in the population. The crossover probability χ is usually set to the standard value of 0.8. Crossover seems to influence the process only slightly. No problem was found so far in which crossover actually has a significant effect. The action set size threshold θ_{as} is more crucial since it determines the set size for the genetic generalization application. If the threshold is set too low, the GA might cause the deletion of important classifiers and consequently disrupt the learning process. If the size is set very high, the system might learn the problem but it will take much longer since the population size will rise a lot. However, the default value of 20 worked very well in all so far applied problems. Finally, the experience threshold θ_{exp} controls when a classifier is usable as a subsumer. A low threshold might cause the incorrect propagation of an over-general classifier. However, no negative effect or major influence has been identified so far. Usually, θ_{exp} is set to 20.

3 Algorithmic Description

The provided description approaches the problem in a top down manner. First, the overall execution cycle is specified. In the subsequent sections, each sub-procedure is specified in further detail.

The following notational constraints are used in the description. Each specified sub-procedure is written in pure capital letters. The interaction with the environment and particularly requests from the environment or the reinforcement program are denoted with a colon. Moreover, to denote a certain parameter of a classifier we use the dot notation. Finally, it is necessary to note that we do not use braces or anything to denote the length of an *if clause* or a *loop* but rather use indentation as the direct control.

3.1 Initialization

In the beginning of an ACS2 run, first, all modules need to be initialized. The environment *env* must be created and the animat represented by ACS2 needs to be set to a certain position or state in the environment and so forth. Also, the reinforcement program *rp* must be initialized. Finally, ACS2 must be initialized itself. Hereby, the parameter settings are determined, the time-step counter, referred to as t, is set, and the (in the beginning usually empty) population is created. After all initialization, which we do not clarify in further detail because of their strong problem and implementation dependence, the main loop is called.

START ACS2:
```
1 initialize environment env
2 initialize reinforcement program rp
3 initialize ACS2
4 RUN EXPERIMENT with population [P] and initial time t
```

3.2 The Main Execution Loop

The main loop *RUN EXPERIMENT* is executed as long as some termination criteria are not met. In the main loop, the current situation is first sensed (perceived as input). Second, the match set $[M]$ is formed from all classifiers that match the situation. If this is not the beginning of a trial, ALP, reinforcement learning, and GA are applied in the previous action set. Next, an action is chosen for execution, the action is executed, and an action set is generated from all classifiers in $[M]$ that specify the chosen action. After some parameter updates, ALP, reinforcement learning, and GA may be applied in $[A]$ if the execution of the action led to the end of one trial. Finally, after $[A]$ is stored for learning in the next step, the loop is redone. In the case of an end of trial, $[A]_{-1}$ needs to be emptied to prevent incorrect learning over a trial barrier (i.e. since the successive situation is unrelated to the previous one).

The main loop specifies many sub-procedures denoted in capital letters which are described below in further details. Some of the procedures are more or less trivial while others are complex and themselves call other sub-procedures. Each of the sub-sections try to specify the general idea and the overall process and then give a more detailed description of single parts in successive paragraphs.

RUN EXPERIMENT([P], t):
```
 1 while(termination criteria are not met)
 2     σ ← env: perceive situation
 3     do
 4         GENERATE MATCH SET [M] out of [P] using σ
 5         if([A]_-1 is not empty)
 6             APPLY ALP in [A]_-1 considering σ_-1, σ, t, and [P]
 7             APPLY REINFORCEMENT LEARNING in [A]_-1 using
```
$$\rho \text{ and } \max_{cl \in [M] \wedge cl.E \neq \{\#\}^L} (cl.q * cl.r)$$
```
 8             APPLY GENETIC GENERALIZATION in [A]_-1 considering t
 9         act ← CHOOSE ACTION with an ε-greedy policy in [M]
10         GENERATE ACTION SET [A] out of [M] according to act
11         env: execute action act
12         t ← t + 1
13         rp: receive reward ρ
14         σ_-1 ← σ
15         σ ← env: perceive situation
16         if(env: is end of one trial)
17             APPLY ALP in [A] considering σ, σ_-1, t, and [P]
18             APPLY REINFORCEMENT LEARNING in [A] using ρ
19             APPLY GENETIC GENERALIZATION in [A] considering t
20         [A]_-1 ← [A]
21     while(not env: is end of one trial)
22     env: reset position
23     [A]_-1 ← empty
```

3.3 Formation of the Match Set

The *GENERATE MATCH SET* procedure gets as input the current population $[P]$ and the current situation σ. The procedure in ACS2 is quite trivial. All classifiers in $[P]$ are simply compared to σ and all matching classifiers are added to the match set. The sub-procedure DOES MATCH is explained below.

GENERATE MATCH SET([P], σ):
```
 1 initialize empty set [M]
 3 for each classifier cl in [P]
 4     if(DOES MATCH classifier cl in situation σ)
 5         add classifier cl to set [M]
 6 return [M]
```

The matching procedure is commonly used in LCSs. A 'don't care'-symbol # in C matches any symbol in the corresponding position of σ. A 'care' or non-# symbol only matches with the exact same symbol at that position. The *DOES MATCH* procedure checks each component in the classifier's condition $cl.C$. If a component is specified (i.e. is not a don't care symbol), it is compared with the corresponding attribute in the current situation σ. Only if all comparisons hold, the classifier matches σ and the procedure returns *true*.

DOES MATCH(cl, σ):
```
1 for each attribute x in cl.C
2     if (x ≠ # and x ≠ the corresponding attribute in σ)
3          return false
4 return true
```

3.4   Choosing an Action

In ACS2 usually an ϵ-greedy method is used for action selection. However, unlike non-generalizing reinforcement learning methods, it is not clear which action is actually the best to choose since one situation-action tuple is mostly represented by several distinct classifiers. In this description we chose to use the simple method that the action of the apparent most promising classifier is chosen. Since ACS2 also evolves classifiers that explicitly predict no change in the environment and there is no such thing as a waiting necessity in the problems addressed, those classifiers are excluded in the consideration. The decision is made in the provided current match set $[M]$.

CHOOSE ACTION([M]):
```
1 if (RandomNumber[0, 1) < ε)
2     return a randomly chosen action possible in env
3 else
4     bestCl ← first cl in [M] with cl.E ≠ {#}^L
5     for all classifiers cl ∈ [M]
6         if (cl.E ≠ {#}^L and cl.q * cl.r > bestCl.q * bestCl.r)
7              bestCl ← cl
8     return cl.A
```

3.5   Formation of the Action Set

After the match set is formed and an action is chosen for execution, the *GENERATE ACTION SET* procedure forms the action set out of the match set. It includes all classifiers in the current match set $[M]$ that propose the chosen action *act* for execution.

GENERATE ACTION SET([M], act):
```
1 initialize empty set [A]
2 for each classifier cl in [M]
3    if(cl.A = act)
4        add classifier cl to set [A]
5 return [A]
```

3.6 Anticipatory Learning Process

The application of the anticipatory learning process is rather delicate. Due to its simultaneous creation and deletion of classifiers, it needs to be assured that newly generated classifiers are added to the current action set but are not reconsidered in the current ALP application. Deleted classifiers need to be deleted from the action set without influencing the update process. The algorithmic description does not address such details. However, it is necessary to be aware of these possible problems.

The *APPLY ALP* procedure successively considers the anticipation of each classifier. If the anticipation is correct or wrong, the *EXPECTED CASE* or UNEXPECTED CASE is called, respectively. In the *UNEXPECTED CASE* procedure the quality is decreased so that it is necessary to check if the quality decreased under the inadequacy threshold θ_i. If the case, the classifier is removed (regardless of its numerosity *num* since all micro-classifiers are actually inadequate). When adding a new classifier, it is necessary to check for identical classifiers and possibly subsuming classifiers. Thus, another sub-procedure is called in this case. Finally, if no classifier in the action set anticipates the encountered change correctly, a covering classifier is generated and added. The method is usually called from the main loop. Inputs are the action set $[A]$ in which the ALP is applied, the situation σ_{-1} - action *act* tuple from which $[A]$ was generated, the resulting situation σ, the time t the action was applied, and the current population $[P]$.

Application Average. The *UPDATE APPLICATION AVERAGE* procedure uses the moyenne adaptive modifée technique to reach an accurate value of the application average as soon as possible. Also the ALP time stamp t_{alp} is set in this procedure. The procedure gets the to be updated classifier *cl* and the current time t as input.

APPLY ALP([A], σ_{-1}, act, σ, t, [P]):
```
1 wasExpectedCase ← 0
2 for each classifier cl in [A]
3    cl.exp++
4    UPDATE APPLICATION AVERAGE of cl with respect to t
5    if(cl DOES ANTICIPATE CORRECTLY σ in σ_−1)
6        newCl ← EXPECTED CASE of cl in σ, σ_−1
```

```
7            wasExpectedCase ← 1
8      else
9            newCl ←  UNEXPECTED CASE of cl in σ, σ₋₁
10           if(cl.q < θᵢ)
11                 remove classifier cl from [P] and [A]
12     if(newCl is not empty)
13           newCl.tₘₐ ← t
14           ADD ALP CLASSIFIER newCl to [P] and [A]
15 if(wasExpectedCase = 0)
16     newCl ← COVER TRIPLE σ₋₁, act, σ  with time t
17     ADD ALP CLASSIFIER newCl to [P] and [A]
```

UPDATE APPLICATION AVERAGE(cl, t):
```
1 if(cl.exp < 1/β)
2     cl.aav ← cl.aav + (t − cl.tₐₗₚ − cl.aav) / cl.exp
3 else
4     cl.aav ← cl.aav + β * (t − cl.tₐₗₚ − cl.aav)
5 cl.tₐₗₚ ← t
```

Check Anticipation. While the pass-through symbols in the effect part of a classifier directly anticipate that these attributes stay the same after the execution of an action, the specified attributes anticipate a change to the specified value. Thus, if the perceived value did not change to the anticipated value but actually stayed at the value, the classifier anticipates incorrectly. This is considered in the *DOES ANTICIPATE CORRECTLY* procedure. Inputs are the to be investigated classifier cl, the situation σ_{-1} where cl was applied in, and the resulting situation σ.

DOES ANTICIPATE CORRECTLY(cl, σ_{-1}, σ):
```
1 for each position i
2     if(cl.E[i] = #)
3         if(σ₋₁[i] ≠ σ[i])
4             return false
5     else
6         if(cl.E[i] ≠ σ[i] or sigma₋₁[i] = σ[i])
7             return false
8 return true
```

Expected Case. The structure of the expected case can be separated into two parts in which either a new classifier is generated or not. No classifier is generated if the mark of the investigated classifier cl is either empty or no difference is detected between the mark and the relevant situation σ. In this case, the quality of the successful classifier is increased and no new classifier is returned (denoted by return 'empty'). On the other hand, if differences are detected between mark and situation, offspring is generated. It is important to consider the case where the specialization requests to specialize too many attributes. In this case, generalization of to be specified attributes is necessary. If the offspring without specialization already reached the threshold u_{max}, it is necessary to generalize the offspring to allow specialization of other attributes. The $diff$ attribute has the structure of a condition part. Its creation is specified below in another sub-procedure. The handling of probability-enhanced predictions as published in $Butz, Goldberg, and Stolzmann(2001)$, which we do not address in this description, should be caught in line 3 if the mark is not empty. Moreover, the probabilities in the parental classifier would be updated in this method.

EXPECTED CASE(cl, σ):

```
1  diff ← GET DIFFERENCES of cl.M and σ
2  if(diff = {#}^L)
3      cl.q ← cl.q + β * (1 − cl.q)
4      return empty
5  else
6      spec ← number of non-# symbols in cl.C
7      specNew ← number of non-# symbols in diff
8      child ← copy classifier cl
9      if(spec = u_max)
10         remove randomly specific attribute in child.C
11         spec--
12         while(spec + specNew > u_max)
13             if(spec > 0 and random number [0,1) < 0.5)
14                 remove randomly specific attribute in child.C
15                 spec--
16             else
17                 remove randomly specific attribute in diff
18                 specNew--
19     else
20         while(spec + specNew > u_max)
21             remove randomly specific attribute in diff
22             specNew--
23     specify child.C with diff
24     if(child.q < 0.5)
25         child.q = 0.5
26     child.exp ← 1
27     return child
```

Difference Determination. The difference determination needs to distinguish between two cases. (1) Clear differences are those where one or more attributes in the mark M do not contain the corresponding attribute in the situation σ. (2) Fuzzy differences are those where there is no clear difference but one or more attributes in the mark M specify more than the one value in σ. In the first case, one random clear difference is specified while in the latter case all differences are specified.

GET DIFFERENCES(M, σ):

```
 1 diff ← {#}^L
 2 if(M is not empty)
 3     type1 ← type2 ← 0
 4     for all positions i in σ
 5         if(M[i] does not contain σ[i])
 6             type1++
 7         else if(|M[i]| > 1)
 8             type2++
 9     if(type1 > 0)
10         type1 ← random number [0,1) * type1
11         for all positions i in σ
12             if(M[i] does not contain σ[i])
13                 if(type1 = 0)
14                     diff[i] ← σ[i]
15                 type1--
16     else if(type2 > 0)
17         for all positions i in σ
18             if(|M[i]| > 1)
19                 diff[i] ← σ[i]
20 return diff
```

Unexpected Case. The unexpected case is rather simply structured. Important is the criterion for generating an offspring classifier. An offspring is generated only if the effect part of the to be investigated classifier *cl* can be modified to anticipate the change from σ_{-1} to σ correctly by only *specializing* attributes. If this is the case, an offspring classifier is generated that is specialized in condition and effect part where necessary. The experience of the offspring classifier is set to one.

UNEXPECTED CASE(cl, σ_{-1}, σ):

```
 1 cl.q ← cl.q − β * (cl.q)
 2 SET MARK cl.M with σ_{-1}
 3 for all positions i in σ
 4     if(cl.E[i] ≠ #)
 5         if(cl.E[i] ≠ σ[i] or σ_{-1}[i] = σ[i])
 6             return empty
 7 child ← copy classifier cl
 8 for all positions i in σ
 9     if(cl.E[i] = # and σ_{-1}[i] ≠ σ[i])
10         child.C[i] ← σ_{-1}[i]
11         child.E[i] ← σ[i]
12 if(cl.q < 0.5)
13     cl.q = 0.5
14 child.exp ← 1
15 return child
```

Covering. The idea behind covering is that ACS2 intends to cover all possible situation-action-effect triples. In the ALP, if such a triple was not represented by any classifier in the action set, covering is invoked. Covering generates a classifier that specifies all changes from the previous situation σ_{-1} to situation σ in condition and effect part. The action part A of the new classifier is set to the executed action *act*. The time is set to the current time t. An empty classifier is referred to as a classifier that consists only of #-symbols in condition and effect part. Note, since the experience counter is set to 0, the application average parameter *aav* will be directly set to the delay til its first application in its first application, so that the initialization is not particularly important. Moreover, the quality *cl.q* is set to 0.5 and the reward prediction *cl.r* is set to zero to prevent 'reward bubbles' in the environmental model.

COVER TRIPLE(σ_{-1}, act, σ, t):
```
 1 child ← generate empty classifier with action act
 2 for all positions i in σ
 3     if(σ₋₁[i] ≠ σ[i])
 4         child.C[i] ← σ₋₁[i]
 5         child.E[i] ← σ[i]
 6 child.exp ← child.r ← child.aav ← 0
 7 child.t_alp ← child.t_ga ← t
 8 child.q ← 0.5
 9 child.num ← 1
10 return child
```

Insertion in the ALP. If the ALP generates offspring, insertion distinguishes between several cases. First, the method checks if there is a classifier that subsumes the insertion candidate *cl*. If there is none, the method looks for equal classifiers. If none was found, classifier *cl* is inserted as a new classifier in the population $[P]$ and the current action set $[A]$. However, if a subsumer or equal classifier was found, the quality of the old classifier is increased and the new one is discarded. The subsumption method is described in section 3.9 since the GA application uses the same method. Note, in the equality check it is not necessary to check for the identical action since all classifiers in $[A]$ have the same action.

ADD ALP CLASSIFIER(cl, [A], [P]):
```
 1 oldCl ← empty
 2 for all classifiers c in [A]
 3     if(c IS SUBSUMER of cl)
 4         if(oldCl is empty or c.C is more general than oldCl.C)
 5             oldCl ← c
 6 if(oldCl is empty)
```

```
7     for all classifiers c in [A]
8         if(c is equal to cl in condition and effect part)
9             oldCl ← c
10 if(oldCl is empty)
11    insert cl in [A] and [P]
12 else
13    oldCl.q ← oldCl.q + beta * (1 − oldCl.q)
14    discard classifier cl
```

3.7 Reinforcement Learning

The reinforcement portion of the update procedure follows the idea of Q-learning (Watkins, 1989). Classifier's reward predictions are updated using the immediate reward ρ and the discounted maximum payoff predicted in the next time-step $maxP$. The major difference is that ACS2 does not store an explicit model but only more or less generalized classifiers that represent the model. Thus, for the reinforcement learning procedure to work successfully, it is mandatory that the model is specific enough for the reinforcement distribution. Lanzi (2000) formulizes this insight in a general classifier system framework. The procedure updates the reward predictions r as well as the immediate reward predictions ir of all classifiers in the action set $[A]$.

APPLY REINFORCEMENT LEARNING([A], ρ, maxP):
```
1 for each classifier cl in [A]
2     cl.r ← cl.r + β * (ρ + γmaxP − cl.r)
3     cl.ir ← cl.ir + β * (ρ − cl.ir)
```

3.8 Genetic Generalization

The GA in ACS2 is a genetic generalization of condition parts. Due to the modified generalizing mutation and the evolutionary pressures, the generalizing nature of the GA is realized. The method starts by determining if a GA should actually take place, controlled by the t_{ga} time stamp and the actual time t. If a GA takes place, preferable accurate, over-specified classifiers are selected, mutated, and crossed. Before the insertion, excess classifiers are deleted in $[A]$. Several parts of the processes are specified by sub-procedures which are described after the description of the main GA procedure.

APPLY GENETIC GENERALIZATION ([A], t):
```
1 if(t − ∑_{cl∈[A]} cl.t_{ga}  cl.num/ ∑_{cl∈[A]} cl.num > θ_{GA})
2     for each classifier cl in [A]
3         cl.t_{ga} ← actual time t
4     parent_1 ← SELECT OFFSPRING in [A]
5     parent_2 ← SELECT OFFSPRING in [A]
```

```
 6     child₁ ← copy classifier parent₁
 7     child₂ ← copy classifier parent₂
 8     child₁.num ← child₂.num ← 1
 9     child₁.exp ← child₂.exp ← 1
10     APPLY GENERALIZING MUTATION on child₁
11     APPLY GENERALIZING MUTATION on child₂
12     if(RandomNumber[0,1) < χ)
13         APPLY CROSSOVER on child₁ and child₂
14         child₁.r ← child₂.r ← (parent₁.r + parent₂.r)/2
15         child₁.q ← child₂.q ← (parent₁.q + parent₂.q)/2
16     child₁.q ← child₁.q/2
17     child₂.q ← child₂.q/2
18     DELETE CLASSIFIERS in [A],[P] to allow the insertion
                          of 2 children
19     for each child
20         if(child.C equals {#}ᴸ)
21             next child
22         else
23             ADD GA CLASSIFIER child to [P] and [A]
```

Offspring Selection. Offspring in the GA is selected by a Roulette-Wheel Selection. The process chooses a classifier for reproduction in set [A] proportional to its quality to the power three. First, the sum of all values in set [A] is computed. Next, the roulette-wheel is spun. Finally, the classifier is chosen according to the roulette-wheel result.

SELECT OFFSPRING([A]):
```
1 qualitySum ← 0
2 for each classifier cl in [A]
3    qualitySum ← qualitySum + cl.q³
4 choicePoint ← RandomNumber[0,1) * qualitySum
5 qualitySum ← 0
6 for each classifier cl in [A]
7    qualitySum ← qualitySum + cl.q³
8    if(qualitySum > choicePoint)
9        return cl
```

Mutation. As has been noted before, the mutation process in ACS2 is a generalizing mutation of the condition part $cl.C$. Specific attributes in the conditions are changed to #-symbols with a certain probability μ. The process works as follows:

APPLY GENERALIZING MUTATION (cl):
```
1 for all positions i in cl.C
2 if(cl.C[i] ≠ #)
3     if(RandomNumber[0,1) < μ)
4         cl.C[i] ← #
```

Crossover. The crossover application, as mutation, is only applied to the condition part. Crossover is only applied, if the two offspring classifiers $cl1$ and $cl2$ anticipate the same change. This restriction further assures the combination of classifiers that inhabit the same environmental niche. Our description shows two-point crossover.

```
APPLY CROSSOVER (cl1, cl2):
 1 if(cl1.E ≠ cl2.E)
 2     return
 3 x ← RandomNumber[0, 1) (length of cl₁.C +1)
 4 do
 5     y ← RandomNumber[0, 1) (length of cl₁.C +1)
 6 while(x = y)
 7 if(x > y)
 8     switch x and y
 9 i ← 0
10 do
11     if(x ≤ i and i < y)
12         switch cl₁.C[i] and cl₂.C[i]
13     i++
14 while(i < y)
```

GA Deletion. While the reproduction process uses a form of roulette wheel selection, GA deletion in ACS2 applies a modified tournament selection process. Approximately a third of the action set size takes part in the tournament. The classifier is deleted that has a significantly lower quality than the others. If all classifiers have a similar quality, marked classifiers are preferred for deletion before unmarked classifiers and the least applied classifier is preferred among only marked or only unmarked classifiers. First, however, the method controls if and how long classifiers need to be deleted in $[A]$. The parameter $inSize$ specifies the number of children that will still be inserted in the GA process. Note, the tournament is held among the micro-classifiers. If a classifier is removed from the population, that is, if its numerosity reaches zero, the classifier needs to be removed from the action set $[A]$ as well as from the whole population $[P]$.

```
DELETE CLASSIFIERS([A], [P], inSize):
 1 while(inSize + ∑_{cl∈[A]} cl.num > θ_{as})
 2     clDel ← empty
 3     for each micro-classifier cl in [P]
 4         if(RandomNumber[0, 1) < 1/3)
 5             if(clDel is empty)
 6                 clDel ← cl
 7             else
```

```
8              if(cl.q − clDel.q < −0.1)
9                  clDel ← cl
10             if(|cl.q − clDel.q| ≤ 0.1)
11                 if(cl.M is not empty and clDel.M is empty)
12                     clDel ← cl
13                 else if(cl.M is not empty or clDel.M is empty)
14                     if(cl.aav > clDel.aav)
15                         clDel ← cl
16     if(clDel is not empty)
17         if(clDel.num > 1)
18             clDel.num--
19         else
20             remove classifier cl from [P] and [A]
```

Insertion in the GA. Although quite similar to the ALP insertion, the insertion method in the GA differs in two important points. First, the numerosity *num* rather than the quality *q* of an old, subsuming or identical classifier is increased. Second, the numerosity of an identical classifier is only increased if the identical classifier is not marked. Parameters are as before the to be inserted classifier *cl*, the action set [A] classifier *cl* was generated from, and the current population [P].

ADD GA CLASSIFIER(cl, [A], [P]):
```
1 oldCl ← empty
2 for all classifiers c in [A]
3     if(c IS SUBSUMER of cl)
4         if(oldCl is empty or c.C is more general than oldCl.C)
5             oldCl ← c
6 if(oldCl is empty)
7     for all classifiers c in [A]
8         if(c is equal to cl in condition and effect part)
9             oldCl ← c
10 if(oldCl is empty)
11     insert cl in [A] and [P]
12 else
13     if(oldCl is not marked)
14         oldCl.num++
15     discard classifier cl
```

3.9   Subsumption

ACS2 looks for subsuming classifiers in the GA application as well as in the ALP application. For a classifier cl_{sub} to subsume another classifier cl_{tos}, the subsumer needs to be experienced, reliable, and not marked. Moreover, the subsumer's condition part needs to be syntactically more general and the effect part needs to be identical. Note again, an identical action check is not necessary since both classifiers occupy the same action set. The procedure returns if classifier cl_{tos} is subsumed by cl_{sub} but does not apply any consequent parameter changes.

IS SUBSUMER(cl_{sub}, cl_{tos}):
```
1 if(cl_sub.exp > θ_exp and cl_sub.q > θ_r and cl_sub.M is empty)
2     if (the number of # in cl_sub.C ≤ the number of # in cl_tos.C)
3         if(cl_sub.E is equal to cl_tos.E)
4             return true
5 return false
```

4   Summary

This chapter gave a precise overview over the ACS2 system. Interaction, knowledge representation, and parameter identification should serve as a basic reference book when implementing a new problem and applying ACS2 to it. The algorithmic description revealed all processes inside ACS2 and should serve as a helpful guide to program an own version of ACS2 or develop an enhanced anticipatory learning classifier system out of the ACS2 framework. The description did not include any implementation details so that the system should be programmable in any programming language with the help of this description.

Acknowledgments

We would like to thank the Department of Cognitive Psychology at the University of Würzburg for their support. The work was sponsored by the German Research Foundation DFG.

References

[Butz (2001a] Butz, M.V. (2001a). *Anticipatory learning classifier systems.* Genetic Algorithms and Evolutionary Computation. Boston, MA: Kluwer Academic Publishers.

[Butz (2001b] Butz, M.V. (2001b). *An implementation of the anticipatory classifier system ACS2 in C++* (IlliGAL report 2001026). University of Illinois at Urbana-Champaign: Illinois Genetic Algorithms Laboratory. http://www-illigal.ge.uiuc.edu/sourcecd.html.

[Butz (2002] Butz, M.V. (2002). Biasing exploration in an anticipatory learning classifier system. In Lanzi, P. L., Stolzmann, W., and Wilson, S. W. (Eds.), *Proceedings of the Fourth International Workshop on Learning Classifier Systems (IWLCS-2001)* Berlin Heidelberg: Springer-Verlag.

[Butz, Goldberg, and Stolzmann (2000] Butz, M.V., Goldberg, D.E., and Stolzmann, W. (2000). Introducing a genetic generalization pressure to the anticipatory classifier system: Part 1 - theoretical approach. In Whitely, D., Goldberg, D.E., Cantu-Paz, E., Spector, L., Parmee, I., and Beyer, H.-G. (Eds.), *Proceedings of the Genetic and Evolutionary Computation Conference (GECCO-2000)* pp. 34–41. San Francisco, CA: Morgan Kaufmann.

[Butz, Goldberg, and Stolzmann (2001] Butz, M.V., Goldberg, D.E., and Stolzmann, W. (2001). Probability-enhanced predictions in the anticipatory classifier system. In Lanzi, P.L., Stolzmann, W., and Wilson, S.W. (Eds.), *Advances in Learning Classifier Systems, LNAI 1996* pp. 37–51. Berlin Heidelberg: Springer-Verlag.

[Dorigo and Colombetti (1997] Dorigo, M., and Colombetti, M. (1997). *Robot Shaping, an experiment in behavior engineering.* Intelligent Robotics and Autonomous Agents. Cambridge, MA: MIT Press.

[Lanzi (2000] Lanzi, P.L. (2000). *Learning classifier systems from a reinforcement learning perspective* (Technical Report 00-03). Dipartimento di Elettronica e Informazione, Politecnico di Milano.

[Stolzmann (1997] Stolzmann, W. (1997). *Antizipative Classifier Systems [Anticipatory classifier systems].* Aachen, Germany: Shaker Verlag.

[Stolzmann (1998] Stolzmann, W. (1998). Anticipatory classifier systems. In Koza, J.R., Banzhaf, W., Chellapilla, K., Deb, K., Dorigo, M., Fogel, D., Grazon, M., Goldberg, D., Iba, H., and Riolo, R. (Eds.), *Genetic Programming 1998: Proceedings of the Third Annual Conference* pp. 658–664. San Francisco, CA: Morgan Kaufmann.

[Stolzmann, Butz, Hoffmann, and Goldberg (2000] Stolzmann, W., Butz, M. V., Hoffmann, J., and Goldberg, D. E. (2000). First cognitive capabilities in the anticipatory classifier system. In Meyer, J.-A., Berthoz, A., Floreano, D., Roitblat, H., and Wilson, S. W. (Eds.), *From Animals to Animats 6: Proceedings of the Sixth International Conference on Simulation of Adaptive Behavior* pp. 287–296. Cambridge, MA: MIT Press.

[Watkins (1989] Watkins, C.J.C.H. (1989). *Learning from delayed rewards.* Doctoral dissertation, King's College, Cambridge, UK.

Author Index